THE GIRL WHO ATE BOOKS

Nilanjana Roy is an internationally acclaimed journalist, columnist and writer. Her books include *The Wildings* (2012), which won the Shakti Bhatt First Book Award in 2013, and *The Hundred Names of Darkness* (2013). She lives in New Delhi.

THE GIRL WHO ATE BOOKS

ADVENTURES IN READING

NILANJANA ROY

First published in India in 2016 by Fourth Estate
An imprint of HarperCollins *Publishers* India

Copyright © Nilanjana Roy 2016

P-ISBN: 978-93-5029-711-7
E-ISBN: 978-93-5029-712-4

2 4 6 8 10 9 7 5 3 1

Nilanjana Roy asserts the moral right to be identified
as the author of this work.

The views and opinions expressed in this book
are the author's own and the facts are as reported by her,
and the publishers are not in any way liable for the same.

HarperCollins *Publishers*
A-75, Sector 57, Noida, Uttar Pradesh 201301, India
1 London Bridge Street, London, SE1 9GF, United Kingdom
Hazelton Lanes, 55 Avenue Road, Suite 2900, Toronto, Ontario M5R 3L2
and 1995 Markham Road, Scarborough, Ontario M1B 5M8, Canada
25 Ryde Road, Pymble, Sydney, NSW 2073, Australia
195 Broadway, New York, NY 10007, USA

Typeset in 11/14 Bembo by
R. Ajith Kumar

Printed and bound at
Thomson Press (India) Ltd.

For those ace storytellers, Ma and Baba,
who never once said, 'You're too young to read this.'

Contents

Prologue

'We're done,' I said.

It had taken almost two weeks of sweat—all too literal, in Delhi's humidity—to clean up our bookshelves, and I was staring at the end result. The Holy Grail of bookshelves, the ultimate shrine, the sanctum sanctorum, the point where every booklover and hoarder's pilgrimage ends: an empty shelf. Two of them. A gift from the gods, a sign, allowing us to continue on the manic, ruinous path of collecting books that marks a reader forever, setting him or her apart from the rest of the community as surely as you wearing a silver bell that rings: 'Hoarder! Hoarder!'

Booklove is a dangerous thing. Those of us who have it do not joke about it or take it lightly, because booklove is all-consuming. You move houses with an eye to wall space, and you covet other people's bookshelves, especially if they had more skilful carpenters than you.

My partner and I both inherited moderately large libraries, and perhaps we had fallen into the trap of thinking of these only as 'family books'. The inheritance had come in a mass, as one solid bookshelf worth of things to be read and dusted and looked after. But as I sorted these books, I suddenly found myself back in touch with people whom I could never have known, because they had died before I was born.

As we pulled them out from the bookshelves, looking at the names inscribed in faded fountain-pen ink on the fly-leaf, I began to see more clearly the individual readers behind the 'collection'.

Here was the doctor from two generations ago who loved history, here was the boy straight out of his village who built a broader world by reading in three languages, here were the reformers whose hopes for a better world were encased in their lectures, and the essays they collected.

My grandmother on one side brought in cookbooks, women's magazines, Mills & Boons, and sometimes, the anguished memoirs of pioneering Bengali women. Her handwritten ledgers reminded me that none of my other grandmother's books had survived—her collections of almanacs, volumes of Bengali literature and even her own short stories had disappeared after her death. I could almost see the gap in the bookshelves, remember the way her presence in our house had allowed us to float comfortably from English to Bengali, demanding and receiving stories in both languages.

Over the years of our marriage, these books had been buried underneath the inevitable layers of more and more books, the objects that haunt professional readers and reviewers. Discovering them made me wonder how we had sorted our shelves in the first place. The present had dislodged much of what was really important and meaningful, and there was a special pleasure in rescuing and re-reading what had been allowed to slip to the back.

The slow accumulation of books in any reader's life testifies to many things, but chiefly, to hope. There is nothing more optimistic than a shelf-ful of books you have not yet read, but that you mean to get down to someday. And yet, too much booklove, and what you have is a disease; the books you do not love and would not normally read or keep or treasure, or tell friends about, accumulate thickly, like fungus, like mold, around the books that you truly love and will come back to, again and again.

As we assessed the books, perhaps we seemed ruthless, in the way that we discarded perfectly good writers and anthologies. But as I placed each book on the donations pile, I also sent up a silent prayer for it, hoping that it would find its readers.

Books, like people, like children, should always be certain of a warm welcome, wherever they go next. Few books survive in their physical form beyond 150–200 years; in that time, perhaps they should exchange readers a lot, perhaps they should be shared until their beautiful bound leaves start to drop and shed. They deserve to be loved, especially the old ones, that were hand-sewn, hand-bound, made with care.

As we cleaned each of those shelves, I inhaled dust for three weeks, and became sick from the past. We sniffed the pages of encyclopaedias and dictionaries so far beyond the restorer's art that they fragmented at the lightest touch, exploding into the air like enchanted objects. But whenever I looked upon the books, mine and my partner's, I felt a sense of kinship that went beyond the blood ties of family. The people who had bought and collected these books, our ancestors, were ordinary readers.

The two of us loved books and reading and authors for no good reason except that it had been encoded in our DNA by the previous generations, because we had lived in homes where everyone read books, as a matter of course. My father had grown up in a small town with a tiny library; in later years, he bought books expansively, with the same joy of the forbidden that was reserved for things like expensive, imported chocolates.

When I look more closely at the 'family' books, one thing stands out. You don't collect books to demonstrate how much you know about the world; instead, these small libraries represent every reader's acknowledgement of how little you know about the world, and how much you reach out for it anyway.

Collecting books is the same as looking up at the stars: you don't want to own the stars, any more than you want to own books or the knowledge in them. All you hope to do is to brush the surface of wonder, to acknowledge that there is still, as an adult, some part of you that is always in awe of, and in love with, the world and the word.

★

This book is chiefly about the love of reading, and about a reading childhood in India. It is not intended to be a history of Indian writing in English (though you'll find some excellent histories of Indian writing and publishing in the Bibliography) or a history of contemporary Indian writers. Instead, these essays track one reader's journey—sometimes awkward, often magical—into becoming a writer. Most of these essays were written for the general reader; my apologies in advance to those academics and scholars who are already familiar with Dean Mahomet and the rest of the gang of Indians who wrote in English in the eighteenth and nineteenth centuries and who will not find much here that is revelatory. Because I love reading in Bengali and grew up in Delhi and Kolkata, these essays centre on English, Bengali and those two cities; I can only hope that readers incensed by this evidence of gross bias will redress the balance by writing their own memoirs of reading in other parts of India.

Some pieces originally intended for this edition were omitted, on reflection: three long essays on reading Indian writers in translation, on memoirs and writings about caste in India, and on cookbooks and on food writing seemed incomplete, and besides I wasn't sure I was in any way qualified to speak on Dalit writers. Book reviews were left out for the most part because I prefer writing them to re-reading them. An ambitious essay on a subject close to my heart, the libraries and reading habits of prominent Indians in the national movement, has been set aside until I can find time to read the little magazines and journals of those decades.

The first two essays, 'The Girl Who Ate Books' and 'Finding Dean', are about reading, and the slow, tentative shift towards becoming a writer and finding my 'family': a bunch of excitable, eccentric and voluble Indians from the eighteenth and nineteenth century. 'How To Read In Indian' collects assorted profiles on the pioneers of Indian writing in English, from enterprising eighteenth-century spa proprietors armed with pamphlets and chutzpah, to the early twentieth-century woman who set up schools for Muslim girls and imagined a classic feminist Utopia. From the novels written after and about 1857 to a glimpse of the language debates over Indian English to a previous generation's obsession with the Encyclopaedia Britannica, this section touches very lightly on the history of Indian writing in English across three centuries.

'Coffee Break' compiles short interviews with writers: from Kiran Desai and Pico Iyer to Nayantara Sahgal and Ved Mehta, most of these conducted for *Business Standard* over the last two decades, and includes two brief appraisals of the works of Rohinton Mistry and V.S. Naipaul. The subsequent sections, 'Booklove' and 'Booklovers', are a tribute to fellow bibliophiles, and roams from childhood reading in the era when Soviet books flooded Indian libraries to reminiscences of houses built of books, and short memorial pieces to five stalwarts of the publishing and bookselling world. 'Plagiarism' and 'Expression' are explorations of faultlines of two kinds: the trouble that greed and carelessness can get writers into and the dangers of silence and censorship. 'Crossing Over', the last essay in this volume, is for everyone who wants, in their secret hearts, to be a writer.

I have only one suggestion to add: despite the title of this book, I can guarantee from personal experience that reading books will cause less heartburn and acidity than eating them. If you remain undeterred, choose books with crisp pages and matt rather than glossy covers, and remember that hardbacks (and poetry) are better for your health than pulp fiction.

ONE

Early Days

1

The Girl Who Ate Books

On long road trips, I often dream of Kolkata, especially in the mountains when the air is thin enough to switch on the mind's most vivid hallucinations. It is always the same dream. I am a child, young enough to be carried past the whitewashed walls where graffiti and political slogans ran from one end of a street to another, my eyes level with the spiky palm-frond tops of the letters. Sometimes I am in a car, looking out. But the feeling remains the same: of travelling through a city built in sentences and slogans, where rivers of words flowed through its lanes.

Each neighbourhood's walls were allocated to political parties. The *parar chele* were the gangs of boys who ran each patch of territory, who lounged on the street corners lighting their cigarettes from the end of a burning twist of rope as the rains came down. As the muggy summer heat rose up from the cramped pavements, they saw to it that few walls were left pristine white or cream.

The calligraphy of the graffiti artists was superb, sometimes as beautiful as the brushstroked Bengali words that adorned posters and book covers. The hammer and sickle, the political symbol of the communist left parties, is the first punctuation mark I remember; also

3

the bearded trio of Marx, Lenin and (fading into historical distance) Stalin. Sometimes the fragile framework of the Howrah Bridge sketched in black and green paint sounded a more wistful note. In my dreams, the walls and their words are alive and the black slashes and rounded stomachs of the Bengali letters undulate, pushing and shoving past me like crowds shouting worn, familiar slogans: '*Amader daabi maantey hobe! Cholbe na, cholbe na!*' Our demands must be heard! This won't do, this won't do!

Later, as a student in the city, I grew used to the walls and took their chatter for granted; they were as verbal as the rest of Kolkata. You walked and drove among colourful and carefully calligraphed slogans, Bengali advertisements, as though the pages of magazines and flapping banners had been frozen in stone and brick, as if the city itself was a large, living, illustrated book.

Kolkata is a good city for walkers, for though the pavements are crowded and the flagstones broken, the traffic moves too slowly to cause much harm. It is crowded; people can't help jostling you, yet when they push past, they are usually gentle, unthreatening. As students, we walked as much as we could, except in the monsoons when we waded through the filthy streets, honing a skill that was useful in much of India and absolutely essential in Kolkata—the ability to not think about the muck and tamped-down dirt that was as much part of the city's texture as the floating butterfly skeleton of the Howrah Bridge was a part of its imagined, loved skyline.

We walked through street and maidan cricket and football matches. Intricate paper shrines would be constructed during World Cups and Eden Garden matches at the roundabouts and the intersections, honouring the small but powerful gods who really mattered, the gods of fours and sixes, of googlies and wickets.

There were some constants. The political graffiti was punctuated by the *jhalmuri* sellers perching their grubby, spicy, irresistible paper packets of stomach-churning, mouth-tingling goodness on stork-legged wooden contraptions. And always, on the pavements and on the stoops, if you looked up, on the long, low roofs, there were the silhouettes and shapes of men, reading. In the back lanes of the slums of Garia or Jadavpur, no one-room or half-room shack was so poor that its inhabitants could not afford books or magazines. Bengali publishers produced cheap paperbacks and clothbound books at ridiculously low prices.

In the lanes of North Kolkata, you would see these cheap books by the score, lying face down on a tin trunk that had been converted into a sofa in one of those open balcony-verandahs where metal railings protected the house from thieves and cast slanted diamond shadows onto the hot tarmac below. The pages were so translucent that on summer days, a man reading, his checked gamcha slung over his shoulder, his belly bare so that he could scratch it with greater ease in between short stories, could hold his book up to the sunlight and read two pages of text at once.

Women read too, perhaps as much if not more than the men, but, for some reason, rarely in public, except on the buses with the wooden seats covered in rexine where the mini-bus conductors sang out the names of stops as though they were rousing Bengali hymns: Shyambajaar, Grey Stritt, Beadon Stritt, Bow Bajaar, Bhictoria Hauze, 'Splanade. It was not uncommon for the conductor to read, too, and in the slow trams that clattered over the cobblestones, I once saw the driver rustle the pages of a magazine, turning them idly as the tram made its stately, inch-by-inch progress along the ancient tracks. He was pronouncing each word aloud, with wonder, as though these were the very first sentences he had ever read in his life, but when you listened carefully, he was only reading the report of a cricket Test match that had ended in a draw.

★

Of the two most distinctive Kolkata sounds I remember, the first is the clamour of the traffic roaring over Howrah Bridge, counterpointed by the warning boom of the sooty steamers that passed on the river down below on their way to the rapid tugging treacherous tides of Diamond Harbour. The second was the clang of the gate to a red-brick house with green shutters that no longer exists.

The gate, a solid unbroken sheet of steel rattling over white gravel, was so heavy that it took some effort to swing it open or shut on the iron rollers, and in the monsoons, the iron track beneath rusted, making it harder to open. Cocooned inside, from behind the peeling green wooden shutters, we could hear the clang and the judder when guests or relatives arrived, the gate decanting more cousins, uncles, aunts and friends into the noisy, full world of my childhood.

My grandmother's house on Rowland Road was set far back from the busy main thoroughfare where Kolkata's buses juddered down Lansdowne Road, coughing and honking their complaints, and the gossiping clamour of car horns in the crowded lane outside. Inside the house it was cool and dark with the louvred shutters drawn, as they were every afternoon against the heat and humidity. The voices of adults above my head sounded like a flock of chattering parakeets as they went from the formal drawing room into the open verandah. The adults, and us cousins, wound in and out between the house and the garden; the separation between the two was indistinct, with three flights of stone stairs leading down into the lawn where a tyre swing hung enticingly from the mango tree.

In the years to come, through four decades, that would be the only house to lay claim to my imagination. (This was not from the lack of other houses in my life. From my parents, I have inherited a tendency of rapid and sudden jolts of movement from one rented place to another in the same city.)

It is as though living in the home my grandmother, Archana Roy, had created—gracious, warm, welcoming, the red stone floors polished to a high gleam by generations of old retainers, someone at the piano, and laughter or the strains of Radio Ceylon in the large, inviting enclosed verandah most evenings—had spoiled us for settling in a more permanent way anywhere else.

We were exceptionally lucky to have the house and the gift of its many graces; it took me time to see just how much of a gift that kind of spaciousness was in a city as crowded and teeming with people, as dogged by poverty, the ghosts of famine still alive in my grandmother's stories. It took a lot of effort—almost none of it expended by the families who lived in these mansions—to keep the many graces going, too: a small army of staff was required to polish the silver, and the wooden banisters, and keep the cobwebs away, and the roofs tiled and waterproofed, and the napkins starched, and the serried rows of books sorted and free of dust. We were lucky indeed, though neither my mother's generation nor mine had done much to earn their good fortune.

All this was the product of the hard work of the previous generation, many of them rooted in village life until they came out to the cities to explore the opportunities of a new, modern age. One ancestor, Bidhan Chandra Roy, had borrowed money from an Armenian family he was close to in order to fund his education as a medical student in the UK. He had returned to a changing India and made a name for himself as a doctor who was also, like so many in his time, immersed in the new Freedom Movement started by a lawyer from South Africa called Mohandas Karamchand Gandhi.

My grandfather, Subimal Chandra Roy, had died relatively young, but he had made a career for himself in the law. Between him and my great-uncle, they had left the next generation a sizeable, unearned inheritance, but no one understood estates, taxes and other such practicalities.

Many Bengali families were similarly ornamental and utterly useless, and the fortunes that one generation had worked so hard to put together rushed upon inheritors like flood waters, receding in time, leaving the unwary marooned in the muck of crumbling houses and unpaid taxes, bewildered by the loss of what they had not earned in the first place.

But for a child unaware of the tangled politics of class, or the pride mingled with resentment that the bhadralok—the gentlefolk—commanded, the red-brick house was a sanctuary and a haven. As a toddler, I loved being there, wobbling around in bare feet, dodging the commands of parents and an assortment of uncles and aunts, seeking its unexpected gifts. The pleasures of that house were mysterious and personal to each one of us, like the softly lit light fixtures that hung like warm globes from black lacquered iron chains suspended from painted wooden beams. These small surprises mattered more to me than the obvious graces of company and fragile china, the solid comfort of the Burma teak furniture.

Staircases, for instance: there was a winding one in the 'tower', a tiny stone column that led off one of the bathrooms and had a separate, elvish door nestled among the mango trees outside. The stairs to the roof were steep and grey and ominous, like the crumbling ones inside the minarets of the Qutub Minar in Delhi that make the undersides of your soles curl in fear that you will fall. The tower had narrow slits for windows, where I dreamt of the archers of the *Mahabharata* and of Robin Hood's merry men, often mixing up the two bands of brothers.

Inside my grandmother's bedroom, small, snug, the branches of the grapefruit tree tapping at her window in the morning, there was a flight of precarious stairs behind the desk where she kept her hisaab kitaab and the daily expense accounts, all written in her neat, cursive hand.

The stairs led to the wonders of a tiny attic stuffed with papers, old trunks and other junk. Once, during one of our many jaunts, we found a bowl of painted mangoes, bananas and apples, all carved out of wood. The paint had peeled on the pink apples, the bright yellow bananas, but we had read enough fairy tales by then to know that the bowl of fruit was magical. We kept the bowl a little apart from the miniature cane doll's house-furniture and the copies of *Abol Tabol* and Bugs Bunny comics, as though its magic, whatever form that took, might be contagious. And at the back of the house where the gutters added a layer of acrid guano to the air—if you woke up to the strains of birdsong from the jamun and mango trees, some sort of payment was due—a wrought-iron staircase like rusted lace curved up the length of the house. My sister kept that staircase for years after the old house had finally come down.

There was one more thing about the Rowland Road house, though it seemed unremarkable at the time. It was built of books, or rather, the bookcases streamed across the house; the window alcoves had fitted bookcases, the staircases had book cupboards built under them, and it was taken for granted that every room would have either wall-mounted bookracks or standalone bookshelves.

There was nothing unusual about this; most Kolkata homes were furnished in books, regardless of the size of the house or the income of the owner. The ones large enough to have furniture 'sets' and antimacassars ran to full sets of Bengali classics, from Saratchandra to Sharadindu, Jibanananda, Mahasweta, Bankimchandra and co. to Parashuram, Nabarun Bhattacharya, Bani Basu, Moti Nandy. The only assured constants in these homes would be the Holy Trinity of almanacs, back issues of the Bengali literary magazine *Desh* and the complete works of the inescapable, ubiquitous Tagore. The mansions of the boxwallahs, and judges and lawyers' homes, and the Anglicized Brahmos added bound copies of *Time, National Geographic* and Nobel Prize winners to their collection. Years later, I would wince in mortified but inescapable recognition at an essay by Amitav Ghosh where he explored (and deflated) the Bengali obsession with the Nobel Prize for literature.

Didima's house betrayed the same obsession; but then the interests of each of the ancestors asserted itself, taking the collection in the verandah beyond the Tagore–Nobel canon. The high shelves with a special black iron grappling hook-and-slider arrangement contained her husband's law books and the leather-bound volumes prized by a succession of ancestors: the predictable old issues of *Punch* and the collected works of Rabindranath Tagore found themselves alongside military histories, Urdu classics, medical encyclopaedias and always, an eclectic range of biographies, in English and Bengali.

The house was capacious enough to accommodate mild murmurs of protest against the burden of canons and Books of Knowledge. Didima, who had studied Sanskrit and occasionally put me in my place with a judicious quote from the Upanishads when I pushed at her boundaries as a balky adolescent, dedicated herself to amassing a stupendously varied collection of Mills & Boons.

You could trace the historical development of women's romances by studying the gradual shift from outback love and doctor-and-nurse romances through the Greek millionaire and Italian count phase up to the modern phenomenon of softcore erotica and doctor–doctor romances. Didima disapproved of the erotica on the Umberto Eco principle that porn got in the way of a good story, but she liked the egalitarianism of doctors dating, rather than doctors hitting on nurses. In his office and his bedroom, my uncle maintained an eclectic collection of paperbacks on subjects as varied as Tibetan Buddhism, physics via The Dancing Wu Li Masters, classical music and jazz, and his passion, architecture.

These paperbacks formed a thin line of defence against the previous generation's insistence on hoarding all those *How The World Works* books, those confident encyclopaedias of everything. In retrospect, the almanacs, dictionaries and encyclopaedias so common in homes of that era were telling in their belief (most clearly expressed in English libraries, but mirrored in their Bengali counterparts) that the world could be contained and explained, and was amenable to cross-examination.

In the Rowland Road house, the books for children were placed judiciously around every room, in the low window alcoves, in the cupboards under the stairs. It was typical of my grandmother's intuitive understanding of children and her deep-rooted belief that their needs were just as important as those of adults. She scattered the books that children would like around the house in the same accidental fashion as she left large blue plastic bowls filled with *sandesh* or jam tarts from Kolkata Club and chicken patties from Nahoum's or plain puffed rice or grapefruit from the tree near her window, out on the massive dining table. We were supposed to help ourselves to either kind of nourishment, as and when hunger pangs struck us.

This was the city and this was the house where I ate my first book.

★

At the age of three, I was already a pest. This was mostly my mother's fault, though it is possible that I was born believing that the purpose of everyone who showed up in my life—the multitudes of beloved and loving uncles and aunts in particular—was to entertain me. In our equally rambunctious home in Delhi, another place that overflowed with books and assorted guests, my sister and I were only persuaded to go to bed—rather than interrupt the adult revels—because my mother bribed us with bedtime stories.

Everyone's mothers and grandmothers tell the best bedtime stories; this is an article of faith. They didn't have my mother, though.

'Once upon a time, between the mooli patch and the sugarcane fields that you see in the back garden, there lived a . . .'

My mother plucked stories off the cartoon figures on the cheap but colourful bedroom curtains, and made the tiny rows of sheep or the stars on our night suits come alive as she wove them into her tales. She had the canon at her fingertips, and each night, she brought them all out, the wolves from the old dark German fairy tales, the bunyips and the goryos from around the world, the home-grown rakshasas and wizened crones who populated Bengali folk tales.

Red Riding Hood tiptoed down the corridor on her way out to the forest. The Baba Yaga sat at the foot of my bed, and Pooh Bear dangled his paws over the headboard, leaving a jar of honey behind to provide me sustenance through my dreams. Brer Rabbit and the Tar Baby, who would both be politically incorrect today, visited at bedtime just as Tuntuni, the gossipy little bird from Bengal, hopped out of the window. But the best stories were the ones that my mother made up using just her imagination, where the lights would go off and we would be left with only her voice, transforming the prints on the curtains, the bedsheets and our everyday nightclothes into the stuff of magic.

Her storytelling created a small, determined and persistent monster. I was notorious for toddling up to my father's seniors—stodgy ministers, ultra-respectable bureaucrats from an age before scams rotted the name of government servants—and waylaying them with demands if my parents were unwary enough to let me into the room: 'Tell me a story.' If they didn't have a story, I would tell them my long-playing, revisionist version of Cinderella.

If this sounds cute, it was not meant to. I was the kind of child who made people think that perhaps Herod was justified in his massacre of the innocents—they must have asked him for a story.

By the age of three, my relatives had learned to either flee or set me to errands in a vain attempt to ward off demands for more stories. One was never enough, and it was many years later, reading about Vijaydan Detha's insatiable appetite for stories, and the tale-collecting instincts of Gabriel Garcia Marquez or Italo Calvino, that I felt a belated prickle of validation. The gods of storytelling did it; I was just following in their footsteps.

I do not think that Eco, Detha and Marquez hounded their victims in quite the same way, though. The old stories had to be told just right, with the appropriate embellishments. It wasn't enough to hear about Arjuna stringing the bow at the swayamvar.

What did you make bowstrings out of, and did they have to be waxed?

How loudly did the bowstring twang?

If he broke the bowstring accidentally, did he have another at hand?

Did quivers have a separate space for bowstrings?

Why did the prince in Cinderella have to measure her feet, hadn't he been looking at her face?

Why was the coach that took Cinderella to the ball a pumpkin (such an unromantic vegetable)?

Why couldn't it have been a strawberry, to which I was partial, or a grapefruit?

The person at the receiving end of all of this was the kindest and gentlest soul in the house, the only uncle tolerant enough and patient enough to spend most of his waking hours being shadowed by a creature who came up to his knees and wanted story after story after story. (Even my grandmother had a three-story limit, after which she would retire to play Patience or to get some work done for the Women's Voluntary Service and the Time and Talents Club.)

The family version of the small pestering person in their midst is a funny story; my memories of the age of illiteracy are surprisingly dark. I must have been three when I realized that books contained stories, the way tins (if you were lucky) contained biscuits, and from the time that I made that connection, my mind was not at peace.

So much of childhood is a balancing act between the first, indelible rush of astonishment and discovery—and the inevitable grappling with frustration. When he was three, my young nephew named the shiny thing in the sky a 'star', using the word importantly, and I could see the satisfaction in his eyes, the glory of naming everything in the world for the very first time, ever, as though no human being had done this before him and no one would do this again.

Those first thrills of discovery are fierce and unforgettable. So are the first discoveries of frustration, being denied something that you want so very badly—and that is readily available to everyone who towers over you and belongs to the remote world of adulthood.

I would stare at the ranks of leather-bound and cloth-bound books with a hunger so intense that the memory of it is as palpable as the memory of cold, or thirst, or grave injury. Here were books, within reach, many of them. They contained the stories I wanted so badly. And when I opened the books and the magazines, one after another, black ants crawled across the page, silently, saying nothing to me, indifferent to my presence and my need.

My uncle took pity on me and decided to teach me how to read. It is possible that he wanted to be able to retreat and draw plans of buildings without his niece attached to his leg, bawling because the story he was telling had ended and there would be no more stories, ever, but it was kind of him all the same.

I have no recollection at three of tracing the alphabets or learning the English letters, though from another time and place, I do remember learning both the Bengali and the Hindi alphabets. There must have been a stage when I went through the ABCs the same way as the *kaws* and *khaws*, but it has slipped the net of memory. By the time I turned four, my uncle's lessons must have taken hold somewhere in that hungry-for-stories mind of mine.

I remember the first words I read the way I remember nearly drowning in the sea off Goa once, the shock of the water rushing into my nostrils; or the way I remember reaching the top of a hill in Bhutan and stumbling breathless into the high monastery only to come face-to-face with a statue of the Buddha among the clouds and the jagged peaks. It is that sharp, and that electric.

The book was in hardboard, handsomely covered, a miscellany of poems and stories by writers so out of date that even their names are dusty today. The landscape on the front cover was uncompromisingly English, the meadows and polite rows of sheep and the cottage in the background with a stream running by it all completely unrelated to the cities I lived in and knew, Delhi and Kolkata. The pages were thick and creamy, the illustrations embossed in ink that did not smear across the opposite page even in the full heat of summer. And as I turned first one page and then the other, the black ants marched up and down, up and down, waving their antennae mockingly at me.

Then they slowed.

Then the words swam into focus and I could see them, and hear them as clearly as though someone had said the words in my mind.

Slowly, silently, now the moon
Walks the night in her tender shoon.

I said the line over and over to myself, some part of me knowing even then that Walter de la Mare's 'Silver' was terrible poetry, but what I was revelling in was not the words, or even the images behind them— the moon, peering out through a fringe of trees, in a dark night sky. It was the sense of power, of owning some words at last after having to beg them from adults for so long.

I turned the page and there were no ants. Only more words, and each word marched alongside another until I had read a complete sentence, and the sentence pulled me into the books and stories I had coveted and desired for so long. 'Shoon,' I said to myself, not knowing that it was merely the word for shoes, and a pretentious one at that. 'Shoon shoon shoon.' It was magic, being in that house filled with books, wondering how long it would take for me to read all the stories that all of them contained.

The celebrations in my family when they realized I was reading were heartfelt, most of all from my uncle. Part of it was the altruistic welcome that seasoned readers offer to a new initiate; most of it was relief.

When I was alone in the room, I said 'Shoon' again to myself, wanting to celebrate. Then I checked to see that no adults were watching, and hefted the book off the divan. I took it under the dining table, sat on the cool pink mosaic tiles, and hugged the book closer. If the words sounded that good, I thought, how would they taste?

Tentatively, I licked the page. I would discover later, through a process of trial and error, that Bengali books seldom tasted good, that paperbacks were dry and crumbly, and that exercise books were watery and disappointing. But the words 'shoon' and 'silver' and 'moon' had a tiny acrid bite to them. Like a practiced thief, I turned to another page in the book and tasted the text there, just to see. Close up, the paper smelled a little like cookies, or like the waxed paper frill around loaves of plain cake. I let my teeth slide over the edges, stopping when Romen, the chef, came in and rummaged through the cutlery in the sideboard.

When he left, I bent my head to the book and with my teeth, tore off a corner of the page. It went down well, though it didn't taste of much except unsweetened porridge. Boldly, I tried a little more, pleased at the thought of eating what I had just read. Then I looked at the page more closely and panicked: instead of the tiny corner I thought I had torn off, there was a gap, a large tear, a perceptibly ragged edge. Silverfish darted through the older books like illegal sub-tenants, but even at that age, I knew I couldn't pass this off as a silverfish hole. The page was palpably gnawed.

From the bedroom, I heard my mother's voice. The adults would soon be up and about, the lid of the piano would be raised, Didima would play Scott Joplin or old Tagore songs, maybe Mamu would go from jazz to Simon & Garfunkel, and the house would rumble with laughter and chatter; and in the middle of all of this, I would be discovered for the miserable gnawer of books I now knew myself to be.

With trembling hands, I did what I had to do. Ripping out the page, I ate the telltale shreds inside the book, and then, piece by piece, I ate the entire page corner to corner. Then I quietly returned the book to the shelves, pushing it all the way to the back, and joined the household for tea, a little subdued. My conscience was troubling me, and so was my stomach, though this would hardly be the last time I would find the printed word difficult to digest.

(Written in 2009 with additions in 2014.)

2

Finding Dean

It happened several years ago, on the road from Edinburgh to London. It had been a magical week of writers—Harold Pinter, Arthur Conan Doyle, Irvine Welsh, musicians and Qigong enthusiasts doing their thing on the streets, an afternoon spent with no one but the seagulls, a chance encounter with an Irish doctor who showed me around the Canongate and told stories about his favourite writers the way other people tell stories about their favourite aunts, some apple-and-cheese lunches, jazz one blustery night near Arthur's Seat, and then it was time to leave Edinburgh.

The Norwegian mime troupe who'd offered me a ride in the van hadn't bargained for the double bass player who had hooked up with the driver. I said, no problem, I'd make my own way back to London. The flights and trains were too expensive, so I booked a bus ticket, and from thereon, everything—naturally—went wrong.

The wheels on my suitcase locked, so it had to be dragged and carried down the street. It was a grey, drenched morning. 'Here, luv, 'av an apple on me, you're too early for breakfuss,' the lady at the desk had said kindly when I was leaving the hotel. But the apple and my tiny cache of spare cash had disappeared through a hole in the lining of my coat by the time I wrestled the suitcase into the bus.

The bus was packed; two hours into the journey, I woke to find the guy in the seat next to me breathing his halitosis—stale beer, fried fish—into my face; when we stopped at a gas station, the loos had been pre-puked in by the previous busload.

Both the Edinburgh Festival and London were indulgences I couldn't really afford, even with the generosity of the British Council, which had sprung for the cost of air tickets and the stay in Edinburgh. This was a rare treat for the small band of Indian reviewers and authors who had been invited to see what the fuss over the Edinburgh International Book Festival and the writers who massed at Charlotte Square Gardens was like.

This was 2002, four years before the Jaipur Literature Festival kicked off in Diggi Palace, inaugurating festival fever in India. Most of us book lovers had spent the 1990s with our noses pressed up to the thick-glassed window that separated home and abroad, knowing that if you lived in India, you would rarely meet the foreign writers whose books you loved so much. As a fledgling book reviewer at the *Business Standard* newspaper in Delhi, I couldn't believe my luck when the British Council made the offer of a scholarship.

My husband and I did some frantic calculations—he had just quit his job in order to kickstart a career in freelance writing, and we had just spent the year's furniture allowance on, predictably, books—and worked out that if I was very sensible, I would be able to afford meals in Edinburgh as well as a few days in London, if I cast myself upon the charity of friends.

It was a common dilemma: book reviewing didn't pay much, though few of us in the profession minded. Perhaps it had been foolish of me to try to squeeze in a trip to London, but it had been irresistible. Who could possibly come so far and not visit Daunt's, imagine the streets where Charles Dickens had taken his brisk, long, restless walks, try to see the city through the eyes of the generations of Indians who had visited and sometimes settled in, from unknown, unnamed convicts and labourers, to Dean Mahomet, Toru Dutt and closer to our time, Salman Rushdie?

But in the bus, five hours into the ride, I was miserably hungry.

It was only genteel starvation, but I'd blown my cash in Edinburgh on music tickets and books and had skipped meals for two or three days. This was a common problem for the small group from India—all of us went a little crazy when we saw the abundance of books in the stores, compared to the relatively thin stacks back in Delhi, and we went unwisely, but so deliciously, from famine to feast, spending far more than any of us could afford.

London was an indulgence, I knew that right from the start, but it's only at this point that I'm wondering if I made a big, big mistake. Broke, cold, wet, miserable, hungry, sleepy—perhaps I should have just gone back home.

That's when Leaflet Boy appears.

He's young, probably in his early twenties, a thin, brown-skinned figure wearing too large spectacles that he has to keep pushing up his nose. He's standing at a corner watching the slow progress of traffic and offering leaflets with a grave, courtly gesture to Londoners who clearly couldn't give a damn about him or his leaflets. I don't know how long he's been standing there, handing out leaflets no one wants, but his eyes are watery in the wind and his cheeks are blue with cold.

I know it's rude to stare, but he's such a small, brave, pathetic figure. I'm about to look away politely when he catches my eye and waves.

The bus has stopped in traffic. I'm at the window; I'm sure he's waving to someone else, so I look around instinctively.

He's smiling now. He waves again.

At me? I'm confused.

He points a finger in my direction and sketches a wide bow. *Yes, you.*

Tentatively, I wave back.

He puts a hand on his heart and sketches an even lower bow.

Hello! he mimes.

I smile, uncertainly.

He draws a huge smiley face with a flourish in the air.

Cold! he mimes, shivering exaggeratedly.

This I can do. I mime 'cold' back with absolutely no trouble. I'm guessing this is just a brownface meets brown-face encounter.

He does a complicated mime. He smiles, jumps up and down, waves to passers-by.

The pedestrians hurrying by seem startled at the antics of this skinny exuberant kid.

I'm puzzled. He mimes again, sketching an overcoat in the London air and jumping on the spot again: *if you smile, wave, jump and down, flap your hands, it makes you feel warmer.* Then he bows, a big extravagant bow.

I start laughing. By now, others in the bus are beginning to grin at the kid, wave to him. And people on the street aren't edging past him; they're stopping, briefly, turning around to smile at the loony Indian kid.

The bus starts up again. Leaflet Boy looks sad, but only for a second. He crumples one of the leaflets deftly, working fast, shaping it into a rough paper rose. Puts it between his teeth, puts his hand on his heart, gets down on his knees and starts singing. '*Musafir hoon yaaron . . .*' It's a cracked, adolescent voice, and the old Kishore Kumar song grows fainter and fainter until it's lost in traffic.

Soon I can't see him. In the bus, people go back to sleep, rustle their papers, look for mints, stretch and get back to their individual cocoons of silence.

I never saw Leaflet Boy again, and we probably wouldn't recognize each other if we met on the street. But over the next few years, I travelled a lot, and each journey brought its own adventures: lonely roads, unsafe trains, fleabag hotels, muggings, magic, great meals, strange pilgrims, the works. This was the first time I'd travelled abroad alone as an adult, though, or experienced a small sliver of what it might be to feel a little lost in a strange country, and I send up a small prayer of thanks for Leaflet Boy. As I wrestle the giant Third World suitcase with its many extension pockets, inadequate zips and that classy pre-ripped look off the bus, I know that no matter how often I travel in the future, whether it's coach or first-class, I'll never be welcomed as warmly, as gloriously, to a city as Leaflet Boy welcomed me to London. Bless him, wherever he is.

★

Writers adopt writers. As with chefs and artists, this is a kind, warm-hearted community, given to opening their homes to friends and strangers without reservation. The strangeness of being abroad disappeared in the warmth of the house of Ruchir Joshi, Gita Sahgal and their two boys, and as I leaned against the kitchen counter, listening, their conversation washed over me in comforting waves. It switched easily from politics, the history of the Southhall Black Sisters, public radio, to quick sketches of mutual friends, most of them writers or filmmakers or human rights activists. The boys, bright, confident, outgoing, helped with dinner.

These gifts—the boys' instantly extended friendliness, Ruchir's home-cooked food, Gita's tactful tips for getting around London—were priceless, and immensely reassuring. I had not realized until they made me feel so welcome in their home that I had been feeling so out of place, an awkward, first-time traveller who didn't even know how to press the right buttons on the Walk/Don't Walk signs.

In Edinburgh, confused by the buses, afraid of taking the wrong one and squandering the fare I'd set aside for the day, I'd finally walked back to the hotel in the falling darkness, trudging along unfamiliar streets for some hours in a complex blend of trepidation and exasperation at my helplessness. The independence I was so proud of back home in Delhi seemed to have been left behind at the UK Customs counter, leaving me awash in drifts of small humiliations of my own creation.

My passage to England was so unlike the swashbuckling approach of a man I had started to adore, across the passage of centuries. I wished I had half the resilience of Sake Dean Mahomet, the first Indian writer to attempt a full-fledged book in English and the intrepid founder of first a coffee-house and then an unabashedly Orientalist spa in Brighton.

★

Saik Deen Mahomad, manufacturer of the real currie powder, takes the earliest opportunity to inform the nobility and gentry, that he has, under the patronage of the first men of quality who have resided in India, established at his house, 34 George Street, Portman-Square, the Hindostanee Dinner and Hooka Smoking Club. Apartments are fitted up for their entertainment in the Eastern style, where dinners, composed of genuine Hindostanee dishes, are served up at the shortest notice ... Such ladies and gentlemen as may desirous of having India Dinners dressed and sent to their own houses will be punctually attended to by giving previous notice ...

The Morning Post, 2 February 1810

Dean Mahomet was an enterprising young man who grew up at the height of the rule of the East India Company, coming out of Orissa after one of its great famines. His portrait startled me when I saw it. He has a contemporary look about him, an air of competitive alertness and enterprise. It's a blend of the determination of young UPSC aspirants from Patna with the business minded Marwari boys I grew up with in Kolkata, who stuck to their family businesses but loved a dashing start-up story.

Mahomet wrote his *Travels* as a manuscript-length visiting card: he would use these memoirs to pry open the world of English patrons, setting himself up with unabashed shrewdness as an explainer of India:

As you may not understand those terms, I shall thus explain them to you.

    Comedan signifies – Captain

    Subidar – Lieutenant

    Jemidar – Ensign

    Howaldar – Serjeant

    Homaldar – Corporal

    Seapoy – Private soldier

    Tombourwalla – Drummer

    Basleewalla – Fife

    Trooheewalla – Trumpeter

The 'Travels' are often read only by academics, because of their slightly repetitive style, and because of Mahomet's over-careful eye on the English patrons whom he hoped to please. The first Indian writer in English wrote explicitly for a foreign audience, probably plagiarized his recollections of India and life as a Company man from a variety of sources, and committed the (present-day) cardinal sins of Explaining India and omitting the authentic India. He mentions the famine, and brushes it aside; his patrons will not be interested, he intuits, in the sufferings of Indians. (Mahomet was quite correct; in *Mookerjee's Magazine*, a popular periodical of the 19th century, one of the most controversial articles was a running series on the great Indian famines—written, the author explains, to correct the British silence on the subject.)

The critic Amardeep Singh writes:'It must have taken a considerable feat of the imagination for an Indian, however curious and intrepid, in that day and age to consider writing in a foreign tongue, in an age when one's country was observed and the observations set down almost exclusively by outsiders.'

Mahomet's subsequent career would have been of great interest to an Indian audience, but this pioneering desi writer had discovered for himself the sad truth of publishing—the local audience for his travels, Indians back home, didn't exist in numbers sufficient to make it worth his while.

And yet, as Amardeep notes, his story might have been a classic of early immigration. There is nothing that tells us how he felt when the ambitiously named Hindustani Coffee House failed, or whether he missed the monsoons, walking in Ireland's damp and London's grey fogs, wondering whether he could set up his own practice as a specialist in Oriental medicine. He did; he made a startling success of himself as a 'shampooing surgeon' in Brighton.

But having explained *bhishtis* and *oliphaunts*, he is silent on how he felt when he married his Anglo-Irish wife, whether he mourned the coffee—served South Indian style, by the yard, or in contemporary style, by the dish?—he had served at his Hindostanee Coffee House, whether he missed India's heat and dust, or preferred the placid hedgerows of the English countryside, the Brighton pavilions.

A year after Mahomet had tried his hand at providing fine Indian dining for patrons, he switched tack—perhaps because most old India hands and well-heeled Indian visitors to England imported their own cooks to make the rich curries they craved, and had no need to outsource banquets and biryanis.

Hindostanee Coffee-House, No. 34 George-street, Portman square-Mahomed, East-Indian, informs the Nobility and Gentry, he has fitted up the above house, neatly and elegantly, for the entertainment of Indian gentlemen, where they may enjoy the Hoakha, with real Chilm tobacco, and Indian dishes, in the highest perfection, and allowed by the greatest epicures to be unequalled to any curries ever made in England with choice wines, and every accommodation, and now looks up to them for their future patronage and support, and gratefully acknowledges himself indebted for their former favours, and trusts it will merit the highest satisfaction when made known to the public

The Times, 27 March 1811

Reading these lines today, I admire his ambition—Dean Mahomet was aiming higher than you would guess. Coffee houses were not the equivalent of today's cafes; they were a cross between the addas of Kolkata, informal versions of gentlemen's clubs or New York nightclubs, and which coffee house you patronized said a great deal about your politics, your interests and your social standing. In John Timbs's history of London's coffee houses, he charts their bumpy start: in 1657, James Farr, a barber-turned-owner of a coffee house, was called up at St. Dunstan's, for instance. The charge against him was that 'he annoyeth his neighbors by evil smells', incurred in the making and selling of a drink called coffee. Moreover, his chimney had a tendency to catch fire, to the understandable 'affrightment of his neighbors'.

Just two decades later, these minor inconveniences had been tempered by familiarity, and Timbs includes a song from Jordan's 'Triumphs of London', 1675:

You that delight in wit and mirth,
And love to hear such news
That come from all parts of the earth,
Turks, Dutch, and Danes, and Jews:
I'll send ye to the rendezvous,
Where it is smoking new;
Go hear it at a coffee-house,
It cannot but be true.
There battails and sea-fights are fought,
And bloudy plots displaid;
They know more things than e'er was thought,
Or ever was bewray'd:
No money in the minting-house
Is half so bright and new;
And coming from the Coffee-House,
It cannot but be true.

By 1715, there were two thousand coffee houses in London. The *National Review* had a description of how they functioned, which sounded a lot like the reminiscences I'd grown up with in Kolkata, of the equally popular addas where the intellectuals and thinkers of the day presided over discussions fuelled by kabiraji omelettes and endless cups of tea. London's coffee houses were divided by profession, trade, class and political affiliation. The lawyers had their favourite haunts near the Temple, the 'young bloods' patronized more fashionable places where they could drop in after theatre.

I was delighted to learn that it wasn't just the lawyers, the artists, the journalists and the 'Cits'—the bankers and stock market brokers of the era—who gathered over a cup of coffee; parsons went to Truby's or Child's. 'The gamesters shook their elbows in White's and the Chocolate-houses round Covent Garden,' the *National Review* writes. 'And the leading wits gathered at Will's, Button's, or Tom's, in Great Russell-street, where after the theatre was playing at piquet and the best of conversation till midnight.'

It was a surprisingly familiar scene. Starting work as a journalist in Delhi, I had been puzzled by the city's lack of Kolkata-style addas until one of South Delhi's more seasoned troupers explained the city to me. In those days, civil servants and lawyers frequented the Gymkhana Club; journalists huddled over cheap and endless pegs of rum at the Press Club; old Punjabi Partition-era families went to the Chelmsford; the Golf Club (notorious today for its steep membership fees) was home to golfers, but also diplomats, dashing businessmen and rising politicians. Artists and activists preferred the more humble Triveni Kala Sangam, rising to the dizzy heights of The Cellar when they were in funds, and intellectuals had long since stormed the Bastille of the India International Centre, where everyone under fifty was considered young and you had to be a septuagenarian to command any respect.

The Delhi clubs of the 1990s might have had a startling affinity with the London coffee houses of the 1720s, but it would have been far easier for Dean Mahomet to find acceptance in the England of the 1770s rather than in the racially segregated India of that period. I began to see where his chutzpah stemmed from: the barriers that were so insurmountable in India, where a soldier in the Bengal Army could not cross certain lines, were slightly more porous in England.

Ambitious to walk into this world as a rank outsider to England, and assuming that he could make a dent in it, Dean Mahomet over-reached himself. And yet, everything about his writing exudes confidence, from his careful but offhand inclusion of his own climb up the ranks of the Indian army, to the cheerful way in which he unpacked the mystic East. He laid down his chapters in the way a Kashmiri merchant unrolls his carpets, spreading out the wonders, the colourful patterns, the ancient weaves, and that is no doubt what he intended to do in London.

The Hindostanee Coffee House failed well; it was by accident or design the first Indian curry-house in London, and I felt a sudden stab of renewed fondness for Dean Mahomet when I saw its little plaque at George Street. It may have been too much, even for a man of his charm and obvious salesmanship, to rival the great coffee houses of the time. Michael Fisher records his sad advertisement, placed in the papers after his first venture ran aground:

MAHOMED, late of HINDOSTANEE Coffee House,
WANTS a SITUATION,
as BUTLER, in a Gentleman's Family, or as Valet to a Single
Gentleman.

But by 1814, he and his wife, Jane, had shifted to Bath, and taken up jobs as bathhouse keepers. And by 1838 he had established himself as a kind of superior spa owner.

He wrote only one other book, and that was a pamphlet: *Shampooing, or Benefits Resulting from the Use of Indian Medicated Vapour Bath, as introduced into this country by S.D. Mahomed (A Native of India)*. The bulk of the pamphlet is given over to testimonials from grateful clients cured of plumbago, nervous disorders, gouty affection and contraction, torpid livers and in the case of Mr Phillips, comedian, cured of loss of voice and violent hoarseness.

These testimonials were enlivened by odes to 'Mahomed, The Brighton Shampooing Surgeon', written by Mrs Kent and others. It was dreadful poetry—'O thou dark sage, whose vapour bath/ Makes muscular as his of Gath/ Limbs erst relaxed and limber'—but the poems, odes and letters testify to Mahomet's remarkable genius for marketing himself, as a writer or as the introducer of Indian massage techniques. (Shampoo, at that time, was a reference to *champi*, a massage, rather than head-baths.)

I imagine him, content with his Irish wife, rising up through the world of Bath, getting to know the gentry with the same ease in which he appeals to his British patrons in the Introduction to his memoirs, making himself indispensable. His Shampooing Salon promised novelty, gossip and wholesomeness, the three qualities easily discernible in his memoirs.

The salons were enormous, as elaborate as a Hindi film set and as gorgeously baroque; they took the English idea of taking the waters to a sybaritic, exotic, glamorously Oriental extreme. And they fulfilled a small part of the dream he'd had when he started his Coffee House. The *Brighton Gazette* recorded that ladies would make appointments to meet at Dean Mahomet's salon, and would 'often pass seven or eight hours together in the carpeted salon, telling stories, eating sweetmeats'.

Mahomet's salon appears to have inspired a brief vogue in henna body-painting: ladies would have their 'fair bodies' decorated in these traceries. The *Gazette* reporter was scandalized: 'This sort of pencil-work spreads over the bosom, and continues as low down as the navel ... all of this is displayed by their style of dress, every garment of which, even to the light gauze chemise, being open from the neck to that point: a singular taste, and certainly more barbarous than becoming.'

By the time of his death, his memoirs had almost been forgotten, except by scholars of Indian writing in English who marked it down as the first of its kind by an Indian author. But his legend has a gilded edge to it in Bath; Mr Mahomet, the former Company soldier, who rose through the ranks to become one of England's best-known purveyors of hospitality and entertainment, even perhaps a leader of fashion. It is an appealing story, in many ways true to the subsequent history of Indian writing in English: this first book, written by a man shaped by India, who would become an NRI, who was published abroad (still the height of many Indian writers' ambitions).

It seems even more fitting that Dean Mahomet had no special privileges; not the cushion of a rich family, nor did he inherit an easy, lazy network of friends abroad, as many Indians did and continue to do so through the accident of birth. Adventurer, entrepreneur, slick talker, a soldier-turned-businessman: his purpose was not grandiose, nor was he a pompous man. His words, and his memoir, were intended to pry open a new country.

The first book in Indian writing in English was nothing more or less than an advertisement for Mr Mahomet, a knock on the door that opened to the hard work, prosperity and larger opportunities offered by Brighton, London and Ireland.

★

I spend some time in George Street, trying to imagine what his coffee house would have been like in 1811, years before the Bangladeshi cooks turned a bastard dish called chicken tikka masala into the UK's favourite takeaway. I look at the plaque so long that one of London's policemen comes up to make gentle inquiries, and I fumble, trying to explain about Dean, and why he's so important to me.

Unless you study English at the MA level in Delhi University, the history of Indian writing in English—along with the contemporary histories of other Indian literatures—is invisible to most Indians today. Two centuries of rambunctious argument, scurrilous and serious periodicals, the eddies and jugalbandis between English in India and Bengali, Marathi, Gujarati, Tamil and a dozen other Indian languages have been elided and forgotten. Many people have a patchy, moth-eaten sense of how Indian writing in English developed: Dean Mahomet begat Raja Rao who begat Mulk Raj Anand, then there came G.V. Desani who begat Salman Rushdie, who begat Arundhati Roy and (each age gets the writers it deserves) so on, to the best-selling pulp fiction novelist Chetan Bhagat.

But no literature grows in isolation, and looking at the history of Indian writing in English is like looking at a silent movie made up of static postcards of Delhi, or Mumbai, or any other thronged Indian city: the life, the colour, the hubbub of hundreds of eager new writers and high-minded editors, peacocking poets and fiery-eyed pamphleteers, all of that has been bled out of collective memory. In the same year that Dean Mahomet wrote his *Travels*, the *Madras Hircarrah* (1794) started up, joining Hicky's *Bengal Gazette* (1780) and the *India Gazette* (1781); the first in a flood of periodicals and journals that would breathlessly, urgently take the news of India running along from one province to another.

The languages were thickly braided, right from the start—the *Awadh Punch*, brought out in Urdu, the *Modern Review*, an English periodical, and an assortment of papers in other Indian languages were equally influential, often addressing each other's editorials and articles in the casually Indian bi-or-tri-lingual manner.

Between 1823, when Raja Rammohan Roy wrote his 'Open Letter to King George' on free speech, and 1907, when Ramananda Chatterjee founded the *Modern Review*, here is a partial and incomplete list of books published and moments of literary importance:

1828 : Derozio, *The Fakeer of Jungheera*

1830 : Kashiprasad Ghose, *The Shair or Minstrel and Other Poems*

1831 : Krishna Mohan Banerjea, *The Persecuted*

1831 : K.M. Banerjea co-founds *The Enquirer*

1835 : Kylas Chunder Dutt, *A Journal of Forty Eight Hours of the Year 1945*

1835 : Macaulay's *Minute on Education*

1841 : Rajnarain Dutt, *Osmyn: an Arabian Tale*

1845 : Shoshee Chunder Dutt, *The Republic of Orissa*

1848 : Shoshee Chunder Dutt, *Miscellaneous Poems*

1849 : Michael Madhusudan Dutt, *The Captive Ladie*

1858 : Michael Madhusudan Dutt, *Sermista*

1861 : Michael Madhusudan Dutt, *Krishna Kumari*

1861 : *Mookerjee's Magazine* starts publication

1864 : Bankimchandra Chatterjee, *Rajmohan's Wife*

1866 : R.K. Pant, *The Boy of Bengal*

1868 : Tara Chand Mookerjee, *The Scorpions, or Eastern Thoughts*

1870 : *The Family Album: Dutts, Govin Chunder, Hur Chunder, Greece Chunder, Omesh Chunder*

1876 : Raj Lakshmi Deb, *The Hindu Wife*

1876 : *Mookerjee's Magazine* ceases publication

1877 : Toru Dutt dies

1877 : *Awadh Punch* begins operations

1878 : Anand Prasad Dutta, *The Indolence*

1879 : Toru Dutt (posthumous), *Bianca, or A Young Spanish Maiden*

1880 : Lal Behari Dey, *Bengal Peasant Life or History of a Bengal Raiyat*

1882 : Toru and Aru Dutt, *Ancient Ballads and Legends of Hindustan*

1882 : Behram Malabari, *Gujrat and the Gujratis*

1882	:	Bankimchandra Chatterjee, *Ananda Math*
1888	:	M. Dutta, Bijoy Chand, *An Indian Tale*
1894	:	Nagesh Vishwanath Pai, *Stray Sketches in Chakmapore from the Note-Book of an Idle Citizen*
1895	:	Kamala Satthianandhan, *Saguna: A Story of Native Christian Life*
1898	:	K. Chakravarti, *Sarla and Hinganal*
1901	:	Cornelia Sorabji, *Love and Life Behind The Purdah*
1902	:	Romesh Chunder Dutt, *An Economic History of India* (Vol. I)
1903	:	T. Ramakrishna Pillai, *Padmini*
1904	:	Romesh Chunder Dutt, *An Economic History of India* (Vol. II)
1905	:	Rokeya Sakhawat Hussein, *Sultana's Dream*
1905	:	S.K. Ghose, *1001 Indian Nights*

The past is an inheritance, and how it reaches you depends on many things—how conscientious your family is, the presence or absence of public libraries, what they teach in schools, whether you're from a caste whose privileges include owning their history or from a caste low on the totem pole, deprived of its own history along with so much else. My Bengali inheritance had arrived more or less in one piece; the history of Bengali literature was easily available on bookshelves, and it was drummed into the heads of students in school.

If that wasn't enough, a particularly formidable aunt sent me spinning defensively towards Saratchandra and Bankimchandra early on, by sneering at us *injiri* (English-speaking) types, and betting that I knew more Shakespeare than Sarat. My father's parents, my Thakurda and Thakurma, were kinder, but thanks to their frequent and long stays at our home, Bengali remained a living language to us, its soft, rippling cadences a welcome relief after the crisp apple of English, and the earthier sitaphal strains of Delhi's Hindi.

But no one had given my generation the keys to Indian writing in English, the newest of India's languages, barely three hundred years resident in a country where the oldest spoken languages could be traced back to a thousand years and more. Or, for that matter, the keys to our own classics, in a multitude of languages.

I had come across the poems of the *Therigatha* in my student years in a moment of idle browsing on the sparsely stocked library shelves. Mutta's lines caught my ear:

> So free am I
> So gloriously free
> Free from three petty things—
> From mortar, from pestle and from my twisted lord.

She startled me, the sudden sharp bite of that last phrase—'my twisted lord'—setting out all the bitterness of all the women through all the ages who had not been allowed to choose their own lives or marriages for themselves.

I had read on and on, and it was only when I finished reading the verses of Mutta and Ubbiri and the rest that it occurred to me to ask what it was that I held in my hands: the poems of the First Buddhist Women, sometimes claimed as the oldest collection of written poems by women anywhere in the world. How strongly Mutta's voice had echoed from the sixth century down to ours, as though there had been no passage of time in between. Her anger carried down the ages, and so did her rejoicing; no silverfish had nibbled at her poems, nothing had blunted her voice, in those 2,500 years since she had lived, written and died. English, in comparison, was an infant among India's babble of tongues.

I wanted to tell the policeman all this, and to tell him how the hidden histories of Indian writing in English had unfolded slowly for people like me, book reviewers outside the academy. There were no public libraries and few archives open to the curious reader who was not a scholar; the past had to be reshaped from private collections and each generation seemed to forget and re-remember its own past all over again.

For me, Arvind Krishna Mehrotra's *An Illustrated History of Indian Writing in English* had opened up part of such a past, and Amit Chaudhuri's *The Picador Book of Modern Indian Literature* had placed it in context. There was the birdcage lift that led to Adil Jussawala's eagle's nest of a home in Mumbai where the poet lived, perched high above the city, and where he had become the memory-keeper for his generation of Indian poets. When you walked into rooms, brushing against piles of books, papers and photocopied manuscripts, you were walking down the aisles of a history that no one else thought valuable enough to record—the lives of the poets, including (but not limited to) Arun Kolatkar, Nissim Ezekiel, Dom Moraes, Jeet Thayil, Eunice de Souza, Melanie Silgardo.

The Internet had brought archives of old Indian newspapers online, and I stared at their quaint mastheads, watching as the images slowly downloaded in another era, forming themselves into running messengers or proud lions, or figures of Saraswati, the goddess of learning herself, with Bengal's greatest writers (Bankimchandra, R.C. Dutt, Tagore and company), swathed comfortably into the folds of her Oriental-Occidental robe. But none of these time-travelling excursions would have been undertaken without Dean Mahomet's memoirs, the book that lit the fuse of my curiosity.

It is impossible to say all of this to a policeman, even one as kind and patient as that London bobby was; so instead, I explain about Dean Mahomet's coffee house, and add that he was the first writer from India to publish a full-length book in English.

'Is that so?' says the policeman. 'And you wouldn't be after being a writer yourself, would you?'

I am susceptible to Irish accents and wish I could say yes, so as not to disappoint him. But it will be a full decade or more before I wrote my first two novels. The ink-stained, pottering life of the professional book reviewer has closed comfortably around me. I like meeting writers and listening to them, but there is a sixteen-foot high boundary wall between their lives and mine.

'No,' I say. 'I'm a reader, mostly; I review books.'

The policeman leans over and looks at me, very hard. His eyes are a piercing green, like the eyes of a very kind cat I happen to know back home.

'Is that so?' he says.

Something serious in his voice brings forth an answering seriousness from me. I look at the plaque, commemorating a man who stepped accidentally into history with his one published book, and I say: 'But some day, I'll write my own.'

And hurrying back to the house of my friends, I forget all about the policeman until many years later, when in another place and another time, I begin writing the first, shaky sentences of *The Wildings*.

Back then, it took less than half a chapter before I stalled, falling out of the sky of writing like a biplane whose propellers had stopped whirring, and I wondered what had made me think I could be a writer.

Unbidden, in Delhi's rising April heat, the flat mizzling rain of London drums on our small verandah and the slate-grey skies above George Street replaced the harsh blaring light above Nizamuddin, and I heard in my mind the policeman's kind, steadying reply: 'Young lady,' he'd said, 'I have no doubt that you will.'

I held those words to me like a talisman over the next few years, as I stumbled into the strange new world of writing with as little grace and as much curiosity as I had first stumbled into London all that time ago.

(Written between 2005 and 2014.)

3

How To Read in Indian

Outside the heavy wooden gates that guard the Neemrana
Fort-Palace against unwanted day visitors, local villagers and
the curious, a dusty, winding path leads back to the highway.
In 2003, this path was no more than a narrow lane, so narrow that
two vehicles could not pass side-by-side, and to find it blocked by the
carcass of a dead pig brought a caravan of writers to an unexpected halt.

The writers had been brought to Neemrana by the Indian Council
for Cultural Relations (ICCR) and by a team of enthusiasts—current
Jaipur Literature Festival co-director Namita Gokhale among them—
who felt that India needed a festival of its own.

Delhi in particular, and India in general, was no stranger to these
events. The Mughals held their grand mushairas, so splendid, so
challenging and so famous that the writer Farhatullah Baig could
create an imaginary *Last Mushaira* of poets from across the country,
with imaginary sawaal-jawaabs, in the court of the last Mughal, Bahadur
Shah Zafar.

The tradition continued, as Nirad C. Chaudhuri recorded in 1937:
'I had a joyous feeling at the prospect of going to the conference at
Patna. Such gatherings were a typical cultural recreation of the Bengalis
working and settled outside Bengal, the expatriate Bengalis as they

were called: the Bengali Diaspora, who never forgot their Zion in
Kolkata. Thus, in every important city or town in northern India there
was a cultural club to keep alive the traditions of Kolkata life. Patna
was a big city, the capital of Bihar and Orissa, and it also had a large
Bengali population ... The sessions of the conference were very well
attended, actually in hundreds. In India, lectures always attract very
large audiences, however abstruse the subjects.'

One of the big questions at any gathering of this sort is a simple
but unsettling one: what does this curiosity mean? The audience at
Neemrana was missing—the idea was to allow writers to spend time
with each other, undisturbed by the voices of the masses. They would
go back to Delhi and spend another two days discussing versions of
the topics they had already discussed, this time with the public in
respectful attendance.

In twenty-first century Delhi, book launches and festivals like the
one at Neemrana were not precisely the kind of 'cultural recreation'
Nirad C. Chaudhuri spoke of, which had its roots in the tradition
of the adda, the teahouse discussions for which cities like Kolkata
and Mumbai had once been famous. Book launches were symbolic
displays of an author's importance, often displays of status and power,
in a city ruled by the need for both; they were, geographically, held
almost exclusively in South Delhi, and areas like Pitampura, Badarpur,
Shahdara and Shalimar Bagh lay well outside the charmed circles of
the India Habitat Centre and Aqua at The Park hotel.

As the writer Amit Chaudhuri said, Delhi's incestuousness had
infected literary circles as well; the capital, notoriously an insiders'
city, had bred a culture where everyone in publishing knew everyone
in the media and everyone on the writers' circuit. It was the joint
family approach to literature, and while it had an upside—a newcomer
could find his or her feet quite quickly, transitioning to insider status
in less than a year—it was also, in many ways, damaging, masking a
hollowness that showed in the shrinking spaces for book reviews. Often,
instead of substantial literary debates, we made do with manufactured
controversies and warmed-over gossip.

Publishing in English had flourished in the last fifteen years,

generating an appetite for what often seemed the wrong things—the
spurious fame of the ten-second TV appearance, the appearance of
a world where literary importance was measured by column inches,
prizes won and sales figures. By 2003, there were two small but telling
signs that a certain kind of literary culture was on the wane—many of
the great critics of their time, the poet and translator Arvind Krishna
Mehrotra, the scholar Alok Rai, the editor and author Mrinal Pande,
and the poet and critic Rukmini Bhaya Nair among them, had almost
stopped writing for book review pages. The space for translations and
for the voices of writers who wrote outside the gates of English, had
also diminished in the world of the English language media.

The flame of the mushairas of Lucknow and Allahabad had flickered
out, the few that remained were pale imitations of the gatherings
of the past. In the 1990s and 2000s, though India had never had an
Edinburgh-style festival of its own, the Sahitya Akademi was adept at
combining large audiences with very abstruse subjects.

Parle or Britannia Glucose biscuits would be served with chai, and
the appearance of greasy samosas or pakoras would mark the presence
of speakers of great significance. In fact, the Sahitya Akademi held its
own festival of writing, focusing on regional literature, while Neemrana
2003 was under way, in a subtle underlining of the tensions between
the Indian writers in English and the Rest of Indian Literature. (This
was often, much to everyone's annoyance, abbreviated as the IWE
versus the Bhasha School, Bhasha being inaccurate shorthand for 'all
Indian regional languages except for English'.)

For two days, then, Neemrana played host to the Indian literary
pantheon. The writers, separated from their audiences back in Delhi,
squabbled, doodled and argued their way through an endless series
of panel discussions. A heated argument between Naipaul and the
German ambassador's wife had the Nobel laureate threatening to
leave; a clash between Naipaul and Nayantara Sahgal fuelled further
gossip; Khushwant Singh slammed regional writing for failing to
produce biographies and innovative non-fiction; Srilal Shukla watched
sardonically as another version of *Raag Darbari*, his classic satire of
intrigues and power plays in post-Independence India, played itself out.

In an interview elsewhere, Kiran Nagarkar said: 'At that Neemrana conference there were about ten sessions, and all of them essentially became incarnations of the theme of Indianness. All they could think of was this question of being an Indian writer. And it pissed me off no end! For the simple reason that I am not setting out to be an Indian author. But at the same time I cannot for one moment forget that whatever I write comes from an Indian consciousness.'

The debates could swing from amity to bitterness in a second, and then back again; the argument between English versus the Rest of India has roots that go back almost two centuries.

'Who is an Indian writer?'

In the late nineteenth century, Bankimchandra Chatterjee, author of India's first novel in English (*Rajmohan's Wife*), had a political change of heart. He had enthusiastically learned to write in English, the language that had brought him and many others in Bengal a refreshing sense of a wider world and of Europe's debates over civil liberties. The switch he made to Bengali when he chose to return to Bengali was first a political, and then progressively an emotional, choice.

He had struggled with *Rajmohan's Wife*, encountering almost all the problems that Indian writers in English would subsequently face. Novels in English by non-white authors were treated as charming curiosities well into the 1970s, in fact, where a reviewer in England would call V.S. Naipaul's *The Mystic Masseur* a 'little savory from the colonial islands'. For Bankim, the strongest reasons to remain a Bengali writer intertwined patriotism and a love of the mother tongue. He had spent time on indigo plantations, recording the casual and savage oppressions of British rule. He had fallen out of love with a way of looking at the world, as much as he had fallen out of love with English; and the question of who he was writing for became urgent in his mind. He could not, he felt, write unless he was addressing his people, his countrymen, in their tongue.

He never published again in English after *Rajmohan's Wife*, and a few years after that novel came out, Bankim would gently rebuke the economic historian R.C. Dutt for wanting to write in a language that neither writer could ever claim, truly, as their own. (Even their names offer evidence of confusion: Bankimchandra's full name was Bankimchandra Chatterjee, but many Bengalis will use the original version of the surname—Chattopadhyaya—repudiating the Anglicization, and R.C. Dutt's second and third names are similarly compromised, Anglicizations of Chandra and Datta.)

A century after Bankimchandra, Mulk Raj Anand (the novelist died in 2004) would make a very Indian complaint against the Ur-novel that signalled the beginning of the success story of Indian literature—Salman Rushdie's *Midnight's Children*, which has sparked more ambition, unfortunately, than discussion of Rushdie's anguished and subversive retelling of contemporary Indian history. *Midnight's Children* covers two Partitions—the creation of India and the bloody birth of Bangladesh—but in popular imagination, it has been reduced to a series of banalities, all of them prefaced by the adjective 'Booker-winning'.

Mulk Raj Anand's complaint against *Midnight's Children* is worth re-reading; his letter, written in 1982, begins with dismissal, and one can imagine how he would have approached the gathering that took place at Neemrana. He also appears to completely miss the point of *Midnight's Children*, and that too is part of the history of misreadings and misunderstandings that are woven into the history of Indian writing in English.

The question of Salman Rushdie's novel does not arise as far as I am concerned. Rushdie is a clever young man (perhaps too clever by half as the English say). He writes very eloquently in the English language but in *Midnight's Children*, he is aping the recent Americans by disembowelling his mother, painting his grandmother as a scheming old witch, his grandfather as a burglar, his father as a mere crook, and he himself as superior to all his colleagues. I suppose he is brighter than the others, but in the kind of way in which the average advertising copywriter is brighter than every other copywriter. India appears to be a spittoon to Salman

Rushdie. I suppose it is as it was a vast sewage to Katherine Mayo
before the war, or it is the 'Continent of Circe' to that third-grade
actor Nirad Chaudhuri, as it is 'an Area of Darkness' to V.S. Naipaul,
as it is 'Heat and Dust' to Ruth Jhabvala . . .

That sweeping condemnation is interesting on two counts. It attacks
the outsider's account of India—Naipaul, who travelled extensively in
the country, and Rushdie, who grew up here and whose book is steeped
in nostalgia for Mumbai, are clubbed with Katherine Mayo (whose
'drain inspector's report' is still, inexplicably, on the list of books banned
in India), with Nirad C. Chaudhuri, proud dhoti-wearing imperialist,
and Ruth Jhabvala, another writer often seen as an outsider despite
her years of residence in Delhi.

I found it fascinating that Mulk Raj Anand pilloried Rushdie for
the crime of disrespect to the family, that he complained—as critics
often do, of Rushdie and other writers on India—that the writer
hadn't been polite enough, that they shouldn't have written so openly,
or so critically, of family, or community, or country. There is a deep
area of discomfort here, in these critiques, in the constant battle over
authenticity and viewpoint that is summarized in the crime of being
rude to one's elders.

As the authors sat in the cool conference rooms and shaded alcoves
of Neemrana, discussing the burning questions of the day—'Who
Is An Indian Writer?'—tensions had been growing between the
village and the hotel management, not an uncommon situation in
today's India.

The hotel had come up out of the tired, worn-out remains of a
derelict fort hotelier and restorer Aman Nath and his partner, the
late Francis Wacziarg had poured love, imagination and cold cash into
revamping the place and running it as one of India's earliest boutique
hotels. But the village that shared the hill with the fort had its own
set of demands (some unreasonable, for sums of money that were
neither owed nor justified, some reasonable, such as the complaint
that the lives of the villagers were interrupted by the comings and
goings of the hotel guests). Neemrana's villagers knew the simmering

resentment that accompanies being on the wrong side of a pair of gates that will always be locked against you and your kind.

And so as the writers left, Amitav Ghosh, the still-ruffled Naipaul, Sitanshu Yashaschandra, Shashi Deshpande, they were brought to a halt, by the tensions and demands of the world outside. A pig had met its untimely end under the wheels of some visitor's car, probably one of the media caravans who had descended, in Ruchir Joshi's merciless phrase, 'like flies on the dead carcass of the moment' as Neemrana erupted in the last fiery but ultimately irrelevant literary dispute of the conference. (Most Indian literary disputes in the closely-knit and the sometimes airless world of Indian writing in English were of this nature—they generated intense heat, passionate argument and were of ephemeral consequence.)

An argument erupted over who was responsible for the pig-murder, and who—the hotel, the guests, our car—would pay compensation. It continued until someone found a plastic bag, picked up the pig's carcass and deposited it on the side of the road, an action so baffling in its disregard for ritual pollution that the arguments stopped short, and our vehicles were allowed to go on, back to Delhi. The pig lay on the side of the road, a thin line of blood lipsticking its jaw, the only evidence of the accidental violence that had occurred; it looked serene and oddly composed.

Writing for the West: Dean's Descendants

Almost all the arguments that came up at Neemrana had come up before, in the messy and amnesia-ridden history of Indian writing in English. Veterans of Delhi's book launches—events that had grown from slightly dour lectures at the venerable India International Centre to gossip-fuelled Page 3 dos hosted at a five-star hotel poolside, or one of the city's flashier restaurants—knew that at some point during the Q&A, the author du jour would be asked: 'Who are you writing for?' The implication was often made even more explicit: 'Are you writing for us in India or for foreign readers?'

It would come up again and again; for years, the way in which

Naipaul's works were discussed in India was infected with this viral anxiety. His India books were rarely discussed as part of his general oeuvre of travel writing, where he had been equally provocative and just as willing to offer sharp, unvarnished, if not always accurate opinions. The few historians and critics who offered more nuanced criticisms of Naipaul's writing—asking whether his view of Indian history was even accurate, for instance—were drowned out by the many who saw him just as another chronicler of India's heat and dust and filth.

In the 1990s and the 2000s, discussions of that twinned-in-opposition pair, Naipaul and Rushdie, degenerated under the weight of gossip. Except for a few considered pieces by cultural critics like Amitava Kumar or historians such as Ramachandra Guha and William Dalrymple, the shape of what we argued about when we take Naipaul's view of history versus Rushdie's perspective on India shimmered and disappeared under an avalanche of stories about spats and divorces, short-lived feuds; they had been turned into performers in a circus act, not writers.

In a sense, Indians had always been sensitive as a nation to what was written about them; non-fiction about the US, for instance, seldom drew as many reactions, fuelled equally by anxiety and exasperation. The anxiety came, in the reading of many, from seeing any narrative that interrupted the neatly seductive story of India Shining. And the exasperation came from a smaller band of Indians who were tired of having what they already knew and considered familiar explained to them in exhausting and unnecessary detail.

This debate would resurface in 2011, as Pankaj Mishra attacked Patrick French for missing the real India stories in his 'intimate biography of India'. French and Mishra skirmished for a while in the pages of *Outlook*. The broad thrust of Mishra's argument was that French had overlooked, or provided superficial accounts of, the darker side of contemporary Indian history—the poverty, the real hungers and tragedies behind the Maoist conflict. French contested Mishra's reading of his book, and it became clear that the real argument was over divergent views of India—was this a country progressing despite the burden of history and the indifference of the middle classes, or was this a country still mired in ancient inequities?

As the debate overflowed onto other editorial pages, it seemed that there could be no meeting ground here. One part of the debate—a small but not unimportant part—concerned that original, anxious question, which I'll take the liberty of recasting slightly: who is writing about us? Do they have the right to tell our stories, and are they telling the right ones?

It is clear from the very first work in the corpus of Indian writing in English — Dean Mahomet's *Travels* — that a certain kind of writer wrote explicitly for the West. 'The people of India, in general, are peculiarly favoured by Providence in the possession of all that can cheer the mind and allure the eye, and tho' the situation of Eden is only traced in the Poet's creative fancy, the traveller beholds with admiration the face of this delightful country, on which he discovers tracts that resemble those so finely drawn by the animated pencil of Milton. You will here behold the generous soil crowned with various plenty; the garden beautifully diversified with the gayest flowers diffusing their fragrance on the bosom of the air; and the very bowels of the earth enriched with inestimable mines of gold and diamonds . . . As I have now given you a sketch of the manners of my country; I shall proceed to give you some account of myself.'

Every sin in the list of charges flung at the heads of Indian writers in English is represented in the *Travels*: Dean Mahomet explains words like purdah and chik ('purdoe' and 'cheeque', in his spelling), uses Anglicized spellings for names of places and people (Bightaconna for Baithakkhana, Bestys for bheeshti), is guilty of exoticism, devoting three paragraphs to a description of a Nabob who enters in grand style, provides a glossary (two, actually) and makes sweeping generalizations about the customs of the Hindoos and Mohametans.

But Dean Mahomet's travels, despite frequent accusations that he had borrowed large chunks from other writers' tales, have one merit: they claim to be an insider's account. Previous travellers to India, from Thomas Roe to Hiuen Tsang, may have become insiders after their years in the country; in India's vast array of regional languages, the theme of the wanderer and the curious traveller has a centuries-old tradition, especially in religious and spiritual writing.

In the 1790s, what Dean Mahomet managed to sell in the grand bazaar of English writing was not just his exoticism; it was also his position as an insider, as an Indian who knew the country in a way that the Angrez may not. He was probably the first Indian writer to act, unselfconsciously, as travel guide.

Before 1857: A Million Mutinies

The next two major accounts by Indian writers in English were significantly different from Mahomet's travelogue. In 1835, K.C. Dutt wrote *A Journal of Forty Eight Hours of The Year 1945*, a slim, early attempt at a speculative novel set over a hundred years in the future. In 1845, just a little under two decades before Bankimchandra published *Rajmohan's Wife*, S.C. Dutt wrote a similarly slim but ambitious work of fiction, *The Republic of Orissa: Annals from the Pages of the Twentieth Century*. Both works were published in the *Kolkata Literary Gazette*; established in the 1780s, this periodical also had the distinction of publishing writers like the poet and playwright Michael Madhusudan Dutt, another pioneer who struggled to find a balance between the seductions of English and the more solid, comforting attractions of his mother tongue, Bengali.

Indeed, between Dean Mahomet and Bankimchandra, there lay an ocean of Dutts. The most famous was Toru, the poet whose verses drew abundant admirers, especially the one about Sita, forlorn after her abduction by Ravana, languishing in the gardens of Lanka. It paved the way for many of Sarojini Naidu's effusions. Toru's promise was precocious, and she died very young, at an age youthful enough to embalm her legend forever.

Though much of her poetry seems agonizingly laboured to a modern eye, she was strikingly modern by the standards of her day— far less prolix than, say, Aurobindo, and at least as sensitive in some of her lines as Derozio. But she was just one member of a family that, in many ways, embodied the new breed of Anglicized Bengalis (and other Indians) who were reading the works of Empire—at first with unstinting admiration, and shortly with a far more critical eye.

Toru's father Govin Chunder Dutt, her uncles Hur and Greece and their nephew Omesh compiled poems for *The Dutt Family Album* (1870). Some of these poems were reasonably good; some were breathtakingly terrible:

> Home bounded little Edward,
> With loud and joyous cries,
> The rose-red deepened on his cheeks
> And triumph lit his eyes . . .

Some poems were demonstrations of the pitfalls that await those who write for 'The West':

> And should an English landscape ever pall . . .
> Where shall we wander?
> In the fields of France?
> Or classic Italy's wave-saluted shores?
> Or dearer Scotland's barren heaths and moors?

Toru's poetry was considerably better than her uncles' attempts. She, Shoshee Chunder Dutt, Kylas Chunder Dutt were cousins from different branches of the family. Toru's writings were published much later than Kylas or Shoshee's books—her first book, *A Sheaf Gleaned In French Fields*, came out in 1876, a year before she died. Her second book, *Le Journal de Mademoiselle d'Arver*, was published posthumously in 1879. The family home was in Rambagan, a part of Kolkata, and the Dutts were collectively dubbed the 'Rambagan nest of singing birds' for their love of poetry and fashionable dabbling in literature.

Her cousins Shoshee and Kylas were prescient, their slim books drawing on the undercurrents of unrest and discontent with British rule that marked the decades that led up to the 1857 war of independence. Shoshee and Kylas were in many ways truly Macaulay's children, from

Shoshee's glad embrace of Christianity to their mutually shared belief that English was far superior to their native Bengali.

Indeed, Macaulay's infamous *Minute on Indian Education* ('we have to educate a people who cannot at present be educated in their mother-tongue') came out in 1835, the same year that Kylas Chunder Dutt's work of speculative fiction was published. 'The languages of western Europe civilized Russia. I cannot doubt that they will do for the Hindoo what they have done for the Tartar,' Macaulay observed.

And yet, the first serious work of fiction, speculative or otherwise, in English by an Indian writer was Kylas's destabilizing vision of an India in 1945, rising up against the 'subaltern oppression' of British rule, where 'the dagger and the bowl were dealt out with a merciless hand' by the 'British barbarians'. His projected rebellion fails; but the man who leads the Indians against Governor Lord Fell Butcher is a graduate fluent in English, using his education against the British. In the light of the way in which the Revolt of 1857 garnered public support in India just twenty-two years after Kylas penned his fantasy, it's interesting that he imagines a rebellion supported by 'many of the most distinguished men—Babus, Rajas and Nababs'. And he is prescient when he writes that the 'contagion of Rebellion would probably have infested every city in the kingdom, had it only had time to perfect its machinations'.

Ten years later, Shoshee could imagine a happier ending for those who would rise up in revolt. 'The Republic of Orissa' is written as a page from the imagined annals of the twentieth century, an alternate history imagined as the truth. Orissa is independent, and extending its borders into British India, ruled by 'untamed men', tribes who combine great strength with intrepid courage. If K.C. Dutt's fantasy was about language-enabled rebellion, S.C. Dutt's fantasy, set in the twentieth century, went much further: imagining a future India where the British have been defeated, and an independent democratic republic has been established in the state of Orissa. This fantasy of political independence followed on the heels of K.C. Dutt's dream of linguistic independence, both anticipating the events of 1857.

In Shoshee Chunder Dutt's reworking of the noble savage theme, the tribes—freely exoticized—rise up against the British after a

Slavery Act is passed in 1916. They are goaded into final action by the imprisonment of publishers, printers and the suppression of a free press. (Present-day governments might want to take note of Dutt's assumption that the curbing of free expression would bring on rebellion faster than a Slavery Act, in his vision of India.) As the fierce and courageous Bheekoo Barik confronts 'drunken John Bull', the question the tribals aim to answer is crucial: are the Juggomohuns and Gocooldosses, the Opertees and Bindabun Sirdars fit persons to be intrusted with the management of a vast empire?

Shoshee's answer is a stirring yes, and the rest of *The Republic of Orissa* introduces a full-scale tribal rebellion, aided by beautiful women disguised as fakirs and other little flourishes of the novelist's art.

'The Baboo's style is clear and good,' said *The Englishman*, kindly. 'It will be a grand thing indeed for India when all her most influential families can be as much Anglicized as this Hindu gentleman,' wrote the *Kolkata Literary Gazette*. They were responding, however, to Shoshee Chunder Dutt's poetry, and his articles on Hindu caste and practices— not to this vision of triumphant native rebellion that ends with the overthrow of the British.

In many ways, Shoshee had started out as exactly the kind of Baboo Macaulay had imagined—in a rant that praised the superiority of English over Bengali literature, he also refers to the native press as 'servile, low and indecent'.

But as time went by, his writings made the British who had praised him for being such a good Baboo more and more uncomfortable, whether it was his diary of a Kerani (published in *Mookerjee's Magazine*, a famous periodical of the time run by the flamboyant, opium-smoking Shambhu Chander Mukherjee), or this subtly subversive early work. The natives had taken to English, as Macaulay had hoped, but they were restless. As the first two works of speculative fiction in Indian writing in English prove, what they had to say in that tongue was not just prescient, anticipating the events of 1857, but also unabashedly subversive.

The lure of English was complex. Shoshee Chunder Dutt's arguments extolling the superiority of English are not unfamiliar ones.

English was the gateway language to the wider Western world, Bengali had once been a great literature but had stagnated, and because English had received so much from so many countries, we could not expect Indian languages to match its breadth and scope.

Thomas Babington Macaulay would have been pleased at Shoshee's willingness to raise English higher than any Asian language, though he would have missed the subtle but key differences in their arguments. Macaulay belonged to the school of Englishmen who believed, never having read seriously in any Indian language, that all of Indian and perhaps Asian literature could be replaced by one good bookcase of English writers. Shoshee's argument, repeated down the decades and centuries by Indian writers all the way to Nirad C. Chaudhuri and beyond, was that Indian languages and literatures had been of immense importance, but they were now waning.

Behind the baroque prose, the rolling, impassioned sentences, you might sense two things: Shoshee's excitement about this new language has a great deal to do with the ideas he encountered via English, ideas of sovereignty and the dignity of man, of revolution and freedom. And second, he makes the argument for himself as much as for his readers; he wants to be convinced that the language in which he now writes and thinks is the one that will carry him beyond the provincial, hidebound world of old Bengal.

The Little Magazines

He and his cousins were part of an avalanche of Indians—in Bengal, but also in Maharashtra, Gujarat, Tamil Nadu, anywhere that the printing press thrived—who had discovered the lure of the little magazines.

The printing press was the latest in new technology at that time, as freshly minted as the Kindle might be today, and far more revolutionary in its impact. It's hard to imagine the excitement Indians felt, and how joyously they took to the new professions—typesetter, printer, newspaper proprietor, pamphleteer, often bringing to the imported form of the essay or the travelogue a distinctly Indian spin. Most of the new Indian writers arrived at English via the broad rivers of their own rich languages and literatures.

The printing press may have been one of the most unintentionally subversive articles of trade ever imported into India. Brought into the country to print Bibles and spread the missionary message, the presses across the country were soon set to other uses. In these fledgling little magazines, mixed in with the extraordinary effusions of the early Indo-Anglian poets (Kasiprasad Ghose's unintentionally funny elegy 'To A Dead Crow', etc.), imported ideas of liberation and home-grown appeals to revolution and sedition thrived, from South India to Bengal and then in the cross-hatchings of the Western Ghats on the other side.

The intense and immediate love that the educated Indian bore the printing press finds an extreme expression in Rabindranath Tagore's *Nashta Neer* (The Nest Destroyed), which Satyajit Ray made into the classic film *Charulata*. The other woman in Charu's relationship with her husband, Bhupati, is the printing press that ultimately bankrupts him. As Bhupati focuses on his journals—very similar in description to the *Indian Messenger* or the *Modern Review*, the argumentative Bengali Indian's preferred field of battle—he neglects his young, restless wife to the point where he knows nothing about her writing ambitions, her very modern short stories. I admit this is a minority point of view, but to me, the real sadness of Charulata was not the sterility of the marriage, or Charu's stormy brush with extramarital love. It was that if only Bhupati and Charu had known each other better, they might have found happiness as a Woolfeian literary couple—love among the leading and the typos.

Many of the Indian printing presses had mildly deviant histories. The presses set up by the Portuguese in Goa started off well, but died out because of the refusal of the Portuguese to print in the local languages. In about three generations, all that was left of them was rusting iron, corroded and pitted by saltwater, and a collection of Bibles and dictionaries. (Dictionaries, or language primers, were at one time intensely prized and fought over. One of the details James Clavell gets right in *Shogun* is the jealous zeal with which the missionaries guarded their dictionaries and lists of words—those were the keys to a country, a treasury, a court, not to be traded lightly.)

The best-known and most influential press after the Portuguese ones closed down was set up in Tranquebar, now Tharangambadi in Tamil Nadu's Nagapattinam district. The printing press narrowly survived piracy on the high seas; the East India Company ship, despatched in 1711, was taken prisoner by the French off the coast of Brazil and plundered. The press, some books and paper were in the hold—in those days, printing presses were greatly coveted and were often pirated from one ship to another—and journeyed on to India after the ship was released. Jonas Finke, the teacher who had accompanied the press to pass on what he knew of printing, was not so lucky: after being held as a prisoner of war, he was released, but died of a fever around the Cape of Good Hope.

It is unclear whether the Danish missionaries knew about the fate of the jealously guarded Portuguese presses, now silenced from their excessive linguistic caution, but by 1712, they had begun printing in Tamil. The mission in Tranquebar had the blessings of the king of Denmark: in a letter, he bestowed on them the privilege of printing without supervision from the Danish Censor, so that they might more speedily convert 'the heathen'. Bartholomäus Ziegenbalg, who headed the Tranquebar mission, had developed some respect for the local love of learning and sourced books in Tamil from the interiors whenever he could.

Local legend goes that Ziegenbalg learned his Tamil letters on the black, rocky coast of Tranquebar; he married the woman who taught him how to tell her that he loved her, tracing one alphabet after another into the fine-grained sand on that golden, pebbled beach. (A less romantic version suggests that the local schoolmaster taught him the alphabet, and that he learned to read from his interpreter, Aleppa.) By 1709, Ziegenbalg could boast: 'I have scarcely read a German or Latin book, but have given up all my time to reading Malabar books, have talked diligently with the heathen . . . I have been enabled to write several books in Tamil.' Among the first books the Tranquebar press produced was a Tamil Bible; among the second was a Tamil language primer.

When I visited some years ago, I found that the area still loves the smell of printing. In the port town of Karaikal, about fifteen kilometres away from Tranquebar, a collective of enterprising women run India's only all-woman printing press. They used old lead handset type to print out my name as a gift—Nila Writer in blue letters as wavy and graceful as a sarus crane's footprint—and nodded when we asked about Ziegenbalg. Tamil Selvi, the manager of the Women's Press, showed me the heavy rollers of their press and said, 'Just the same as the Danish one, same kind of machine', and the centuries that separated her and the Danish printers rolled away as though no time had passed.

In the nineteenth century, the little magazines gladly gave space to impassioned broadsides, and much more besides. The zest of the journals and periodicals that flourished a century ago still jumps off their crumbling pages, shining out despite the pompous phrases. Political commentary, fledgling literature and (admittedly terrible) poetry reigned.

Many magazine proprietors took for their model a British original, subverting it in the way of wily Orientals. About 140 years ago, the *Indian Charivari* joined a long and distinguished list of magazines inspired by the satirical eye of *Punch*. The *Parsi Punch*, one of the earliest imitators of the original, was to transmute itself into the *Hindi Punch*, and Muhammad Sajjad Hussain was to make the *Oudh Punch* famous as an 'Indian vernacular serio-comic paper, the first of its kind ever published in Northern India'.

The *Indian Charivari* began by reviewing, often favourably, such subjects as the efforts of British painters at the Simla Exhibition, but moved rapidly into political commentary. It was famous for bringing an Indian style to its lampoons, using references to Raja Ravi Varma's paintings and local folk art in its caricatures—including a celebrated one of Lord Curzon, depicted as the goddess Saraswati, in a commentary on educational reform.

Mookerjee's Magazine was founded slightly earlier, in 1861, and was among a score of emerging journals published across the country, from

Bengal to Madras, that allowed themselves extraordinary licence. Its stated aim was to cover 'Politics, Literature, Sociology and Art', and within a few years, it had drawn criticism. This was not for its poetry, which was in the best traditions of splendidly awful Indo-Anglian verse (Song of the Indian Conservative, for instance, or an ode to Mohinee, the Hindu Maiden), but for its politics.

In its pages, a defender writes: 'That *Mookerjee's Magazine* should be deemed notorious, and the quality of its articles depreciated by certain Anglo-Indian writers who see nothing commendable in any independent Native undertaking is not at all surprising. Chime in with their views and write yourself down a humble admirer of Hugrut and his oracles, and you are sure to be petted and fondled as a very respectable Hottentot . . .'

The contents of Mookerjee's ranged from the comfortably obscure—a plaintive essay asking 'Where Shall the Baboo Go', much pedantry about Indian religious texts—to the surprisingly contemporary.

In the present-day obsession with memoirs from the 'insider', it's worth remembering that *Mookerjee's Magazine* published Shoshee's drily critical *Reminiscences of a Kerani's Life* in serial form, which skewered Baboo and Sahib alike. The Indian fascination with long-form journalism showed up in its pages as well—the current affairs magazines at the turn of the century thought nothing of carrying a roughly forty-page history of famines in India, for instance, as *Mookerjee's Magazine* did. This article, 'Indian Famines in the Past', was just one of the many instances where Indians spoke out against the erasure of their history—in this case, British India's perceived indifference to the plight of the famine-stricken. The piece was written just after the famines in the Upper Doab, Orissa and Rajputana, and just before the great famines in Bihar, parts of South India and the Ganjam famine.

By the 1890s, the figure of the intellectual, especially the Bengali Baboo, was a familiar enough one to be caricatured—both by fellow Bengalis and by writers like F. Anstey, whose Baboo Hurry Bungshu Jabberjee B.A. was immortalized in 1897.

About 105 years ago, after *Mookerjee's Magazine* had quietly folded up its shamiana, another journal would become one of the most influential Indian English periodicals of its time. The *Modern Review*, started by the journalist and reformer Ramananda Chatterjee, would have among its contributors M.K. Gandhi, Lala Lajpat Rai, Subhash Bose, Rabindranath Tagore, Sir Jadunath Sarkar, Verrier Elwin, Sister Nivedita and many others. Ramananda Chatterjee was my husband's great-grandfather. My acquaintance with the *Modern Review* began when I reached into a crate of books, sent from Kolkata, and pulled out Ramananda Chatterjee's head: my mother-in-law had thoughtfully packed a plaster bust of the editor along with my husband's science fiction and military-history collection.

It felt impolite to dust an ancestor without reading the magazines he'd started, and I soon became an old-magazine addict: both of Ramananda Chatterjee's magazines, the *Modern Review* and the Bengali magazine, *Prabasi*, brought the decades before Independence in 1947 to far more vivid life than had any of my history textbooks. I read them in sequence, like thrillers, wanting urgently to know what Lala Lajpat Rai had said about Home Rule to Gokhale and Gandhi, waiting for the next instalment in the dingdong political argument between Subhash Chandra Bose and Nehru, reading Tagore's poems as though they had been freshly written.

Ramachandra Guha rummaged through back issues of the *Modern Review* to discover that Jawaharlal Nehru—a frequent contributor who utilized the time he spent in the jails of the British to catch up with his reading and writing—had also written a splendid rant against himself under the pen-name Chanakya. Chatterjee, like many of the intellectuals of the age, was comfortably bilingual, and edited the Bengali journal *Prabasi* as well as the *Review*, which may also have given the *Modern Review* its inclusiveness and eclecticism.

Most of these journals, and the early pamphlets and periodicals published in Madras, Gujarat, Tamil Nadu and other printing hubs around India, are almost forgotten, rarely archived. Some of this indifference to the past may be changing—for instance, *The Best of Quest*, edited by Laeeq Futehally, Arshia Sattar and Achal Prabhala, brought back a sense of the intellectual debates of the 1950s.

But few remember *Mookerjee's Magazine* or the *Oudh Punch*, or the biting wit of the Hindi nationalist journals of the previous century. It's a pity that these were so easily forgotten; to read them is to be reminded that the history of Indian writing in English was not a simple one, any more than the history of pre-Independence India. The textbook versions, the comic book Amar Chitra Katha versions, the cartoon versions of history, and today the RSS's insistence on its own versions—these depend for their effect on a kind of stark simplicity, a plain black-and-white, heroes-and-villains account.

Unfortunately, that simplicity erases the past more effectively than any act of censorship, and turns into a set of bald narratives; it is so easy to forget that 'the past' was just as complicated and layered as our own times. One strand sets up the evil British versus the courageous Indian nationalists, ignoring the ambiguities, the intermingling and what both sides took (or rejected) from one another's culture.

More contemporary misrepresentations by the Hindutva right-wing seek to recast many of those who fought for India's freedom, including Nehru, by denying their extraordinary, decades-long struggles and erasing the long arguments and discussions over nationalism between Gandhi, Nehru, Bose, Jinnah, Sardar Patel, Maulana Azad, Lala Lajpat Rai, Gopal Krishna Gokhale, Aruna Asaf Ali, Sarojini Naidu and hundreds of others.

If there's a gap, a blank, in history, you would notice, just as you would notice a missing photograph in an album. But it's harder to notice when there is no blank space, just an incomplete version.

To assume, then, that Indian writing in English began only with Bankimchandra's *Rajmohan's Wife* in 1864—the first attempt to write a truly Indian novel in English—is dangerous. It encourages the amnesia that has been part of the Oriental scene, a smoothening out of the complexities that surrounded the early history of Indian writing in English, where you could begin by writing for a foreign audience and continue with works that were meant to be read by educated, self-aware Indians in search of a revolution. (It also obliterates the fascination that form has always held for Indian writers in English— alongside the novel, and before the novel, Indian authors gravitated to the travelogue, to alternate histories, to essays and broadsides, poems and plays, treatises and novellas.)

Mother and other tongues

The arguments between the writers of the nineteenth century over language were fierce and enthusiastically fought. But just as Persian had wound its way into everyday affairs some centuries before, English and the ways of the Anglicised Indian were insidiously contagious. When Bankimchandra published his journal *Bongobandhu* (Friend of Bengal), he borrowed an odd, hybrid image for the endpapers. They depict Ma Saraswati, the goddess of learning, revered especially in bookish Bengal, towering like a benign mountain across the cardboard covers. She wears, however, not a sari but some sort of gown, curiously like a lawyer's robe, and from its stiffly pleated folds, the bespectacled faces of young Bengal's finest intellectuals peer out—Michael Madhusudan Dutt, Romesh Chunder Dutt, Raja Rammohan Roy, Bankim himself.

Dean Mahomet's *Travels* are easy to read compared to *Rajmohan's Wife*, an attempt by Bankimchandra to make the English language his own. The novel was serialised in 1864 and published as a book only in 1935. Reading it is something of a strain, both on his writer's nerves and my worn reader's nerves; the writer who would hold thousands in his palm with the florid drama and hyper-nationalism of *Ananda Math* and with his fiery journalism found that English washed him out. As the late Meenakshi Mukherjee observed, English turned his flowering village creepers and their abundant gourds into a pallid 'garden salad'.

Bankim wrote in translation when he wrote in English, and was sternly scolded by his friends, including Romesh Chunder Dutt, who was Shoshee Chunder's nephew. They took turns to scold each other; Bankim was the one who'd started first, declaring (accurately): 'Gobind Chandra and Shoshi Chandra's [sic] English poems will never live. Madhusudan's Bengali poetry will live so long as the Bengali language will live.'

Dutt's biographer J.N. Gupta records in the *Life and Work of Romesh Chunder Dutt*:

Early in his career, therefore, his thoughts turned to his own mother tongue. He has himself described how he naturally came under the influence of the master mind of the great Bankim Chunder Chatterjea [sic]. Bankim Chunder was a close friend of his father, and since his childhood Mr Dutt had the highest respect and affection for him. On his return from England he discussed his plans and ambitions with Bankim Chunder, and the latter suggested that he should contribute in Bengali to the *Banga Darsana* magazine, then in the noonday of its influence and fame.

'Write in Bengali!' exclaimed Mr Dutt, 'but I hardly know the Bengali literary style.'

'Style!' rejoined Bankim Chunder. 'Whatever a cultured man like you will write will be style. If you have the gift in you, style will come of itself.'

This was a memorable episode in the life of Mr Dutt, for from that day he turned to Bengali literature. His inmost ambitions he always laid bare to his brother, and in a letter written in 1877 he says: 'My own mother tongue must be my line, and before I die I hope to leave what will enrich the language and will continue to please my countrymen after I die.'

These were rousing words, but reality was a shade more complicated. Romesh Chunder Dutt continued to flip back and forth between English and Bengali. In 1879, he published both *Madhabi Kankana* and *Rajput Jivan Sandhya* in Bengali, and in 1885, he came out with his translation of the *Rig Veda* into Bengali. But in 1895, he published *The Literature of Bengal* (in English), and in 1896, collected memories and letters, *Three Years in Europe, 1866–1871*. His *History of Civilization in Ancient India, Based on Sanskrit Scriptures* (1890) carried a brief description of the author that united his two linguistic selves: 'Romesh Chunder Dutt, of the Bengal Civil Service; and of the Middle Temple, Barrister-at-Law; author of a Bengali translation of the RigVeda Sanhita and other works.' He was keenly aware of the ways in which languages could play off each other. In *The Literature of Bengal*, he writes an account of how Madhu Sudan wrote *Tilottoma* in Bengali blank verse:

'But the jingling of the Bengali rhyme was ill suited to such attempts, and he remarked to his friend and adviser Jotindra Mohan Tagore, that there was no great future for Bengali poetry until the chains of rhyme were rent asunder. Jotindra Mohan replied that blank verse was scarcely suited to the Bengali language, and that even in the French language blank verse was not a success. But, replied Madhu Sudan, Bengali is the daughter of Sanscrit, and nothing is impossible for the child of such a mother!'

Bankimchandra took the path that Dutt did not; after the failed flirtation with English, he wrote only in Bengali, in an explosion of creativity. Between 1865 and 1875, for instance, he published *Durgeshnandini*, *Kapalakundala*, *Mrinalini*, *Vishabriksha*, *Indira*, *Jugalanguriya*, essays on society and essays on science—all of this in Bengali. He could not have written with such freedom or such persuasive drama in English. In that language, Bankim's sentences come out sounding overblown and unnecessarily bombastic; in Bengali, they retain the man's singular force, he sounds convincing and his voice retains a sense of drama.

This was to be the way of Indian writers for the next few centuries; for some, English opened a door into a room where they could write with more freedom, because they could think openly, liberated from the silent remonstrances and shibboleths of the mother tongue. For a few, like R.K. Narayan or the poet Arun Kolatkar, English became another native language, if not the mother tongue, then not an alien language either. But Bankimchandra fell into the equally broad category of writers for whom English was a shackle, a leaden weight placed on the tongue.

Beyond English

In Edmund de Waal's *The Hare with Amber Eyes*, there is a wonderful section on the fascination Japonism held at a certain time in Europe, when Japanese bibelots, netsuke, robes and paintings found their way into Parisian salons: 'Anyone would sell you anything. Japan existed as a sort of parallel country of licensed gratification, artistic, commercial and sexual.'

Often, what the collectors of that time picked up from Japan was unremarkable—the dross of everyday life, mass-produced objects d'art mingling with the rare and the exquisite. As de Waal recounts so beautifully, this early hunger was replaced by a refined connoisseurship in the early days, and inevitably, a waning of the interest in Japonism, a return to the less exotic and the more local.

In early 2011, as new books on India by Patrick French and Anand Giridharadas were released, that familiar debate had come back to us, reheated and freshly garnished. Pankaj Mishra's argument with French was over the content of the book—Mishra was unable to recognize or reconcile his vision of India, one of cruel economic inequalities and a dominant, often bullying, state, with French's more upbeat India story.

Reading between the lines, the real anxiety was over French's portrait, not the quality of his reportage: was this the authentic India, or had he missed the big story? Elsewhere, in a joyously savage piece of provocation, Mihir Sharma flayed *India Calling*, by Anand Giridharadas, for shallow journalism, and slammed the stereotypes of India that found their way into the 'foreign correspondent' book.

But the real debate became the one that tore Indian writing in English apart about a decade ago: what makes a book about India the genuine article, and who has the right to 'represent' the country? The 'authenticity argument' was rapidly buried, with a few stray knives in its back, in the world of Indian fiction—few readers, writers or critics wanted to police books to see how their Indianness rated on a scale of one to ten.

One of the most memorable battles in that short-lived war was the skirmish between the late Prof. Meenakshi Mukherjee and the writer Vikram Chandra. It began when Dr Mukherjee questioned the choice of titles for Chandra's short stories, in his collection *Love and Longing in Bombay*. To her, his titles—Artha, Dharma, Kama—were 'necessary to signal Indianness in the West'.

Chandra wrote a riposte that was simultaneously thoughtful and very funny: 'I noticed the constant hum of this rhetoric, this anxiety about the anxiety of Indianness, this notion of a real reality that was being distorted by "Third World cosmopolitans", this fear of an all-devouring and all-distorting West . . . I heard it in conversations, in critical texts, in reviews. And Indians who wrote in English were the one of the prime locations for this rhetoric to test itself, to make its declarations of power and belonging, to announce its possession of certain territories and its right to delineate lines of control . . . The issue was decided not on the basis of the relative merits of the books, but on the perceived Indianness of the authors, and by implication, the degree of their assimilation by the West.'

Chandra won that particular battle, perhaps because to most of his readers, the titles of his short stories seemed not just acceptable, but given the content, entirely appropriate. These were stories of greed, of lust, of the tyranny and the pleasures of duty. They were very Indian stories, if Indianness was the criteria by which you chose to judge them. (They remain an accurate representation of Bombay, but I would suggest here that they have lasted not because of the India they represent, but because they happen to represent taut, compelling storytelling.)

But Dr Mukherjee's suspicion, her distrust of a certain kind of writing, is not so easily dismissed. It remains alive in the parodies that sometimes appear on blogs about Indian writing of the stereotypes on the covers of Indian books in English—insert mangoes, add a sari border, use a suitably Oriental font, bear in mind that pictures of the Himalayas, rivers, sadhus and godmen will always sell a book, even one that has no reference to any of those elements. In a blogpost on the commandments of Indian writing in English, The Buddha Smiled set down the first: 'Thy Book Must Have a Title That is Strange & Wonderful. Also Very Long.' His post should be read alongside a beautiful, deadly piece of parody from I. Allan Sealy's *Trotternama*:

How the Raj is done

I wish to shew how the Raj is done. This is the play of children, good adept, rest easy. You must have the following ingredients. (It matters little if one or another be wanting, nor is the order of essence. Introduce them as you please, and as often.) Let the pot boil of its own.

An elephant, a polo club, a snake, a length of rope, a rajah or
a pearl of price (some use both), a silver moon, a dropped glove,
a railway junction, some pavilions in the distance, a chota peg, a
tent peg, a learned brahmin, a cruel king, a chapati (or chaprasi),
a measure of justice, gunpowder (q.v.), equal portions of law and
order, a greased cartridge, a tamarind seed or else a cavalry regiment,
a moist eye, some high intentions, two pax of Britannica, Glucose
biscuits, an ounce of valour, something in the middle, a Victoria
Cross, a soupcon of suspense (q.v), a bearer, a dhobi (or dhoti), a
chee-chee, a dekchi (or deck-chair), a pinch of dust, a trickle of
perspiration, a backdrop with temples or mosques (some use both),
a church pew, a little fair play, a boar, some tall grass, a tiger, a rain
cloud, a second snake or a mongoose, a flutter of the heart, a sharp
sword, a bared ankle, walnut juice or burnt cork (some use both),
a boy of British blood unsullied, a locket.

In most discussions of Indian writing in English today, we are still
not comfortable, outside of parody, acknowledging what might be
called marketplace realities. In the years when Indian writing was doing
well, like a hardworking honour student, in the West, we were happy
to measure our importance and success not by the literary impact of
a Kiran Desai or a Salman Rushdie but by the sales figures and the
prize shortlists.

What we are all uncomfortable acknowledging is that the West—
shorthand for the complex markets and divergent reading tastes of the
UK, the US and a large swathe of Europe—has a sharply truncated
view of Indian writing. Imagine assessing all of European literature
by reading only works in Polish, or only works in Italian—that, in the
absence of a market for translations of Indian fiction, is the position
the West is in when it reads 'Indian writing'.

And as long as the market is open only, or chiefly, to Indian writing
in English, this blindness cannot be overcome. There is also the
question of economic power—with access to larger audiences abroad,
publishers outside India can and do dictate who has that access, what
kind of stories travel from here to there, what books will be considered

future Indian classics. There is an inequality in the system, inevitable, inescapable and often resented.

Much of the unease expressed by Pankaj Mishra, and in a different form by Mihir Sharma, and earlier, by Allan Sealy and even Prof. Mukherjee, comes from questioning the need for the Big India book—at some level, we understand that these books are very rarely written by Indian journalists, and that the stories they tell, whether simplified or not, are influential even so. Some of the unease comes from a sense of disenfranchisement; it is telling, for instance, that there seems to be little need for the Big India book in Hindi, or Urdu, or Marathi. Outside of English, we lack either the curiosity or the need to explain India to ourselves.

What the West sees of Indian writing would be ridiculous, if that view wasn't so influential; as with the age de Waal describes, where all of Japanese culture and history could be interpreted through the shlock, detritus and masterpieces of the art world. Over the last thirty years, some realities have been inescapable; Indian writing in the Western world is defined largely as Indian writing in English, with very few translations making their way abroad.

Writing from outside the metros and outside the mainstream—Dalit writing, the resurgence in Indian poetry in English, writing from the seven sister-states that make up north-east India—is rarely visible, and when it is visible, it's exoticized, here and abroad. And by its nature, Indian writing in English has been largely privileged writing—if not quite limited to the sons of St. Stephens', most contemporary writers in this language come from the relatively enfranchised middle class, and their work reflects the limitations of their backgrounds.

The Census 2001 figures revealed that English had in effect become India's second language, behind Hindi. Many of the new English speakers come from the small towns, or belong to areas of the metros that lie outside the charmed circles of privilege. English belongs to them now as much as it once did, about two-three decades ago, to the old class of writer-Brahmins.

And as this generation begins to tell and write their stories, they may not need to beguile the souks of the West with their Indiennisme. About

125 million English speakers, out of whom a much higher percentage has made it their first language in the decade since the Census data was collected, is enough to make its own marketplace. If that happens, this new generation of writers might finally be able to step away from the debates that have come down across a century-and-a-half of Indian writing in English.

Or perhaps they will find a new set of things to argue about. In the years before the call-centre phenomenon spread across India, adding an American accent to Indian English, the first signs of the hunger for English—a language that might offer a passport to better jobs, more money, more status—showed up in the India of the 1980s and the 1990s in the ads for the very popular Rapidex English-speaking course.

Their spokesman was the cricketer Kapil Dev, whose contribution to the ad was to speak about its effectiveness, not in a BBC-tinged accent or in the beloved fake-Yank accent, but in heavily accented Indian, Haryanvi English. It was a kind of claiming of the language as our own, the way K.C. Dutt and S.C. Dutt had attempted to claim the right to write for an audience of Indian readers, the way Bankimchandra had struggled in *Rajmohan's Wife* to convey the accents and emotional grammar of Bengal in this alien but covetable tongue.

From that period of Indian history, I retained for many years a small memento, picked up in my travels across the Hindi heartland. A flyer from the Prince School and Education Bureau, distributed at a bus-stand, it offered the familiar 'English Tutions' ('Tuition' is often misspelled, and the Indian version sounds more euphonious to my biased ears), and this beguiling promise:

IN THREE WEEKS, LEARN HOW TO READ IN
GREMAN. HOW TO READ IN ENGLISH. HOW TO
READ IN INDIAN.

I like the enterprise behind that promise. I think, in many ways, we are all still trying to learn how to read in Indian, even if we don't always have the right glossaries.

(First published in Caravan, *2011, with some material added from research and readings between 2011 and 2014.)*

(At the Neemrana Festival: the authors present included Vikram Seth, V.S. Naipaul, Amitav Ghosh, Ved Mehta, Amit Chaudhuri, Khushwant Singh, Dom Moraes, Arvind Krishna Mehrotra, I. Allan Sealy, Farrukh Dhondy, Pico Iyer, Nayantara Sehgal, Shashi Deshpande, Kiran Nagarkar, Keki N. Daruwalla, Githa Hariharan, Ruchir Joshi, Imtiaz Dharker, Mukul Kesavan, Amitava Kumar and Anita Rau Badami. So were U.R. Ananthamurthy, M.T. Vasudevan Nair, Paul Zacharia, Shrilal Shukla, Sukrita P. Kumar, Sunil Gangopadhyay, Ashokamitran and Bhalachandra Nemade, leading the contingent of the eminent authors who wrote in Indian languages other than English.)

4

1857 and All That

Mention the Great Rebellion of 1857 to any educated Indian of a certain generation, and they have the galloping-hoof rhythms of Subhadrakumari Chauhan's ode to the Rani of Jhansi playing in their heads as background music:

Bundeley Harbolon key munh hamney suni kahani thi,
Khoob ladi mardani woh to Jhansi wali Rani thi.

A century-and-a-half after the stirring events of 1857, most Indians have read a wide array of books on what is often called India's first war of independence. These range from Amar Chitra Kathas to revisionist histories and eyewitness accounts. Some have read the few great works of Indian fiction—very few of them contemporary—and a smattering of well-known novels by the likes of John Masters or George MacDonald Fraser.

But in the two to three decades after 1857, novels about the Mutiny (to use the British nomenclature), were almost guaranteed to sell. Most of these works of pulp fiction are remembered now only by scholars, but they tell us at least as much about the complexity of the British response to 1857 as a dozen well-researched histories can.

Barely two years after the massacres and stifled rebellions of 1857, Edward Money published *The Wife and the Ward; A Life's Error*. Money's perspective was almost entirely from the contained, slightly claustrophobic world of the British, but it is a disconcertingly sympathetic work.

The first chapter is set in a regimental mess, where officers exchange banter unaware of the gathering clouds of insurgency around them, and the novel faithfully follows the tragic fortunes of a band of British officers struggling to protect their wives, children and camp followers as Nana Sahib's men close a deadly trap around them.

And yet, in chapter two, Money has one of his characters lament: 'India! How little art thou known to the mass of the English public, and yet who can doubt that thy loss would rob Britain of the brightest jewel in her crown . . . 'Tis strange, this apathy, this ignorance on all Indian subjects . . .' Remember, this is barely a year-and-a-half after the Mutiny; but several of Money's characters express this sense of regret and loss, from the Colonel of the regiment mourning the severing of ties with his men to a sensitive young army officer wincing at the inability of his countrymen—and women—to see India more clearly.

Far more stereotypical was James Grant's *First Love and Last Love*, a baroque, almost rabid three-volume extravaganza published in 1868. Grant included a scene where the sepoys strip and parade Englishwomen, and offers explanations such as this one: 'To the brutal Mussulman and the sensual Hindu, the position occupied by an English lady or any Christian woman, seems absurd and incomprehensible; hence came the mad desire to insult, degrade and torture, here they slay them.'

Just a few years after the Mutiny, pulp fiction had become a genre in its own right; Philip Meadows Taylor added to it with his own mammoth page-turner, *Seeta*. Taylor is an interesting character—a police officer involved closely in the hunting down of the thugs, and his first best-seller, *Confessions of a Thug*, brought the words 'thug' and 'thuggee' into general usage. Taylor's *Seeta* set a love affair between an English army officer and a Hindu widow against the backdrop of the Mutiny. The novel offers some of the usual stereotypes of Indians, what with bloodthirsty Muslims and cunning Hindus, but it also displays Taylor's tremendous interest in India's landscapes, social and geographical, and his romantic vision of a world where Indians and the English might meet without barriers.

Flora Annie Steel's *On the Face of the Waters*, published in 1896, is lushly romantic, but it also displays great ambivalence. The novel begins with the auctioning of the menagerie of 'the lately deposed King of Oude', a suitably surreal opening for a book that will include a registered prostitute and a British officer masquerading as an Afghan horse trader.

She portrays Bahadur Shah Zafar as an ineffectual king (and bad poet) ruled by a wife in equal thrall to opium and dreams of power. But Steel was a sharp observer of both the Anglo-Indian and the Indian scene. Her novel includes portraits of the Gissings, 'who preferred India, where they were received into society, to England, where they would have been out of it' as well as quick but accurate sketches of the 'Bahurupas'—the Bahurupiyas—and the difference between, say, a Gujjar and a Banjara. The book ends, atypically, not with an excoriation of treacherous Indians, but with a paean to the legendary soldier Nicholson.

The ambiguity that writers like Steel or Taylor or even Edward Money displayed so freely, and the affection they showed even in their Mutiny novels for their visions of a particular India or specific Indians didn't last. By 1881, the Mutiny pulp fiction stage was dominated by the likes of the prolific and unstoppable G.A. Henty.

Henty, who churned out more than a hundred boys' adventures in a range of imperial settings, turned to the Mutiny with *In Times of Peril*. The opening chapter is a personal favourite: a fine upstanding English family in India heads off for a jolly evening of pigsticking. ('Hurrah!' says one of the boys at the treat.) It also has illustrations that tell you a great deal about Henty's preferred style, i.e.. 'A tiger stood, with one of the guards in his mouth, growling fiercely'. The dialogue, after these promising signs, does not let the reader down, either:

'Any one hurt?' the major asked.

'I have got a bullet in my shoulder,' said Captain Dunlop.

The rest of the novel is a boy's own adventure where the Warrener brothers pop up in 'Cawnpore' and Lucknow, and Oudh, and Delhi to save a garrison here, rescue a shrinking maiden there. Henty is cheerfully open about the quantity of loot the boys collect during the course of their adventures, and is careful to balance the dastardly treacherous Indians with the occasional portrait of a sympathetic ranee or two.

For Henty and his fellow novelists, many of them like him the most popular writers of the age, India was an exotic backdrop, and Indians were props, no more. Henty's fellow adventure novelist Hume Nisbet, for instance, had his hero Sammy Tompkins disguise himself as an Indian to spy on the sepoys. But this was no early forerunner for Rudyard Kipling's *Kim*—unlike the Little Friend To All The World, who slipped with ease between the British and the Indians, at home wherever he went, Sammy Tompkins had no use for the Indians, and no interest in them. Going native was just a way to inject a little excitement into the narrative.

The frenzied dream of vengeance had reached its culmination in 1880, when Jules Verne joined the ranks of Mutiny writers with two books, *The Steam House*, and its sequel, *Tigers and Traitors*. *The Steam House: The Demon of Cawnpore* is an extraordinary early steampunk novel. The premise was just as baroque as you would expect from the author of *Ten Thousand Leagues Under the Sea*. Intent on avenging the slaughter committed by Indians during the Mutiny, a small band of brave British officers set out to hunt down Nana Sahib. They seek the perpetrator of the Cawnpore Massacre by journeying through the jungles of India in the belly of the Steam House—a giant mechanical elephant called Behemoth that drags several houses behind it—so that they can travel in comfort while pursuing justice.

The title of *The Steam House* has been nervously sanitized over the years; later versions carry the subtitle 'The End of Nana Sahib' rather than 'The Demon of Cawnpore'. 'Nana Sahib! This name, the most formidable to which the Revolt of 1857 had given a horrible notoriety, was there once more, flung like a haughty challenge at the conquerors of India.' In Verne's hands, Nana Sahib lives and has not lost his bloodlust: '. . . this railroad, the accursed work of the invaders' hands, shall ere long be drenched in blood!'

And what is the reaction of the British in this Mutiny novel written by a man who saw the events of 1857 from a great distance, both physical and intellectual? Their dream is to build first a steam horse (and then the Steam House), that would travel the highways and byways of India, penetrate the jungles, plunge into the forests: 'Venturing even into the haunts of lions, tigers, bears, panthers and leopards, while we, safe within its walls, are dealing destruction on all and sundry!'

Only Verne could have dreamed this up—a revenge fantasy that was also a safe retreat back to the womb of a mechanical elephant.

It would take an insider to write perhaps the best of the post-1857 novels; Flora Annie Steel had lived in the Punjab as the wife of a civil servant for years, and brought an original perspective to the sometimes deplorable school of memsahib writing. Her memoirs of her life are thoughtful and lively; her engagement with India closer to the deep attachment felt by the couple in *Staying On*, Paul Scott's novel of the twilight of the Raj. In her 1896 novel, *On the Face of the Waters*, her protagonist lurks in the heart of occupied Delhi in the guise of an Afghan horse trader, and right from the opening paragraphs, Steel sets out her sympathies.

'GOING! Going! Gone!'

The Western phrase echoed over the Eastern scene without a trace of doubt in its calm assumption of finality. It was followed by a pause, during which, despite the crowd thronging the wide plain, the only recognizable sound was the vexed yawning purr of a tiger impatient for its prey. It shuddered through the sunshine, strangely out of keeping with the multitude of men gathered together in silent security. But on that March evening of the year 1856, when the long shadows of the surrounding trees had begun to invade the sunlit levels of grass by the river, the lately deposed King of Oude's menagerie was being auctioned.

Her world is exotic India—filled with cockatoos and opium dens, king's menageries, homesick memsahibs who daren't trust the ayahs; but it is also much more than that. Steel fills the first chapters with heat, dust, and Ye Olde Oriental Charm, and moves briskly on to officials discussing the 'mischievous paragraph' in the *Christian Observer* about widow remarriages, the politics of the 'Sheeahs and Sunnees'.

Steel has a tart tongue: 'In the big dark dining-room also— where Alice Gissing, looking half her years in starched white muslin and blue ribbons, sat at the head of the table—there was no cult of England. Everything was frankly staunchly of the nabob-and-pagoda-tree style, for the Gissings preferred India, where they were received into society, to England, where they would have been out of it.'

And there we go, flashing from suttees and bahurupias to bis-cobras and Englishmen disguised as mendicants, cries of 'Deen! Deen!' in the bloody streets of Meerut. But if Kipling's *Kim* had a forerunner, in its complicated blend of sympathy, reluctant respect and yearning for India, touched with a tinge of British superiority, it may have been in Steel's novel, published four years before *Kim*.

Steel set herself large ambitions, and her words, re-read after all of this colour and drama, are startling: 'I have tried to give a photograph— that is, a picture in which the differentiation caused by colour is left out—of a time which neither the fair race nor the dark race is likely to quite forget or forgive. That they might come nearer the latter is the objective with which this book has been written.'

She makes it easier to go back to photographs of the Great War of Independence, the Revolt, the Rebellion, the Mutiny according to one's preferred nomenclature, and see them with a different eye. Perhaps it wasn't just Steel; perhaps in her time, there were others who looked at the sepia photographs and were comforted (or unsettled) by the way in which they bleached out colour and race.

(Written between 2007 and 2013.)

5

Pioneers: A Line of Unbroken Trust

One of the great perks of reviewing books in the late 1990s and early 2000s has vanished these days, thanks to the ready presence of courier companies: the ritual visits to publishers' offices to collect the fortnight's most interesting titles.

I had joined the Ananda Bazar Patrika group as a junior dogsbody at the *Business Standard*. In less than a week, we had established that I was thoroughly unsuited to work at a business paper—I was mildly dyslexic about numbers, dividing when I should been multiplying figures, and tended to drift into writing scurrilous poetry in my head when the powers that be handed me the Economic Survey or annual reports.

But this was the last of the decades in which every business magazine, and many mainstream journals, was considered incomplete unless they had twelve- or fourteen-page Arts and Books sections, and these could use the only marketable skills I possessed: I could speed-read, and I could touch-type without needing to look at the screen.

That was useful, since the office PCs were antique and given to shuddering blackouts when the brightness keys died. This was the era when we ran commands from the DOS prompt, stored pathetically small amounts of data on 5¼ inch floppy disks, wrote articles on

WordStar or WordPerfect, and talked to colleagues in the Bombay or Kolkata office through Telnet.

The *Business Standard* office on Bahadur Shah Zafar Marg was a short autorickshaw ride away from Daryaganj, where Cambridge University Press, Rupa & Co. and other publishers had their cramped offices that you approached gingerly, walking up rickety flights of stairs. I loved making the trip to collect books, especially if I could squeeze in a visit to the Old Delhi paper market nearby. The publishers were just a few streets away from another Old Delhi attraction, though that had limited appeal for me. But Daryaganj was also famous for its hakims; at renowned institutions such as the Khandani Shafakhana and the Hakim Hari Kishan Lal Shafakhana, their manuals promised to guarantee anxious couples a happy married life if only the gentlemen would follow their advice on how to avoid Nightfall.

Daryaganj had a popular Sunday book bazaar, which sold nineteenth-century Indian writers' books at ridiculously cheap prices: Dhan Gopal Mukerji's *Kari* in a handsome bound edition for Rs 26, a tattered copy of Behramji Malabari's memoirs for Rs 53, Raja Rao's *Kanthapura* more expensive at Rs 110, Nayantara Sahgal's more modern Delhi novels sold at a discount because of their water-stained covers. And if I had time, and sufficient funds, I would stop at the nihari shops adjoining Karim's restaurant near the Jama Masjid in Old Delhi. In 'Dilli ka Dastarkhwan', an essay published in Khushwant Singh's 2001 Delhi anthology, *City Improbable*, Sadia Dehlvi let readers into the secret of a classic nihari. She wrote that a few kilos from each day's leftover nihari were added to the next day's cooking: this was the *taar* that gave the dish its unique flavour. 'There are still some nihari shops in old Delhi which boast of unbroken *taar* going back more than a century.'

I think that writing, too, can have a line of unbroken *taar*, the ideas and insights of one writer stirred into the pot that another puts on the fire to simmer. When I began reading the pioneers of Indian writing in English, that was the image that came to mind (this is probably true for many Indian literatures, not just English). I have neither the breadth of reading nor the academic qualifications to set down the full history of the hundreds of writers, small presses and magazines who filled the nineteenth and early twentieth century with their eager prose, their impassioned essays, flowery poetry and ambitious drama, but here are a few of the pioneers whose books meant the most to me.

Travellers: Romesh Chunder Dutt and Behramji Malabari

Until I came across Dutt's *Three Years in Europe* (1868), I'd thought of him as the Serious Dutt: the formidable R.C. Dutt who turned his hand to economic histories, translations of Sanskrit classics into Bengali, a history of the literature of Bengal that spanned eight centuries, and stern tomes on the causes and prevention of Indian famines.

But there was another side to him, and *Three Years in Europe* brought that out—an unabashed delight in travel (he was the kind of tourist who would have been spamming Instagram today), allied to a remarkable degree of confidence. Seventy-four years after Dean Mahomet had prefaced his book on India with blandishments to the English, Romesh Chunder eyed the West with a curiosity that didn't preclude him from being critical. He had compiled his letters home he wrote, to serve as a guide book to Indian youths containing: 'The views and opinions of a foreigner for the first time coming in contact with the noble institutions of the West.'

His book filled a neat gap in the market, as Dutt smartly points out: 'As it is, none of our countrymen has favoured the public with accounts of their travels in Europe.' The flow of writing had been in the other direction, travellers from the Occident setting down their impressions of the Orient: Dutt was one of the first writers in English from India to reverse the gaze.

He, Surendranath Banerjee and Behari Lal Gupta had run away from home, 'stealthily leaving' in order to travel to London. Their aim was equally adventurous: they planned to sit for the Open Competition examinations that would make them the first Indians, after Satyendranath Tagore, to join the Indian Civil Service. 'We have left our home and our country, unknown to our friends, unknown to those who are nearest and dearest to us, staking our future, staking all, on success in an undertaking which past experience has proved to be more than difficult,' Dutt wrote with patent relish. 'The least hint about our plans would have effectually stopped our departure, our guardians would never have consented to our crossing the seas, our wisest friends would have considered it madness to venture on an impossible undertaking.'

Once they were in England, they settled in quickly: Dutt was a gleeful tourist, visiting Madame Tussaud's, the Crystal Palace, Westminster Abbey, Cambridge, Brighton and any other entertainments that came his way with immense zest. The weather didn't dampen their spirits, though in time-honoured fashion, he registered a complaint: 'The weather is murky and the days are generally half dark, there being plenty of mist with showers every now and then, but they are not our Indian heavy showers, but slight patter, patter, patter, which is very annoying.'

He was far more impressed with the levels of political engagement he saw around him. The 'commonest tailor, the commonest greengrocer, the commonest bootmaker in London' would talk about the national debt or the day-to-day business of Parliament in detail, and Dutt's approval was warm.

In a reversal of the usual exclamations of horror from foreigners who visited India and found the poverty overwhelming, Romesh Chunder declared that the size of the families of the poor in London, and the drunkenness that often accompanied poverty, 'presents a sight of misery compared to which the poorest classes of people in our own country are well off'. It was really painful, he wrote, to reflect on the sufferings of the poor 'in this inclement weather'. He sounds almost exactly like a present-day foreign correspondent when he summarises the English class system—the aristocracy, the landed gentry ('a creature with little education and less general knowledge'), town gentry ('educated, in many case liberals'), tradespeople and labouring classes.

The three friends from Bengal discovered that they had all passed the exam, though Surendranath would later be disqualified on account of questions over his date of birth. 'I cannot describe the transport I felt on that eventful day,' Dutt wrote. Their aim had not been simply to emulate the British, but to open a door for more Indians to join the civil service, breaking the monopoly that the English had maintained over the administration of the country. In 1868, ideas of Independence were far off, but Dutt could still write: 'A path, we ventured to hope, had been opened for our young countrymen.' They set off on a celebratory jaunt around the British Isles, travelling to Scotland and other places. But London had cast its spell on Dutt, and he wrote:

> I must say I was very glad to come back to old London, unromantic as it is, with its busy shops and markets, its huge and unshapely omnibuses, clattering over stony streets, and its thousand haunts of business or pleasure.

Some eighteen years later, in 1886, he went back with his wife and four children to settle briefly in England. Marriage had changed him, and this part of his travels is cozily domestic, filled with notes on the costliness of laundry, the easy availability of good food, and the difficulty of finding domestic help.

'Both the Hindu matron and the Mem Saheb would, I fancy, have more patience with the state of things in India after they have tried house-keeping in London for some time,' Dutt wrote after a week of interviewing potential housekeeping staff. The household sorted, he plunged with his usual enthusiasm into London life. He enjoyed a performance of *The Mikado*, and dropped in at the Wimbledon camp of exercise, where soldiers and volunteers contested for prizes. 'What interested me most was the Lawn Tennis match between the celebrated players Renshaw and Lawford.' He visited Parliament and heard Gladstone speak, but his attention was caught by 'little Churchill, twirling his moustache as he eyed his opponents as if in disdain'.

When the demand for home rule in Ireland swept London, it made Dutt cautiously optimistic. Over two decades, India had changed; it was possible to think of autonomy, at least. 'And is it a bold prophecy to make that the time is not far distant, that some of our young men may live to see it, when it will be considered unwise to govern any country or any people without consulting the people's wishes, without some kind of representative institutions?' he wrote with some hope.

The family travelled further; he met his old professors, some of whom had mentored him in his years at the Temple Inn, and then they visited other towns across England at the invitation of the Colonial and Indian reception committee.

It was the year of the Colonial and Indian Exhibition, and they were received, he writes, 'as the sons of old England, visiting the old country from the ends of the earth', feted, wined, dined, received at galas and balls galore.

But Dutt was no longer a wide-eyed student on his first visit abroad, and his years in India had given him a strong sense of how much was at stake for England. The point of them was 'to display to Europe and to the world the strength which she derives from her connection with various nations to the ends of the world, and to draw closer the bonds of sympathy and fellow-feeling which bind these colonies to her'. He wrote, drily but without rancour, that England desired that these visitors should go back to their countries 'full of sympathy and affection for her'. He listened with interest to the impractical idea of a federation of colonies, and concluded with the hope that the day was not far when India too 'would have a voice and a hand in the management of her own affairs'.

And before leaving Bristol, he visited one of his favourite spots—not a church or an English memorial, but the tomb of the reformer Raja Ram Mohan Roy. Soon after that, the Dutt family boarded their ship, and went home; they would visit Norway on their next trip, they had caught the habit of travel from Romesh Chunder.

Behramji Malabari, Traveller to the Occident

Dutt's travels end in 1871; Behramji Malabari's *The Indian Eye on English Life, or The Rambles of a Pilgrim Reformer*, was published in 1895 at the Apollo Printing Works in Bombay.

It would take an intrepid novelist to invent the life of Behramji Malabari. My own imagination quails at the thought of creating a great Hindu reformer who was born a Parsi in Baroda, educated at an Irish mission school in Surat after the death of his father, where he was adopted by a childless Gujarati spice-trader.

Behramji took his name, Malabari, from the Malabar spices in his adopted father's shop, though his love for writing and for reform was entirely his own. He began his career as a Gujarati poet, switching with dismaying results to English.

His first collection, *The Indian Muse in English Garb*, is grimly awful, as this 1876 ode to The Empress of India, demonstrates:

See! how lordly Nizam glares!
Holkar, Scindia and Benares, Cashmire, Jepur and their heirs
Evincing all their loyalty!
See the gallant Gaicowar, Princes of old Katyawar,
And each dominant Durbar
Increasing thy hilarity!

But two years previously, he had put together a superior collection, the *Niti Vinod* written in Gujarati. The poems here foreshadowed his interests far better than his English verses: odes bewailing the curse of infant marriage, the 'prayer of a Hindu widow' marked the areas where he would argue for reform.

Max Mueller wrote a gentle letter when he received a copy of the younger man's English poems: 'Whether we write English verse or English prose, let us never forget that the best service we can render is to express our truest Indian or German thoughts in English . . .' In subsequent decades, Malabari would translate Mueller's lectures on Hinduism, attempting to justify his own argument that some of the Indian guardians of religion had misinterpreted the Vedas and the Puranas.

It is not Malabari's poems that should be exhumed from their well-earned grave, but his prose. When he wrote *Gujarat and the Gujaratis*, some seven years after his volume of verse, he joined Dutt and others—they were part of the first generation of Indians who wrote about their travels in the West in the spirit of enquiry, seeing the flaws as well as the marvels of the Occident.

Malabar had trained as a journalist at the *Times of India*, and by the time he took over as editor of *The Spectator*, his paper was part of the new, thriving, often robustly combative school of Indian journalism. From the *Hindoo Patriot* and *The Pioneer* to the *Indian Statesman* and the *Indian Mirror*, 'native' Indian journalists had begun to report on their own country.

Gujarat and the Gujaratis reminds me of the very contemporary explorations of their own cities, and of the 'other' India, undertaken by writers such as Aman Sethi, Sonia Faleiro and Amitava Kumar. The gap of a century shows most in terms of craft: Behramji left out the fact that he had walked across large stretches of Gujarat, for instance.

He ruffled several feathers: 'Something ails it now,' he wrote of his 'poor, primitive, peace-loving' Surat. Of Broach he writes: 'The town itself is henpecked by that termagant of a river, the Narbada; the husbands are henpecked by their better halves.'

Malabari published his influential *Notes on Infant Marriage* in 1884. His zeal for reform was successful, winning him the friendship of Florence Nightingale, among others. Writing the foreword to Malabari's biography, she remarks: 'The mission which he led against infant-marriage has stirred up a strong feeling of hostility in some quarters. But . . . the evils he has attacked will be acknowledged to be those which most endanger the physical and moral well-being of the Indian race.'

A few years later, he published *The Indian Eye on English Life*. Malabari, who began by trying to imitate the English, and then by reporting like a tourist on his own country, would close his literary career with this absolutely confident travelogue. He turned as close and as carefully scrutinizing an eye on Britian as any traveller from the West had done on India: this was the Exotic Occident. England's cities were crowded, he reported, their food barbaric; everybody ate too much, walked too fast, and yet, he admired their energy and their political engagement.

The Cockneys on buses and the London bobbies were rendered for comic effect, just as travellers to India had written with patronizing charm about the antics of palkiwallahs and khidmatgars. 'The people seem to be as changeable and restless as the weather,' Malabari writes, and elsewhere, of the English habit of eating in shops, on the streets and in the open: 'Bismillah! How these Firanghis do eat!' He found points of resemblance:'How like our Diwan-i-Khas and Diwan-i-Am of old are these Houses of Parliament!' and of resentment:'Talking of "Babu English", I should like to know how many Englishmen speak Bengali half so well as Bengalis speak English.'

After his return, Malabari was interviewed by a Bombay newspaper. 'How much I wish my countrymen travelled more freely, and that they studied history, modern and ancient, with a tithe of the zeal they devote to barren rhetoric or still more barren speculation.' Over a century later, much has changed in India, but versions of Malabari's complaints—and his optimistic belief in change—survive, side by side.

(From research and columns written between 2004 and 2013.)

Rokeya Begum's Legacy

Around 1904, Rokeya Sakhawat Hossein wrote a stirring essay in Bengali:

> Dear female readers, have you ever thought about the condition of your misfortune? What are we in this civilised world of the twentieth century? Slaves! I hear slavery as a trade has disappeared from this world, but has our servitude ended? No.

'Woman's Downfall' was just one of the essays collected in *String of Pearls*, but it was fairly representative of the persuasive bluntness that Rokeya Begum employed through her busy writing life. She put bilinguals to shame: her articles came out in Urdu, Bengali and English, and the periodicals she wrote for were equally eclectic—*Nabaprabha, Mahila, Nubanur, Sabujpatra, Bangeya, Muslim Sahitya Patrika,* the legendary *Indian Ladies' Magazine* and *The Mussalman*.

I had known of her only as an educationist—she was famous for setting up one of the first schools in Bhagalpur and then in Kolkata for

Muslim girls. She was born in 1880 in Bangladesh, in what was then part of undivided Bengal and the British Indian empire. At home, she was taught Urdu and Arabic as a matter of course; women were not supposed to learn languages that might take them too far out of their households, but her brother Ibrahim and her older sister Karimunnissa secretly taught her Bengali and English.

I had read this detail, and thought of the woman who had written the first autobiography in Bengali, Rassundari Debi, whose *Amar Jiban* was published in 1876, just four years before Rokeya Begum was born. Rassundari Debi had written eloquently of her struggles to teach herself how to read, secretly, furtively, hoping that no one in the family would find out, because in that time and community, it was forbidden for women to learn letters. And yet, she had written of a hunger that would not be appeased, of the snatched attempts to write the letters of the Bengali alphabet from memory in between the endless rounds of kitchen and household tasks.

Visiting Dhaka's Liberation War Museum, before we went upstairs to witness the records that had been kept of the bloodbath and devastation of 1971, I had stopped, startled, before a photograph of Rokeya Begum and her husband Syed Sakhawat Hossain. She had been married at sixteen, and had moved to Bhagalpur, where Syed was deputy magistrate. In her writings, she had often acknowledged his encouragement, with a gratitude so genuine that you could feel it across the intervening decades; in the photograph, they stand beside one another with the ease peculiar to married couples who are also good friends, their smiles unforced and natural. There was a letter in her firm handwriting, and a small, handbound booklet in red cloth that contained one of the treasures of Indian writing in England—*Sultana's Dream*.

Rokeya Hossein had a distinctive voice, and quite a presence: in 1926, she presided over the Bengal Women's Education Conference, for instance. The academic Mrinalini Sinha records that she had come out in support of Katherine Mayo's *Mother India*, writing in the periodical *Masik Mohammadi*: 'I too have been speaking of these evils for the last twenty years, but no one heard my faint voice, today they have all sat up at the roar of Miss Mayo's voice!'

It made her unpopular with her readers, but Rokeya Begum was not the kind of writer who softened her words. In 'The Dawn', another piece of early journalism, she had sounded a war-trumpet:

Wake up, mothers, sisters, daughters; rise, leave your bed and march forward. There, listen, the Muezzin is calling for prayer. Can't you hear that call, that command from God? . . . Whilst women of the rest of the world have awoken and declared war against all kinds of social evils, we, the women of Bengal, are still sleeping on the damp floors of our own homes, where we are being held captives, and dying in thousands as victims of consumption.

And a year later, she had refined her message: 'Only catch them (men) and put them in the zenana.' In 1905, that was the advice Rokeya Sakhawat Hossein offered in her vision of a feminist utopia called 'Ladyland' in *Sultana's Dream*, now considered a minor classic. If Shoshee and Keshab Chunder Dutt had set off Indian writing in English on the path of speculative fiction, it was Rokeya Begum who would return most strongly to that genre.

Rokeya Sakhawat Hossein was actually ahead of her time when she wrote *Sultana's Dream*. The women of her benign utopia don't view men as the enemy, but see them with affection as time-wasting creatures who must be shut up because they can't control their own appetites and urges. Once the men are behind the purdah, women can get on with running things the way they should be. Back in 1905, Rokeya dreamed of a world where women had learned to harness the power of science, had pressed solar energy and rainwater harvesting into service. Her vision contrasted women's 'sentimental' view of science with the masculine 'military' view of science, to fascinating effect.

'Ladyland' was very unlike the female-populated utopia created by another pioneering writer, Charlotte Perkins Gilman, whose *Herland* I found frightening when I read it as a teenager, and did not change my mind when I read it in my forties. It was not a feminist vision of a perfect, manless world so much as a slightly rabid vision of a perfect, Aryan-populated world where the purity of the race was protected by an unbroken line of births through parthenogenesis. In Gilman's book, three male explorers eventually break into *Herland*, with troubling consequences.

But Rokeya Begum's two fantasies, *Sultana's Dream* and *Padmaraag*, have both aged well, standing as precursors to more modern explorations of feminist utopias and dystopias by Indian-origin writers.

When Manjula Padmanabhan's *Escape* came out in 2008, I found myself hoping that readers wouldn't read this intriguing work of dystopian science fiction in isolation. (The sequel, *The Island of Lost Girls*, was published in 2015.)

A brief plot summary: *Escape* is set in a world devoid of women, dubbed the 'Vermin Tribe' by the generals who run the land. There is, however, a single woman left—a young girl called Meiji, who has been raised in isolation by her three uncles, and as she emerges into adulthood, she must escape in order to survive. It's a complex tale, where, as with much of twenty-first-century science fiction, the development and growth of the characters is just as important as the futuristic setting.

To read *Escape* in a vacuum, however, would be to do both the book and yourself a disservice. It should be book-ended by a utopia and a dystopia—both written by Asian women. Ladyland's utopia is a gentle precursor, filled with touches of whimsy—the work day in Ladyland is only two hours long, for instance, because the men used to waste the remaining hours in smoking hookahs. Rokeya Begum continued her exploration of utopia and its challenges in a second novella, *Padmaraag*.

It was almost nine decades after *Sultana's Dream*—and just nineteen years before Padmanabhan's *Escape*—that the feminist scholar and imaginative writer Suniti Namjoshi published *Mothers of Mayadip*, in 1989. This fable was set in a crueller world than Ladyland, and Namjoshi set down a flatly didactic novel: what if a feminist utopia depended on killing off all men? How utopian would it remain, if it rested on a foundation of fear and deliberate cruelty? What would happen if any one of the women decided to save even a single baby boy? Namjoshi's world was the exact opposite of the world Padmanabhan evokes in *Escape*, but they share a common basis: in each, one gender's sense of identity is based on its fear of the other.

Mothers of Mayadip is much shorter and much less ambitious in scope than *Escape*; Namjoshi's interest lay in writing a fable, not a full-length novel. Like Padmanabhan, Namjoshi offered no easy conclusions: a world minus men was not guaranteed to be fair, equal or free of fear, and would inevitably face its own troubles. In *Mothers of Mayadip*, female infanticide has been replaced by the ritual killing of male babies. The vision of the perfect, free, female society has been marred by suspicion, conservatism and paranoia. Nor is Namjoshi convinced that a world without the tyranny of men amounts to the same thing as a world without men.

Escape is far more interested in the question of what form a world inhabited by just one gender would take; Manjula Padmanabhan's predecessors were more interested in the idea of a feminist utopia/ dystopia as a thought experiment.

It took a writer of the calibre of Ursula K. Le Guin to explore the finer shades of gender politics, which she did with particular skill in *The Left Hand of Darkness*. The world she created, where the inhabitants were gender-neutral most of the time, but can become either male or female when their sexual cycle peaks, becomes more and more interesting as gender loosens and gender definitions become less rigid in our time. Le Guin's characters may choose to be male in one season, female in another; aside from human choices, we live in a time where it is perfectly possible for artificial intelligence to be both, or neither, or something far beyond.

The interesting thing about feminist utopias is that even the authors who create them don't appear to want a world ruled by women. They want the opposite of the nightmare vision Margaret Atwood set out in *The Handmaid's Tale*, where she created a world of Wives, Marthas, and Handmaids, in subservient thrall to the men. No more slavery, each generation says to the next; and each generation of women still asks Rokeya Begum's question: 'Has our servitude ended?' The answers are still mixed.

Exactly a hundred years after it was first published in *The Indian Ladies Journal*, *Sultana's Dream* deserves to find a wider audience. For me, it's fascinating to think that a woman born in that age, who had to discreetly learn English and Bengali, would have dreamed of a utopia that rivalled anything her colleagues elsewhere had come up with. Today, it's her gentle but empowering vision that seems the most hope-filled, rather than Gilman's subliminally racist utopia or the fear-filled worlds of women driven into retaliation.

The Restlessness of Dhan Gopal Mukerji

In the 1980s, my grandmother's house yielded steadily diminishing quantities of books that had once represented a library: each year, their numbers were eroded by termites, old age, white ants, dampness and marauding grand-daughters.

Among the fugitive books I rescued were several by a man who was once a celebrity in the US, sought after by the *New York Times* for his opinion on Gandhi, Katherine Mayo's *Mother India*, and other issues of the day.

We had a hometown in common, but Dhan Gopal Mukerji had a love-hate relationship with Kolkata. I wonder whether he realized that some of his books would find their way to one of the houses he so despised: '. . . European houses modelled after the horrible mediocre middle-class homes of the 1870s in Britain and Germany.'

To him, they represented 'the ugliness of British India'; to present-day residents of Kolkata, they represent an era of graciousness and expansiveness now facing the bulldozer, old red-brick and white plastered houses transmuting into block upon block of lookalike flats. When he came back to India to travel around the country, many years after he had settled in the US, he found some consolation and spiritual discourse in Benares, little in his home town: 'Kolkata offends me. Speed and profit, yes, that is the breath and pulse-beat of modern Kolkata.'

I bristled at this, and found his views on 'Mohammedans' repulsive (he wrote of Muslims as one-dimensional conquerers bent on conversion by the sword, expressed fears of India being 'overpopulated by Mohammedan children', declared while living in a chiefly Hindu/

Christian milieu that Muslims were cruel and bloodthirsty by nature),
while recognizing that many of these views were shared by the Bengali
bhadralok of his time.

He had grown up in Tamluk, on the outskirts of Kolkata, and his
love for the jungle at his doorstep would resurface in many of his
books: *Kari, The Elephant; Hari, The Jungle Lad; Ghond, The Hunter*. They
were exotic, studded with phrases such as 'O Beloved of Felicity',
and he would be accused today of the twin modern-day crimes of
appropriation and stereotyping, but re-reading the books, I began to
see what made him so successful: in these times, he would probably
have made an excellent nature writer. In *Ghond, The Hunter*, he argues
passionately against the killing of snakes on the grounds that the worms,
frogs and creatures they live on would multiply. Part of his reasoning is
elegantly modern: 'If we destroy species after species, as we have done
in the past, life will be flat, colourless and monotonous, a spectacle of
unrelieved dullness.'

He had studied to be a priest, and though he jettisoned the ambition,
he retained a lifelong interest in religion and spirituality. Over time, I
judged him less harshly, and more as a product of his age: in his books,
he emerges as a seeker, a restless wanderer who never settled fully
anywhere, an open-minded traveller. His books haven't dated well, but
they stand as a record of his times—Mukerji was born in 1890 and died
in 1936. Books that once moved American critics to rhapsodies, such as
Caste and Outcast, are all but forgotten, as is the relative boldness of his
stand. He identified strongly as a Hindu of Brahmin parentage while
excoriating the caste system and, in retrospect, I think he was astute
in his understanding of caste privilege: 'The only way to abolish caste
would be to renounce the desire even for the highest caste.'

Mukerji had a vivid turn of phrase, and I had nightmares for months
after reading this passage from his autobiography. I cannot see now why
this was so terrifying, but at the time, the image of the eyes of animals
gleaming in the darkness, approaching inexorably, haunted my dreams:

Our house was situated at the edge of the forest not far from the
town. In the evenings, after the lights were out, we used to sit

by the open window looking toward the forest. I remember one evening especially; though I must have been a little child at the time. I was gazing into the darkness outside when I saw something that appeared to me like a huge jewelled hand. This hand, with rings gleaming on all of its fingers, was slowly coming toward me out of the jungle. The movement of the hand in the darkness was intense and terrifying. I cried with fright, and my mother, putting her arms about me, said, 'Fear not, little son. Those are only the eyes of the foxes and jackals and hundreds of other small jungle dwellers coming and going about their business.' I was overawed by the fierce power of life, and I watched in silence the tremendous black masses of dark trees with the emptiness gleaming all around them, and the innumerable fireflies flitting about.

His passage to the US as an adult was not as smooth as it is for many NRIs today: his biographer, Gordon Chang, records that Mukerji washed dishes and harvested crops in order to pay for his education at the University of California in Berkeley. Perhaps this experience coloured his feelings towards America. It was a hospitable country, a place rich with ideas where he made many friends over the years, and found a place for himself as a respected author who lived in New York with his wife and family, and yet he saw it clearly: 'a continent fierce with homelessness'.

Mukerji wrote directly for his American readers, explaining unapologetically in his Foreword to *My Brother's Face* (1924): 'This book deals with the India of to-day from an Indian's standpoint . . . I have written what my brother Indians had to say, hoping that the views of Englishmen in India would be set down by English writers.' He was good at this, setting down a reverse travelogue that turns into a spiritual exploration of the land he had departed from, with a running internal battle between stories from the West and the East.

On 4 April 1925, the *Chicago Tribune* reviewed the book generously: 'Mr Mukerji is a Brahmin well-known to American readers. [He] is an intelligent man who has chosen the hard task, as it were, of being a liaison officer between the warring camps of the east and the west. This last book of his, a very serious attempt to interpret India to Europeans and Americans, is the result of a trip which he made to India after an absence of twelve years. It is the unwritten law of every Hindu that he shall visit the place of his birth at least once in twelve years . . .' The column-length review is placed among advertisements for the best-sellers of the day: P.C.Wren's *Beau Geste* ('a corking good yarn'), A.A. Milne's *When We Were Very Young, The Cave Girl* by Edgar Rice Burroughs.

My Brother's Face begins on an exuberant note. 'India at last! The hills of the western Ghauts gleamed so intensely emerald that it hurt one's eyes to look at them. As the boat was moored and made fast, the crowds ashore shouted "Gandhiji ki Jai!" I had returned to India in the very midst of the Gandhi ferment and during my first week, I found that the sound of his name rang like a refrain to everything I did.'

What he loved about Kolkata was that it returned him to his language, Bengali, the tongue he preferred to speak in, though his books were written in English and his lecture tours in the US were conducted, naturally, in the same language. And it reconnected him with his brother, Jadu Gopal Mukerji, who stayed on in India and became a revolutionary, spending years dodging the police.

He spent his time well, travelling up and down the country. But the core of the book was his reunion with Jadu Gopal. They spoke to one another in Bengali. Jadu Gopal said bluntly that he couldn't stand speaking English: 'It makes us nervous and turns our voices falsetto, which never happens when we speak any tongue native to India.'

Like many expatriates, Mukherji's relationship with the language he wrote in was troubled. He used English well enough, but it was donned like a suit of Western clothes and thrown off gladly for Bengali, which he felt was more picturesque, more lyrical.

His sister felt similarly: she read a story about a dead man's ghost, a young prince and an old fool. 'Is it right to tell a mother that she is unchaste, and all because of the idle talkativeness of a good-for-nothing spirit?' she asks her brother.

'That tale destroyed all my ambition to know English.' And thus, comments Mukherji drily, did they dispose of *Hamlet*.

And one of his anecdotes should be required reading for all expatriate writers struggling to 'translate' their country for the benefit of foreign readers. He and an old lady of seventy are recalling the songs of the palanquin bearers. She recites in Bengali:

Heavy, heavy
Heavy, heavy, heavy;
He ate too much.
My shoulder, my shoulder,
It aches, it aches.

Mukherji expostulates that the English rendering is more beautiful. 'Listen,' he says, and recites Sarojini Naidu's famous lines from *The Palanquin Bearer*:

Lightly, oh lightly
We bear her along
She hangs like a pearl
On the thread of our song.

(In school, we sang a scurrilous third version, truer to the Bengali original: 'Heavily o heavily, we bear her along/ She should have skipped lunch/ The silly fat Bong.')

Dhan Gopal learnt a lot from his older brother, who had spent time travelling in the villages of Bengal and elsewhere: 'I found that every peasant believed the English must go. And why? Because they said the English had abandoned righteousness.' Jadu Gopal had been politically active since 1915. Once when the police came looking for him—they had no image of his face to go by—he met them at the door and said, 'I think the man you want stepped across the way. I will go and call him.' He went into the house opposite, which belonged to his uncle, took a back route and waited in a lane near the police station, guessing correctly that all the streets would be filled with plainclothes men except for that one.

Before he left India, Dhan Gopal met Tagore at Bolpur and also went to the 'jungle country' to find his old friend, Ghond, a hunter and trapper who lived with a pet leopard. They discussed the future of the country, and Mukerji wrote: 'My judgment is that the rich Indian ("bankers, landlords, princes") is more of an enemy to his poorer countrymen than he realizes.'

He had established some contact with Mahatma Gandhi previously; in 1929, Gandhi wrote a letter to him: 'Dear Friend', it began, and then Gandhi excoriated the poor quality of what appeared in the US press about India. 'Journalism seems to be sinking lower and lower and so is diplomacy.' He offered some advice—'Indians outside India should become in their own persona a living demonstration of what a true Indian can be like.'

Their correspondence shows genuine affection and respect on both sides, and Mukerji was quoted in the *New York Times*:

> Author fears India may have civil war; Mukerji, Back From Visit, Sees "No Statesmanship Great Enough to Prevent It". DEPLORES GANDHI'S ARREST He Says British Have Removed Only Restraining Influence That Can Control the Masses. Says We Cannot Know Truth. Marvels at New Youth.

Perhaps Mukerji's books have not lasted because he was not an especially original thinker. His suspicion of Muslims (and also Marwaris) was drawn from Bankimchandra; his views on politics were borrowed from all over the place; at the risk of offending readers who like his Ramakrishna biography, *The Face of Silence*, his spiritual narratives read like a thousand other tales of worship and mysticism.

He is best remembered today for his children's stories, and for a famously outraged response to Katherine Mayo. In the annals of the Newbery Medal, one of the most prestigious awards for children's writing, the only Indian name on the rolls is that of Dhan Gopal Mukherji.

Of the several books he wrote, the only one that is still widely in print today, thanks to the Newbery Medal, is *Gay-Neck: The Story of a Pigeon*. Like many books of the time, it is far less sanitised and far more curious than Disneylit: its feathered protagonist is shot, badly injured, and near death, but recovers and goes on several adventures.

Gay-Neck, a trained carrier-pigeon, wanders the Himalayas before being employed by a Bengal Regiment to carry messages back and forth during the First World War in France. Through his narrative, we get an idea of Mukherji's sense of his country and of foreign lands.

When Katherine Mayo's 'drain-inspector's report', *Mother India*, came out and horrified any self-respecting Indian with its farrago of half-digested nonsense, Mukherji was first off the mark. He wrote a spirited riposte, titled *A Son of Mother India Answers*, which anticipated the criticism that *Mother India* would continue to gather over the years. By the 1930s, he had his share of literary fame, and he was much in demand as a public speaker. But the Depression in the US affected the sales of his twenty-six books, and in his forties, his life may have hit a few bumps. His spiritual quest did not appear to have borne fruit: 'I had spent hard outcast years in America, followed by years in which I was admitted within the precincts of Western caste; I had travelled in England, France and Norway and had felt everywhere a deepening fellowship with men, but instead of lessening, these human contacts intensified, the emptiness that surged within me.' He had become reclusive, sticking to his 72nd Street apartment in New York, and some accounts suggest that there was strain in his marriage to Ethel Dugan.

In July 1936, the *New York Times* carried another headline featuring Dhan Gopal Mukerji, but this was a tragic one: 'Friend of Gandhi dies by hanging.' He was just forty-six.

'My father was aware that all his life so far had been a search for who he was and where he belonged,' his son Dhan Gopal Mukerji II wrote in the Foreword to *The Face of Silence*. He also cited a letter written by one of his father's many friends and well-wishers, Josephine Tantine MacLeod, who wrote on 28 July 1936 from Helsinki to Jadu Gopal in India: 'Dhan Gopal has gone to join the great ones he so loved. His *nostalgie de Dieu* (love of God) took him over . . .'

He left at least one indelible claim on literary historians. Indian authors have won the Booker, the Nobel, the Pulitzer. Seven and a half decades have elapsed since a Bengali immigrant to the US won the Newbery Medal, but no other Indian has claimed Dhan Gopal Mukerji's trophy again.

(From research and columns written between 2004 and 2015.)

Raja Rao: 'We cannot write only as Indians'

'Sainthood is an inconvenient thing,' Raja Rao, who was born in 1908 and witnessed some of India's most politically stirring decades, wrote of Mahatma Gandhi. The saint, to him, was a man who 'would be perfect'; the politician was a man who 'would make the world wholesome, whole'.

Raja Rao understood saints and sainthood perhaps better than he understood politicians and politicking. Over time, especially in the last decades before he died at ninety-eight, Raja Rao would be canonized himself, which is to say that he was praised more and more and read less and less.

That is such a pity, because his first novel, *Kanthapura*, remains one of the most perfect classics of Indian literature. His later works, from *The Serpent and the Rope* to *The Chessmaster and His Moves* and *The Cat and Shakespeare* were critically acclaimed, though none of them achieved the iconic status of *Kanthapura*. None of them was as moving, or as unsettling.

Kanthapura was published in 1938, when Raja Rao was just thirty. Today's college students in India might not understand the impact *Kanthapura* had on students of a decade-and-a-half ago, when the 'Eng' in Eng Lit was taken very seriously. The curriculum was devoted to Dryden and Chaucer and Shakespeare: no Faulkner, no Proust, no Garcia Marquez, and certainly no Indian writers were allowed to pollute those literary waters. Few colleges would have dreamed of placing Mulk Raj Anand or Mahasweta Devi or Salman Rushdie alongside the Silver Poets or E.M. Forster.

Reading *Kanthapura* in college was a liberating experience. It was the key to our own world, and to a wider world. The fierce discussions sparked off by Rao's novel, of a village whose slow life-cycles are savagely interrupted by revolution, led us inevitably to Manohar Malgaonkar, Bankimchandra, O. V. Vijayan. And *Kanthapura* also let us claim the work of other writers, outside both the Indian and the Western canon—such as Mario Vargas Llosa's early Peruvian novels, or Chinua Achebe or Naguib Mahfouz.

Today, when debates over the importance of 'location' and 'audience' overwhelm the actual work of writers, it is worth remembering that the work seen as one of the most quintessentially Indian in the Indian writing in English (IWE) canon was written in a thirteenth-century French castle in the Alps, according to Robert L. Hardgrave. Raja Rao had written in Kannada and then experimented with French before settling into English.

'The telling has not been easy. One has to convey in a language that is not one's own the spirit that is one's own . . . English is the language of our intellectual make-up—like Sanskrit or Persian was before—but not of our emotional make-up . . . We cannot write like the English. We should not. We cannot write only as Indians. We have grown to look at the large world as part of us.'

That prescription, from the Foreword to *Kanthapura*, was written in 1937 and holds true for Indian writers even today. The voice of Achakka, the old woman who narrates Kanthapura's story, is still fresh, seventy years after Raja Rao created her. In Rao's words, the story 'may have been told of an evening, when as the dusk falls . . . stretching her bedding on the verandah', a grandmother might tell a newcomer the sad tale of her village. Gandhi and the freedom struggle swirl around and change Kanthapura.

In a later time, a brasher India, traditional village life—in all its richness and also all its starkness—of the kind that Ananthamurthy or Bibhutibhushan or Mukundan wrote about with such intimate love would be threatened by much: tourism, corporate greed, political indifference or corruption. But Rao's *Kanthapura* chronicles the first invasive wave that would permanently change and shape the lives of the villagers of Kanthapura—an invasion of new unsettling ideas about how to live, the unease that came along with the joy of discovering ideas of independence or freedom.

In 1945, Raja Rao wrote to his friend E.M. Forster: 'I have abandoned literature for good—and gone over to metaphysics. I am not a writer any more . . .' Forster responded in kind: 'You have, you say, abandoned literature for metaphysical inquiry. I have abandoned literature for nothing at all. So please let us meet.'

Raja Rao became a student and teacher of philosophy, but continued to write. David Iglehart, a former student, runs the Raja Rao Publication Project: Rao has left behind four unpublished novels, short stories, essays, poetry in French and correspondence with Indira Gandhi, Octavio Paz, and Andre Malraux. Iglehart has also edited Rao's *Daughter of the Mountain*, the second volume of his trilogy based on *The Chessmaster and His Moves*, to be published soon. He was an active writer, Iglehart reminds us, not someone who should be stifled beneath the camphor of sainthood.

In 1969, Czeslaw Milosz wrote a poem to Raja Rao:

Raja, I wish I knew
The cause of that malady.
For years I could not accept
the place I was in.
I felt I should be somewhere else . . .
I hear you saying that liberation is possible
and that Socratic wisdom is identical with your guru's . . .

Milosz continues, and ends with:

No help, Raja, my part is agony,
struggle, abjection, self-love, and self-hate,
prayer for the Kingdom
and reading Pascal.

Raja Rao's path was very different from Milosz's, much less wracked by pain and doubt. But here, at last, is an image of him that might stand for the author as well as the man: not a saint, not an icon, but the priest in his confessional, listening in silence, offering understanding and absolution.

(From 2006)

G.V. Desani: Who is H Hatterr?

There are literate, widely-read booklovers in this world who have not read *All About H Hatterr*. I know of their existence; I have even met some, but the thought that they exist is chilling. It's like meeting people who have never read *Tristram Shandy*, or *Gormenghast*, or found themselves hallucinating, as Hatterr fans do, about swamis and multiple exclamation marks.

This has nothing to do with literary snobbery. G.V. Desani's 1948 classic appears with dreary regularity on lists of books you must absolutely, positively read in order to be considered truly literary, and his astonishing hero has influenced writers from I. Allan Sealy to Salman Rushdie. But the real reason for anyone to read Hatterr has to do with a quality rarely cited in critical texts—never again will anyone write a book with so much exuberance.

Desani, for instance, didn't. His next work was the mystic *Hali*; and then he retreated into the comfortable life of the author-recluse. And in 2000, in the blurred newsprint of the obituary section of an Indian newspaper, next to the Antim Ardas and In Fond Remembrance notices, a brief postage-stamp sized picture of a blurred, young Desani alongside two brief lines informed us of his death. By then, the image of Desani the writer had blurred along the edges as well, and *All About H Hatterr* had plunged into the obscurity of the remainder bin from which it would need (and receive) repeated rescues from its fans in the publishing and literary world.

Hatterr fans are a lonely breed today. We know not just the famous lines—'Damme, this is the Oriental scene for you!', 'Sir, I identify it (the novel) as a *gesture*. Sir, the rank and file is entitled to know.'—but all the lovely obscure bits about swamis who trade in secondhand clothes stolen off their disciples and the fact that Desani managed to fit thirteen exclamation marks into one paragraph. There is something slightly deranged about us, and a tendency (as you will have noticed) to digress, that we share with H Hatterr Esquire.

'The Issue: The following answers the question: Who is H Hatterr?' unleashes Desani's torrential prose, and his unmatched ability to beguile you into trickster territory, holding your attention for three pages until he answers the question—sort of—on the fourth. Hatterr, born a year after Independence, was an early example of the only kind of Indian protagonist the Indian novel in English could possibly have: a man on the margins, a hero who belonged to two worlds and to neither. 'Biologically, I am fifty-fifty of the species,' writes Hatterr, introducing us to his European, Christian father and his Malay, Oriental mother and swiftly kicking them offstage as he does so.

So there you have it: our first bona-fide homegrown, school-of-Indian-writing-in-English literary character was not Indian at all. Decades later, writing in partial homage to Desani, Salman Rushdie's Saleem Sinai in *Midnight's Children* would also be half-caste—Anglo-Indian, in his case.

Hatterr belonged to the same no-man's-land—territory claimed by three of India's greatest writers, Rushdie, Desani and Saadat Hasan Manto, in works spurred by or written about Independence. And Hatterr, with his permanent logorrhea, his rapidfire, utterly Indian English patter, his frantic capering around a world that includes pukka British clubs and ash-coated fakirs, could also belong to Manto's lonely lunatic asylum. In Manto's iconic short story, 'Toba Tek Singh', the lunatics occupy the no-man's-land between India and the newly created Pakistan; Hatterr's no-man's-land, between the Orient and the Occident, is wider, but no less lonely.

Readers tend to miss the isolation of Hatterr on first reading: the man proceeds from swami to circus act to charlatan fakir with a frenetic speed and an unstoppable energy calculated to short circuit introspection. But it's there in *All About* . . ., Desani's introduction, showcased as the familiar loneliness of a writer without an audience, a voice rendered loquacious by the fear that he might be talking only to himself.

'Planning a rest, I submitted the manuscript to a typist place, to be typed, three copies please. It came back the same week. The rejection slip pronounced it 'Nonsense'. Besides, the lady said, it wasn't the sort of nonsense young girls in the office ought to see. I apologized, postscripting me a mere slave of the critics. Then I passed it elsewhere. And he referred it to a well-known psychiatrist friend of his (at a clinic). The doctor posted it, with an invitation to me to meet him—professionally. It was hawked around, three copies please, and finally kept by a very kind person. She typed a quarter and returned it. Her brother, a clergyman, was coming to stay in the house. Chance might lead him to the manuscript. I apologized again . . .'

This is still the voice of Desani, in character as Desani-the-author, not the voice of Hatterr himself. 'In all my experience,' T.S. Eliot wrote famously of the book, 'I have not quite met anything like it.' (The closest parallel to Hatterr's voice might come not from Eliot, Burgess, or Joyce, or even Laurence Sterne, but from John Kennedy O'Toole's *A Confederacy of Dunces*.)

Here is a small sample, from a conversation between Baw Saw and The Sheikh:

I learnt of the ways of the Occidental people from my master Angus . . . And I possess the *Etiquette-Garter*, the *Honi*! Soot quay *Malay-pence*! Soot quay *Malay-pence*! I am the Sheik of the London County Council, the *Ell See See*! Behold, I am wearing my *Ell See See*! Know, this is the source, the device and the secret of my prosperity! With this neck-wear, this mystic material, I am a burrasahib! A man! I am Eaten! I am Westmoreland! I am Shrewsbury! I am Arrow! I am Charter's House! I am Rugby-Football! I am Gun Co. Winchester! I am all-in-all! And CLC besides! With the aid of this neck-wear, I have helped others, given countless concrete lessons of pukka Occidental wisdom to the needy, as I myself once was! Verily, O beloved, I am a burrasahib!

Listen to me and fathom the world! Pay the fees, and see the world! *Ek dum, och aye! Och aye!*

Exactly ten years before *Hatterr*, Raja Rao had published *Kanthapura*, struggling, as he wrote in the Introduction: 'One has to convey in a language that is not one's own the spirit that is one's own.' In the same decade, Mulk Raj Anand had struggled with the 'unleavened bread' dilemma in his work, from *Untouchable* to *Across the Black Waters*: the complexities of conveying Indian speech, Indian ways of thought, in a language that was at once ours and alien. (Anand often came off sounding like Kipling in reverse, but he did try.) R.K. Narayan, from 1935 when *Swami and Friends* was published to 1948 when *Mr Sampath* came out, had found an easy Indian English that still seems neither forced nor dated. But even in the 1940s, after more than a century of writing in English, most Indian writers struggled to loosen their tongues, to find their own voice.

Hatterr invented his own: a mongrel hybrid that transliterated Indian phrases, borrowed and mauled Greek and Latin tags, mocked English-English, and turned language into a three-ring circus, shifting from juggler to trapeze artist to clown.

It's been over six decades, and *All About H Hatterr* has dated—in the same way that *Tristram Shandy* or Anthony Burgess's *Enderby* quartet has dated, the way any great classic should date. Desani resisted literary ossification—in a brief encounter with a Betty Bloomsbohemia ('the Virtuosa with knobs on') in his introduction, he writes: 'As for the arbitrary choice of words and constructions you mentioned. Not intended by me to invite analysis. They are there because, I think, they are natural to H. Hatterr. But, Madam! Whoever asked a cultivated mind such as yours to submit your intellectual acumen or emotions to this H. Hatterr mind? Suppose you quote me as saying, the book's simple laughing matter? Jot this down, too. I never was involved in the struggle for newer forms of expression, Neo-morality, or any such *thing*! What do you take me for? A busybody?'

But despite his (and Hatterr's) best efforts, the book invited analysis. Saul Bellow found that Desani was one of the few writers he could read while he worked on his own novel. Allan Sealy's *Trotternama*—another classic that bounces dangerously in and out of existence, like Hatterr, revived by one generation, forgotten by the next—romps down the yellow brick road Desani had built for Indian writers back in 1948. 'I learnt a trick or two from him,' Rushdie said once of Desani, and perhaps, more than the linguistic exuberance, what Indian writers received from Hatterr was permission.

The book opens with a 'Warning!' and a conversation between an Indian middle-man and the Author.

'Sir,' says the middle-man, 'if you do not identify your composition a novel, how then do we itemize it? Sir, the rank and file is entitled to know.'

'Sir,' says the Author, 'I identify it as a gesture. Sir, the rank and file is entitled to know.'

But there is, the middle-man explains, no immediate demand for gestures. There is, however, immediate demand for novels, and the Author gives in.

Or perhaps not. Desani's 'novel' is really a breathless, joyful performance, a gesture stretched across 316 pages, and perhaps that's why it remains unforgettable, despite its periodic descents into oblivion. Over the last few decades, Hatterr revivals have depended on the largesse of Western critics and publishers rather than the growing maturity and changing tastes of the Indian reader.

And since the West has its own set of classics, and India is reluctant to claim any story that is not a success story, *All About H Hatterr* remains not so much lost as not yet quite found. Damme, that's the Occidental-Orientale scene for you.

(From March 2010)

6

Goodbye, Britannica

In my home in Delhi, sometimes I'll take one of the old books
off the shelf, dust it, run my finger down the spine, and open it
to be confronted with evidence of that long career as a practising
bibliophagist: a telltale triangular gap on one of the pages of an old
Kaye Webb-edited Puffin edition, a torn-off corner from the collected
Brahmosangeet, the pages sticking together from humidity and
disuse. There must have been an age at which I stopped wanting to
consume the books I loved, and like other bibliophagists, I'm unable
to explain why you want to eat books in the first place or why, having
honed that appetite, you would grow past it into other pleasures.

As an adult, some foods have the ability to take me back to the past:
biting into fresh filo pastry in some cafe in Europe once, I stopped mid-
mouthful, as the papery taste of a particular favourite (*Kids and Cubs*,
Olga Perevskoya) flooded back. Thin pasta will do it; rabri, with its
blotting paper texture; grits; caramelized onion skins; zucchini blossoms;
the first bite of a paper dosa. All of these distinct and different tastes
bring back a rush of unreasonable book love, and the memories of
what we read in the other city where I grew up, a Delhi so mellow,
so village-like, so relatively small, compared to today's megapolis, that

it is a city of the imagination, as fabulous and distant as Pataliputra, as distant as Mohenjodaro.

The Rowland Road house, built of books collected by a previous generation of ancestors, had a curious but not uncommon effect on everyone who lived in it and visited the house: it became hard to buy books, beyond a certain point. We had nothing as grand as a family library, just wall shelves filled with handsome leatherbound volumes, but I sensed back then how a library could be both pleasure and burden, how it could open some doors and close others just as firmly.

Inherit a library, and you inherit wealth; but you also inherit someone else's way of ordering the past. If you lived in the Rowland Road house, fiction was easier to buy than encyclopedias; and while the massive tomes up on the stacks were there to be used, we used them gingerly, aware and fearful of damaging something that was, in the most literal sense, ancestral property. I would find this pattern repeated when, many years later, I watched the inhabitants of grand old houses auction their books off: all too often, the amassed and now unwanted collections had been put together by the generation before, not the generation of now. It is not that easy to make space for new readers in houses built of old books.

In my parents' house in Delhi, there were not that many old books, and there was the parallel luxury of empty bookshelves in the sturdy government bungalows of my childhood. My father, Tarun Roy, was a Cuttack boy, and he told us marvellous stories of cycling for kilometres to his school, of the fact that the local ghosts included ghostly cows (with flaming hooves) among their cohorts. When we visited his hometown many years after we'd heard the Collected Cuttack Tales, I realized how rich he and his three brothers had been: their 'gardens' included the fields, the rivers, the forests in a way we children of the city could not begin to imagine.

My Thakurma, Bibhabati Debi, Baba's mother, was a writer, in an unfussy way, producing short stories in Bengali with the same practiced flick of her wrist that she used to turn out roasted coconut treats and puffed rice and jaggery moas. She kept her writings in a black-leaded tin trunk, her home-made sweets in an old Lactogen tin, both containers equally battered and utilitarian. My Thakurda, Shibesh Roy, Baba's father, had been a manager at Andrew Yule, but he had the instincts and the ink-stained, comforting cheerfulness of a born schoolteacher. The four brothers had grown up reading in their years in the small town of Cuttack, because their parents considered books and reading important, but in my father's memories of his childhood, there was also a thrumming underlying current of hunger. The big libraries—not large, but capacious enough—were in Sambalpur or Behrampur. The school library, as with most school libraries across India, was a one-room sparse affair, and there were few bookshops within walking or cycling distance.

In that earlier, quieter, sleepy Delhi, it was possible for a government official to cycle to the imposing sandstone fortresses of North and South Block, as my father occasionally did. It would be unthinkable in today's more hierarchical bureaucracy, but it was perfectly normal in those days for a panjandrum like a secretary or a joint secretary to invite a humble deputy secretary or under secretary to carpool, so that one fat white Ambassador took all of them to office. Petrol was scarce in Indira's India, but then there weren't that many places where you could live it up in the Delhi of the 1970s and even the 1980s, especially on the meagre salary the sarkar handed out to government servants in those days.

Ice cream at India Gate from the Kwality carts were a big treat; my mother, Sunanda Roy, would drive us out in the ancient big black Ambassador with as many of the neighbourhood children as could be fitted into the back seat, where we squirmed and fought and bounced up and down like puppies. It was the kind of city where people spread white cotton bedsheets over the lawns on hot summer nights and slept outside—no one, not even the President, had air-conditioning. It was also the kind of city where when a family left for vacation, to a reasonably humble hill-station or for a tour of the dak-bungalows (no one could afford the few five-star hotels in existence, except for 'business people', a phrase uttered with the utmost darkness), they bolted the back door but did not lock it, just in case their neighbours might need to check on the house or borrow something from the kitchen in their absence.

Our government house in Delhi did not resemble the Kolkata house in many ways except for one crucial particular. Government houses were built like prisons designed by a very kind architect— enormous lawns and back gardens made up for the structure of the houses themselves: concrete barns with cement floors and to heighten the prison feel, iron-barred windows.

But like the Kolkata home, my parents' Delhi house swarmed with people, and the dividing line between a guest who stayed for dinner and a guest who crashed on the divan for weeks was very blurred. Uncles, cousins, the children of my parents' friends, anyone in need of a billet would find one under my mother's roof. My mother and the man who ruled the household, the chef Harilal, would go from the bedrooms to the drawing room to the back verandah to the small lawn outside just before main meals, counting the heads, and then cut the potatoes smaller or water the dal or in extremis, raid the kitchen garden. The unspoken rule of the house was that no one would be allowed to leave hungry, and that anyone in need of a bed would be offered it, even if the definition of a 'bed' could stretch considerably.

My architect-uncle suffered several shifts in his time as a house-guest; he began well, with a proper bed and bedroom until another uncle arrived pellmell with his family. He was demoted to the big divan in the drawing room, but then my Thakurda and Thakurma, who spent their years shifting from one brother's house to another so that no one felt left out, arrived a little before they were expected. So my uncle was shifted to the other divan, which was little more than a slender plank with an equally slender mattress plunked on top; if he breathed out with too much emphasis, he would fall off, and there wasn't much question of turning over in a space so reminiscent of the cramped upper bunk in Indian railway trains. He survived; there was an easy, bustling hospitality about my parents' house that made it possible for everyone to do the quintessentially Indian thing and 'adjust'.

All would have been well if it hadn't been for two things: my father had to be sent out from time to time to do the shopping, given the pressure on my mother's time, and aside from his early experience of book hunger, he also had an eye for life's little luxuries. The background raga to my childhood was the sound of the parents' bickering. 'Tarun!' my mother yelled, exasperated. 'Where did you put the groceries?' 'On the table,' my father said, shaking out *The Statesman*.

My mother inspected the dining table and found chocolate cake, figs, and Gabriel Garcia Marquez in paperback. 'But where are the dals and the masalas?' My father would treat the query with surprise: surely my mother could see that there were more important things in the world? 'But what are we to have for dinner?' my mother, with Harilal nodding in assent like a Greek chorus of doom, would ask. My father would point out with impeccable logic that he had, technically, come back with food. (The figs were of good quality, and in those days, frightfully expensive.) This was usually the point where my mother flew into a rage and stormed off to see what would be cobbled together from odds and ends, but she was in a minority. The rest of us were on my father's side, especially after I began reading Garcia Marquez: the dal could always be watered, it did no harm to anyone to eat khichdi for a few days, but Macondo, and Fermina Diaz, and the banana companies, and shipwrecked sailors, could not wait.

And then one day, my father came back home with a set of the most beautiful books my sister, my baby brother, and I had ever seen: the *Time-Life* collection of books on the history of the world, on scientific discoveries, and a full, new set of the Encyclopaedia Britannica.

There were versions of these sets in the Rowland Road house, but when I went up to the row of books and inhaled the scent from their brand-new leather spines, it was an experience of the most sacred and the most carnal of loves at the same time. These books were different, because they were new, and because—perhaps my father had intuited this—we did not have to touch them gingerly, worrying that the pages would fragment and fall apart. They changed my life, and my sister's life, and perhaps my brother's life too, though he was more an outdoors person than we were: they brought the wider world of Mayan cultures and contemporary America, of Enlightenment Europe and the great African oral storytelling heritage, right into our bungalow.

There were not that many ways, in that time, for the world to come to your doorstep. All India Radio's calm, reasonable, muted newsreaders gave us the government line on the news. In the verandah of the Rowland Road house, my Didima would twiddle the dial on her ancient radio, until the hissing of the vintage tubes gave way to the tinny, cheerful strains of Radio Ceylon and more distant, whispering Australian radio stations. The boxwallahs and royalty travelled; government servants on deputation to the UN travelled; diplomats travelled; the rest of India stayed mostly at home, and we treasured blue airmail letters as though they were the rarest of rare documents.

Those who did go abroad came back with gifts for the ones marooned at home, and the nature of those gifts is both poignant and telling: plastic ABBA and Beatles badges, tins of yellow Kraft cheese that tasted like dyed plasticine, blue-eyed, thick-lashed, white-skinned dolls draped in clothes that were completely incomprehensible to us. In a slightly later time, after television had arrived in the late 1980s, some travellers brought back videocassettes onto which foreign ads from UK and Australian television had been seamlessly recorded. They were the wistful equivalent of mixed tapes, playlists of products that Indian households did not need, did not have, and coveted anyway.

We grew used to having the world at our fingertips, and to looking it up, without questioning the authority of these encyclopedias. We saw them as the foreign equivalent of the *panjikas* and almanacs in their comfortable pink wrappers that told us the cycles of the moon and kept non-resident Bengalis informed of the dates of important festivals that shifted according to the lunar calendar; these books allowed us to keep a distant, shifting world straight in our heads.

Often, when I met scholars or writers in later years, I would find that they had grown up with the solidity of libraries of reference in their homes, and were so used to being able to consult their bookshelves for information in several Indian and European languages that they did not see how rare and precious the owning of reference books could be. It seemed to me to be a stroke of luck, to see the slow accumulation of knowledge on our shelves, so much more satisfying (and often far more easily available) than money in the bank.

The names on the spines of the Encyclopaedia Britannica form a litany. As a child, I browsed my way from Baltimore to Braila, Extraction to Gambrinus, with a special stop at P-R: Plants to Raymond of Tripoli.

That was from the fourteenth edition, with sombre dark blue spines instead of the brown, blue and gold of later editions; the music of the Britannica's spines would change through each edition. (The first, issued in just three volumes in 1768, went from Aa–Bzo and Caaba–Lythrum to Macao–Zyglophyllum, for those who were wondering.)

For many Indians, the Britannica stood for unassailable authority. The aspiring brown sahib bought a set for his fledgling library, though secretly he envied those who'd inherited theirs, complete with age spots on the pages. The Britannica was the caste mark of the newly Anglicised Indian; a generation later, it would signal the owner's interest in the wider world, stamp him or her as an aspiring global citizen.

Nirad C. Chaudhuri captured the solid place that the Britannica had in many Indian—all right, Bengali—homes in the days when knowledge was pursued with the same acquisitive fervour that we reserve for Gadino white diamond bags or gold-leaf ceilings these days.

'In 1914, I was able to surprise my acquaintances by chattering about the German General Staff, General Briamont and his fortifications, artillery and aeroplanes. To no one did this showing-off of mine give greater pleasure than to an aged uncle, Mr Das . . . who was the father of the cousin who owned the Encyclopaedia Britannica.'

The edition Niradbabu would have read had very few entries by Indian contributors, though in keeping with its imperial spirit, the Britannica included many entries on India. By the 2000s, this had changed, but the first few editions bristled with entries on Benares, Indian currency and the Frontier tribes, most written by retired British generals and old India hands.

One of the early exceptions was the wonderfully named Sir Mancherjee Merwanjee Bhownaggree (Knight Commander of the Indian Empire), one of the very few Indians in the 1890s to be elected to the British House of Commons. Sir Bhownaggree's expertise allowed him to write entries on Aga Khan, Sir C.J. Readymoney, Jeejeebhoy and Takhtsinghji. It was a respectable list, if not quite as interesting as the one curated by George Cordon Coulton, an expert on celibacy, concubinage, indulgence, knighthood and chivalry.

The insistence on the wisdom of experts set the Encyclopaedia Britannica apart from more modern rivals, such as Wikipedia. The Britannica's approach to knowledge is a curated one: the board of editors picks experts on different subjects, and the early bias towards a British, masculine, Christian view of the world has yielded to a more broad and inclusive understanding of history.

The rise of Wiki as an accepted people's encyclopaedia in the last eleven years was unexpected. Few thought that an online open-source 'encyclopaedia' in which entries were contributed and edited by ordinary readers rather than experts would be successful; yet, in its eleven years, Wiki has become as ubiquitous as Google.

But neither institution is free of problems. Many Wiki entries focus on issues of ephemeral value or amplify the present obsession with celebrity. The editing battles on Wiki may be its eventual downfall—entries on more controversial subjects read like constantly overwritten palimpsests. If Wiki can't scrape the barnacles off its hulk, it may not survive. The Britannica is likely to thrive online, if not in print; but the question of who gets to select its panel of experts is likely to become more fraught. Wiki catalogues everything, arriving almost accidentally at accuracy; the Britannica's utility is that it promises to select only the most important.

That is not how the Britannica began, though. The first edition advertised the Encyclopaedia as 'A Dictionary of Arts and Sciences compiled upon a new plan in which the different arts and sciences are digested into distinct treaties and systems'. It was compiled by 'a society of gentlemen in Scotland', and William Smellie, a young scholar, wrote most of the articles. He used a curiously modern method, listing the key sources from Alston's Tyrocinium Botanicum to Ulloa's voyages and Young on composition, liberally borrowing from all of these books.

It was very much the cut-and-paste method that journalists and students use these days, and Smellie made no bones about it: 'With paste pot and scissors I compose it.'

I know that last quote is accurate, because it's there on Wikipedia.

But I have no real reader's relationship with the Wikipedia; the information on it might be useful, but it cannot be held in your hands. Though I'm used to virtual reading, my first relationship with books was inescapably tactile (you cannot, for instance, eat a Wiki page), and that perhaps explains some of the love for old things, for the ancient pink almanacs that remind me of my Thakurma, the black-and-gold leather-bound Britannicas that bring back my Didima's house.

For many bibliofetishists, the thistle-stamped bound volumes were inseparable from the content. In 2012, when it was announced that no further physical editions would be printed—the Britannica will now be available only online and as an app—I went to my bookshelves and looked with some concern at the row of encyclopaedias.

These ones were inherited from the Rowland Road house in Kolkata, not my father's house. They were fragile when I was a toddler, and they are positively frail now. Touching these books is like meeting people you knew in the prime of their lives and realizing that you must now take their papery hands with care, lean forwards to speak so that they can hear you clearly: you must acknowledge that they have grown old.

And as I gently handled the volumes with their peeling leather spines, the delicate, powdery pages, it suddenly seemed unbearable to me to know that someday the pages would fragment and fall apart. Unlike many book lovers, I am not in love with the physical form of books, any more than I like my friends for the clothes they wear or the fashions they adopt; the words matter more than the page.

And yet, kneeling in front of the bookcase, there was that stab of protectiveness, the certain knowledge that if the Britannica was no longer to be printed, something solid and essential would be lost. One small fragment of that loss was there in my hands, in the dust left when I closed the old thistle-embossed volume and part of a sentence crumbled into nothingness.

(Written in 2012)

7

English, Vinglish

How long have Indians been arguing about language? For centuries, in some style.

Shankar Gopal Tulpule, the historian of Indian literature and compiler of a dictionary of Old Marathi, records that it was roughly seven to eight centuries ago that Mukundaraja prefaced his great work, *Vivekasindhu*, with a defiant excuse for using Marathi instead of Sanskrit:

> If common trees can bear fruit on par with the wish-tree,
> Why should they not be planted with growing zeal?
> So also, even if here the language is Marathi,
> The content is the same as that of the Upanishads,
> Why should it not, therefore, be stored in the recesses of the heart?

This was a radical argument, guaranteed to offend the purists with its placing of a local language, Marathi, on the same elevated plinth as Sanskrit. He had, Tulpule writes, 'already anticipated the displeasure of the orthodox Sanskrit pundits' of the day—in their eyes, Indian regional languages were not considered refined enough to be used for serious work. That argument over hierarchy and power between languages ran fiercely in the thirteenth century, some declaring that

Sanskrit was the only language that a serious writer would use, others fiercely spurning it in favour of their own regional tongues.

Another story Tulpule tells is of the time Kesiraja asked the great Mahanubhava preceptor Nagadeva a question in Sanskrit. Nagadeva snubbed Kesiraju: 'Please, I do not follow your *asmat* ('for this reason') and *kasmat* ('why'). The Master preached to me through Marathi. So, ask me in the same language.'

When language wars break out today, with angry arguments and sometimes riots over the question of whether English should take a backseat to Hindi, whether Telugu has received its due, or whether Hindi is cannibalising less prominent local dialects, I think of the long history of these clashes, stretching all the way back to Nagadeva and Mukundaraja.

In many of the present-day arguments over language, English and Hindi dominate the discussion. The arguments over English have not substantially changed over the two centuries that it has been an adopted Indian language: it is an alien tongue (not after 230-plus years), it is unfairly the language of power and jobs (as true of English as it once was of Sanskrit, Persian and sometimes Hindi), it is the carrier of class privilege (an increasingly inaccurate claim as the language spreads, adapts and democratises), it divorces Indians from their root language (this ignores the very large number of Indians who are comfortably bi- or multi-lingual).

The imposition of Hindi is a tricky subject: claims made for the dominance of Hindi speakers often club together the speakers of allied dialects—G.N. Devy, the formidable linguist, points out that over 100 'feeder' languages surround the Hindi belt, and act as the 'roots' of Hindi. And opposition to Hindi as the national language rests on the fact that it is an alien tongue, just as much as English, for large swathes of the country. On the plus side, Hindi is easy to learn, and is considered one of the fastest-growing languages in India today; it has also become more adaptable in the sense of assimilating words from other Indian languages.

But all of the English versus Hindi (or English/Hindi versus The Rest of India) debates in the mainstream, if not in academia, ignore a far bigger question: could India's dominant languages strangle the rest? G.N. Devy and his colleagues conducted the People's Linguistic Survey of India (PLSI), working over a four-year period to track the number of languages still in existence and the number threatened. The Census of India names 122 languages, of which twenty-two are scheduled; the PLSI found over 780 different languages and sixty-six different scripts. In the past fifty years, they discovered that India had lost about 250 languages.

What India should be concerned about, more than the reductive and frankly useless Hindi/English versus The Rest of India debates, is an environmental issue. Given that this is such a radically, almost magically, multilingual country, preserving language diversity is more important than lingering over the angst of the Indian writer who uses English as his primary publishing language.

In a fascinating 2002 paper for UNESCO, Rajeshwari V. Pandharipande offers a simple way to assess power equations between Indian languages: how many domains do they cover? In her analysis, English emerges as powerful because it is used across several domains— business, education, national/international communication and technology. Regional languages, especially state official languages, also have power: they cover private domains (home), but also education, government, law. Tribal languages emerge as the weakest because they are only used in the private domain, and as their power wanes, they are used less and less often at home.

Another historian of Indian literature, Sisir Kumar Das, makes a comparison between the influence of Persian and the influence of English. Persian, used as the 'power' language until it was displaced by English, was, he points out, the language of the elite. But that elite was cross-community, and included both Hindus and Muslims. It had the advantage of being a living tongue, unlike Sanskrit whose reach was more written than oral. And for centuries, Persian served as a medium of translation, receiving texts translated from Indian languages as well as translating other Indian language texts into Persian, from where they spread across the world.

The Persian-versus-Urdu debate raged as strongly some centuries ago as the Hindi versus English one does. However entertaining, these debates should not blind us to a key fact about India: the dominant language in any region has often posed the greatest threat to smaller local and tribal dialects. Even multilingualism does not cut through hierarchies of power. As Das remarks of the eighteenth and nineteenth centuries: 'Bilingualism was an accepted fact of life. Bilingualism, however, did not mean equal prestige for both languages.'

It might be utopian to imagine a time when Indian schoolchildren are encouraged to learn one of the many Indian languages on the endangered list as their third language. Or to imagine a time when English, Hindi, Bengali, Marathi, Gujarati and other dominant languages do not, like bullies, overshadow the many, many other tongues that people call their mother tongues. But as our understanding of the map of Indian languages changes and shifts, so should the old, atrophied arguments yield to newer debates.

*

The annual birthday party for English is held on 25 October, Thomas Babington Macaulay's birth anniversary, and celebrating it might become a new Dalit tradition. Over a century ago, Savitribai Phule, the first woman to teach in the first women's school in India, wrote a classic ode to Mother English:

> Brahman's rule is now in ashes
> Under the English whips and lashes.
> It is all for the good of the poor
> Manu's dead at English Mother's door.

In another, equally well-remembered poem, Phule urges 'Shudras and ati-Shudras' to 'learn and break the chains of caste/ Throw away the Brahmin's scriptures fast'.

It is only fitting that Zareer Masani's biography of Macaulay opens with a description of a birthday party to English, held at the home of the writer Chandra Bhan Prasad. A poet sings, 'O Devi Ma let us learn English/Even the dogs know English!' And Prasad endorses

Phule's prescription, adding, 'Hereafter, the first sounds all newborn Dalit babies will hear from their parents is — abcd.'

Macaulay's *Minute* is famous and infamous in India, where the spread of English cannot be denied, but where its influence and importance are often resented. Many in India still bristle at Macaulay's ignorant dismissal of Indian literature ('a single shelf of a good European library was worth the whole native literature of India and Arabia'), and his intent: 'The languages of Western Europe civilized Russia. I cannot doubt that they will do for the Hindoo what they have done for the Tartar.'

Until Mr Masani's biography (*Macaulay: Pioneer of India's Modernisation*), though, Macaulay had been reduced to a museum portrait—like so many other figures in contemporary Indian history, British and Indian—in the absence of a tradition of biographical writing. In Mr Masani's well-researched and engaging telling, Macaulay emerges from the dust of the past. He had little physical charm— Thomas Carlyle called him 'a short squat thickset man of vulgar but resolute energetic appearance'—but he had a lively, ferocious mind, and a debater's zest for argument.

By 1832, he was secretary to the Board of Control, with an office overlooking the Thames: 'I am already deep in Zemindars, Ryots, Polygars, Courts of Phoujdary and Courts of Nizamut Adawlut . . . Am I not in fair training to be as great a bore as if I had myself been in India?'

Macaulay's interest in India was broad, but not necessarily deep; he advocated 'an enlightened and paternal despotism' for the new Raj. He met Ram Mohan Roy before he and his sister Hannah came out to India on *The Asia*. On board the ship he read his Greek, Latin and Spanish, neglecting his Hindi and Urdu grammars, and his Hindi was of the 'coop tunda' ('khoob thunda' — very cold) variety.

He wrote lyrical passages about the colours and sounds of India, even though he complained that the fish and the fruit were inferior to England's cherries and cod. Macaulay's standards were set by England, and when he met the Mysore Raja, he lamented what the king might have been: 'If he had been put under tuition, if he had been made an accomplished English gentleman . . .' His Kolkata was a racially segregated city, with the natives in Black Town, the Angrezis in power.

Mr Masani does not attempt to excuse Macaulay's prejudices—he was very much a man of his times—but he also draws attention to his brand of enlightened liberal imperialism. 'Almost two centuries later,' Mr Masani says of Macaulay's *Minute*, 'its underlying principles remain the Bible of Anglo-American nation-building in the world's trouble spots.'

Macaulay's aim was to produce 'a class of persons Indian in blood and colour, but English in tastes, in opinions, in morals and in intellect', and for a while, English was indeed the preserve of the babus and the bhadralok in India. As the latest Census figures demonstrate, it is now the fastest growing language in India behind Hindi, and it has become part of the Indian mainstream.

But Macaulay couldn't have predicted that a century after Savitribai Phule and other Dalit intellectuals saw the potential of English as a way out of the caste labyrinth, there would be a temple to Angrezi Devi. When work started on the temple in 2010, Chandra Bhan Prasad was quoted as saying: 'She stands on top of a computer which means we will use English to rise up the ladder and become free forever.' It was not an easy undertaking; the construction of the temple was halted on one ground or another, most of them remarkably flimsy. Some newspapers reported tension in the area, after members of the upper castes objected to a temple built for and by Dalits.

But Macaulay would have approved; his aim was not to replace local languages, but to add the library of English into the 'native tongues'. As Phule wrote in her poems:

In English rule we've found our joy
Bad days gone, Mother English abhoy!
English is the inheritance of none
Persian, Brahman, Yemeni or Hun.

There it stands, 175 years after Macaulay's Minute, ready to be claimed by Angrezi Devi's devotees.

(Based on writings from 2001 to 2014.)

TWO

Poets at Work

These short interviews that appear in the following pages should be consumed like samosas or paapri chaat. They were written in the moment, built around conversations that lasted at most for a few hours, and are useful only in the way that those old black-and-white snapshots by Mahatta are helpful: as snapshots of their time. With great regret, the editor and I left out interviews with authors who write in Indian languages other than English, since this collection of essays is chiefly about the history of Indian writing in English. Book reviews tend not to age well, so only two or three have been included, chiefly when they focus on the work of a writer who should not be ignored.

1

Dom Moraes

(1938–2004)

On the narrow ramparts of Neemrana, while a literary festival swung through its various moods—insularity, belligerence, camaraderie, jealousy—you might have observed a quiet, white-haired figure who managed to stay in the background while being present at every key moment. Dom Moraes, unlike other literary luminaries, enjoyed a position of relative ease on the fringes of the great game, and only his love of conversation and a certain humorous, observant, shrewd gleam in his eye marked him out.

If you wondered what was going through his mind, he had provided a partial answer years ago in *Gone Away*:'I have a little game I play with people, which in my nastier moments I am proud of: I take notes of their mannerisms, chuckling to myself. I was just starting the first invisible chuckle when I noticed [Ajit] Das chuckling too. His eyes rested on me, intelligent, sardonic and seeing, I stopped taking notes hastily.'

Fortunately for readers who enjoy his matchless prose just as much as the poetry on which his reputation rests, Dom Moraes encountered few subjects equipped with Ajit Das's ability to see what he was up to. Over the three volumes that make up *A Variety of Absences: Gone Away, My Son's Father* and *Never at Home*, he is relatively free to get on with his observations, chuckling invisibly all the while. And, spaced apart as they are, these three volumes offer a remarkable insight into the life and times of a singular figure. No novelist could have created a character like Dom Moraes, though most would have given their right arms to be able to do so.

Gone Away was first published in 1960. At the precocious age of twenty, Dom had won the Hawthornden Prize for poetry, launching his career in somewhat premature fashion. Dom was not your average self-conscious twenty-year-old; the son of a famous father (the legendary Frank Moraes), he summed up his curriculum vitae in 'Song':

> I sowed my wild oats
> Before I was twenty
> Drunkards and turncoats
> I knew in plenty.

He had met Stephen Spender, who had praised his poems; been taught by W.H. Auden; met Cyril Connolly, who had criticized his suit; refused to respond to Raymond Chandler's gibes about Nehru; received a magisterial nod of approval from T.S. Eliot. He had travelled, far more than most young men of his generation, and grappled with the complex emotions his mother's progression into madness had evoked.

As the first volume of his memoirs, *Gone Away* works precisely because it was never meant to be a memoir; Dom had been commissioned by Heinemann to write a book about India. 'The book was called a travelogue,' observes Dom, 'but it turned out to be a better picture of me as I was at twenty-one than any more orthodox autobiography.' Nevertheless, he managed to pack in some travel: inside Bombay, gloomily surveying the extremely strange phenomenon that was a cocktail party in a prohibition state (as it was at the time), Dom pushed off to scrutinize the infinitely more fascinating world of Bombay's bootleggers. In Delhi he noted an eternal truth about the capital: 'All the gossip in New Delhi is political.'

Ved Mehta—he accompanied Dom on several other alcohol-fuelled trips with long-suffering phlegmaticism—and he visited Nirad

Chaudhuri and listened in some bewilderment to the Bengali author's extolling of the wonders of England, including Lyons' tea-rooms. With Ved, too, he travelled to Nepal and met 'the last feudal overlords that the world has seen, these Ranas', saw villages and monasteries, recited Edna St.Vincent Millay's 'For Any Dying Poet' to the poet Devkota as he lay, dying of cancer, among the bodies of more dead and dying. With the sardonic Ajit Das for company, he travelled to Nathu La—not, in those days, just another offbeat tourist spot, but a grim forbidding pass guarded by the Chinese—and saw the first Indian troops enter Sikkim.

At thirty, he wrote an autobiography—*My Son's Father*—more personal in tone, his eye for detail and his sense of humour more focused, his critical faculties combative and developed. He sums up the poet Sarojini Naidu in one line—'Naidu, who in her youth had lived in England and written quantities of appalling verse which was praised by Yeats and Gosse'. He fell in love; he wrestled with his mother's nightmares; he became a poet. He was able to look back at the first stirrings of his talent with the clarity and humour that mark his best work:

> My imagination, naturally vivid, was fired and flowered by anything I read . . . I wanted to extend the myth of the book into my own mind, to create new situations for the characters of the book. I told myself stories, therefore, based on the characters I had just read about: Tarzan, Black Bartlemy, Sherlock Holmes, Allan Quatermain, etc. At first I simply told myself these stories in bed: then I began to do it walking up and down my bedroom; finally I wandered through the flat, murmuring to myself, and gesturing fiercely with my hands as the tension of the plot mounted. My father and his friends, sitting on the verandah, often watched astounded as I slowly paced the drawing-room, mouthing and flapping my hands. My father was already worried about my mother's mental health: he now began to worry about mine.

Never at Home is best read as the third volume of a trilogy; it has a sense of closure about it, even though Dom's fans might well ask for a fourth volume. Of Eichmann sitting inside his glass box as the trial wound on and on, he writes: 'I could not feel pity, because of the evidence, and because of his dehumanization by the glass box; for the same reasons I could not feel anger or hatred. The evidence might have caused those; but the evidence had become unconnected with the man.'

He covered Algiers during its war, and Vietnam during its struggle. 'It had been a beautiful country, but it had also been depopulated and deforested; scabbed with napalm, stained with cordite, it lived on in a new incarnation, goddess of boredom and war.' In between there was poetry; then there was writer's block. There were distractions—affairs, other writers, the bizarre figure of Christine Keeler, sponging off journalists without any of the charm of Holly Golightly demanding change from her escorts for 'the powder room'.

In 1982, Dom wrote the first 'real' poem he had produced in seventeen years. It's called 'Absences' and the title of this edition of his collected memoirs is drawn from it: 'No sound would be heard if/So much silence was not heard . . . this/ World only held together/By its variety of absences.' For the moment, he rests—a travelogue through India with Sarayu Srivatsa came out last year, and another book is in the pipeline. He doesn't so much fight his long-term illness as he eyes it sardonically, in between more travels, more wine, more cigarettes. At the end of his memoirs, illuminated by his inimitable raconteur's voice, he leaves 'a little tired, but in the end/Not unhappy to have lived'.

★

His voice was so quiet that you had to lean forward, straining, to catch what he said; until he startled you by summoning up a resonance and a richness from somewhere deep within. 'Writers, if they are good writers, don't talk much about writing,' Dom said the first time we met, and he talked about everything else instead.

I was not one of Dom Moraes' circle of intimates; the few encounters I had with the poet (the writer, the columnist, the reporter, even the cheerful, committed drinker: all these stemmed from this primary version of his self) happened in the evening of his life, after he'd crossed sixty. I didn't see the young Dom, the precocious boy-poet who shared his anecdotes of Stephen Spender and Henry Moore in a London long since gone.

I never met the Dom Moraes who grappled with his mother's importunate demons, who struggled with the formidable shadow cast by his father, the legendary Frank Moraes, who told his wife, Henrietta, that he was just going out to buy cigarettes and walked out of the house and the marriage.

I was a little too young to hear about the Dom Moraes who married Leela Naidu (to say that Naidu is celebrated chiefly for her beauty may seem condescending, unless you remember the extraordinary quality of that beauty). The marriage didn't last; Dom's friendships survived better than his relationships.

His appetite for good whiskey almost matched his relish for a good story: he consumed both in generous quantities. E.M. Forster once asked for 'a non-alcoholic edition' of Dom's early memoir-travelogue, *Gone Away*.

In the last few years, Dom had cut back; his cancer had been diagnosed (according to Jeet Thayil, he had nicknamed his tumour 'Gorgi'). But there is something essentially wrong, naggingly incomplete, about any memory of Dom that doesn't include the whiskey. In 'Song', he continues, after the mention of drunkards and turncoats:

Then with the weather worse
To the cold river
I came reciting verse
With a hangover.

I remember it was a Wednesday night when the phonecalls and the emails came in. One friend wrote: 'Dom's dead. I'm off to drink to his shade.' I no longer drank, so I saluted him with plain orange juice. But many others must have instinctively done the right thing, raising a glass to his memory.

Any toast to Dom would have to commemorate his great gift, a singular, unmistakable talent that never reached the heights he aspired to, but that never fell below a certain level either. I cannot remember a single poem by Dom that stands out or that would be anthologized repeatedly, which may be just as well.

Too many lay readers remember Nissim Ezekiel only for 'The Night of the Scorpion', Gieve Patel only for 'On Killing a Tree'. But with Dom's verse, you read on, never running out of new lines to fall in love with. He published over thirty books in his lifetime, some in collaboration with his companion, architect and writer Sarayu Srivatsa, who saw him through his twilight years with a marvellous blend of grace, humour, exasperation and affection.

By dying peacefully at sixty-five, he won a kind of victory over cancer: Dom retired for his afternoon nap, had a heart attack, and never woke up. He never had to suffer what he and Sarayu had feared—the long hospital stay, complicated operations, a slow descent into pain. 'He died without indignity,' Sarayu said, and she was grateful for that small mercy, of the perfect ordinariness that could make him spend the day before he died choosing aquariums for the house, Japanese fighting fish, turtles.

At one stage, his poetry dried up for seventeen years, belying the early promise of the sensitive, frighteningly bright youth who'd precociously won the Hawthornden. In 1982, Dom wrote the first 'real' poem after that long gap: 'Absences'.

Last year, he released *Typed With One Finger*, a collection of poems; among the plenitude of book projects occupying his time was an idea for a new collection of poems. No writer could find the perfect word better, or faster, than Dom; no one could so accurately capture a moment, whether it concerned Sir Vidia throwing a fit at Neemrana (Dom disapproved, but gleefully captured every unspoken nuance in the situation) or Ginsberg discoursing on his vision of William Blake. 'I inquired what Blake had worn to the interview. "Oh, like a toga, man," Ginsberg said, "the kind of clothes all the people wore in those days."'

Dom was always in place, and always out of place: after so many long years in India and his travels around the world, he never learned to speak any language except English. But India was the country he kept coming back to; England, which sometimes had the greater claim on him, was never home. It didn't seem to bother him; he had the calm assurance of an eternal passenger, the knowledge that he could put his bedroll down anywhere and find a space for himself.

There are as many Dom anecdotes as the man had friends and fellow travellers. One of the best comes from Jeet Thayil, now an immensely talented poet in his own right. He met Dom when he was a young poet, just starting out; Dom was in his late-forties. As he rose to leave, Dom took his hand, and told him about 'the handshake'.

Jeet recalled Dom saying: 'Well, this handshake goes all the way back to Shakespeare, the first poet. You see, just as you're shaking my hand, I shook Eliot's hand, he shook Yeats' hand, Yeats shook Tennyson's hand, Tennyson shook Keats' hand . . .'

Dom Moraes passed it on, whatever it was that he had: sometimes it was kindness, sometimes stories, sometimes just a drink, sometimes his ability to remember uncomfortable things, sometimes the promise that other poets would come along who would share his gift, and shape it.

(Based on interviews with Dom Moraes between 1998 and 2004.)

2

Arun Kolatkar
(1932–2004)

Years ago, when I interviewed my first Indian poet, I thought longingly of Arun Kolatkar. The poet in question was a woman only too eager to expound on the meaning and beauty of her verse, which had little of either, unfortunately.

I'd just finished reading *Jejuri*, Kolatkar's cycle of poems set in a temple town where the narrator finds moments of beauty among darkness and squalor, devotion not in the sanctum sanctorum, but an awareness that, as the poet would say in an interview, 'wherever a bitch gives birth is probably a holy place'. To move from Sarojini Naidu and Toru Dutt to this was an epiphany.

And as the woman poet droned on and on, I thought of all the questions I wanted so desperately to ask Kolatkar about his poems, his images; questions that I and most ordinary readers would never be able to ask him, even by proxy, because of his contempt for and resistance to the whole process of mythmaking around poetry.

I can't ask Kolatkar these questions any more—he died, it was cancer—but it doesn't matter. His poems and writings, from *Jejuri* to the recently released *Kala Ghoda* poems and *Sarpa Satra* poems, were dismissive of questions and critical notes, intolerant of footnotes, contemptuous of explanatory essays. If you didn't find what you were looking for in the poetry itself, you had no business reading it. He wasn't quite as reclusive as reputation had it; resistant to intrusion, certainly, as his notorious refusal to install a telephone in his house demonstrated.

But his friends knew where to find him: the former adman (he worked at Lintas for a long while) had a favourite restaurant in Kala Ghoda, and no doubt, future devotees of his work will make pilgrimages there to go and genuflect at the tables. I imagine his ghost will look on sardonically.

My favourite Arun Kolatkar story concerns his response to an interviewer who asked him the standard question: 'Who are your favourite poets and writers?' The question infuriated Kolatkar, but then most questions did: he was the master of the freezing silence, the riposte in the form of another question, the non sequitur, the bland digression. This time, he let rip.

'There are a lot of poets and writers I have liked. You want me to give you a list? Whitman, Mardhekar, Manmohan, Eliot, Pound, Auden, Hart Crane, Dylan Thomas, Kafka, Baudelaire, Heine, Catullus, Villon, Jynaneshwar, Namdev, Janabai, Eknath, Tukaram, Wang Wei, Tu Fu, Han Shan, Ramjoshi, Honaji, Mandelstam, Dostoevsky, Gogol, Isaac Bashevis Singer, Babel, Apollinaire, Breton, Brecht, Neruda, Ginsberg, Barth, Duras, Joseph Heller . . . Gunter Grass, Norman Mailer, Henry Miller, Nabokov, Namdeo Dhasal, Patthe Bapurav, Rabelais, Apuleius, Rex Stout, Agatha Christie, Robert Shakley, Harlan Ellison, Balchandra Nemade, Durrenmatt, Aarp, Cummings, Lewis Carroll, John Lennon, Bob Dylan, Sylvia Plath, Ted Hughes, Godse Bhatji, Morgenstern, Chakradhar, Gerard Manley Hopkins, Balwantbuva, Kierkegaard, Lenny Bruce, Bahinabai Chaudhari, Kabir, Robert Johnson, Muddy Waters, Leadbelly, Howling Wolf, Jon Lee Hooker, Leiber and Stoller, Larry Williams, Lightning Hopkins, Andre Vajda, Kurosawa, Eisenstein, Truffaut, Woody Guthrie, Laurel and Hardy.'

I look at those names now, and I think, okay, that's a poem right there. It speaks for all of us, for our hybrid heritage, our right to claim everything that comes from our 'roots', everything that comes from 'elsewhere' and to put the two together in one defiant, all-inclusive category.

Osip Mandelstam sculpts his protests against a repressive regime alongside Namdeo Dhasal, the defiant poet speaking for the downtrodden, the Dalits, in a language he claimed as his own, alongside Lenny Bruce's anarchist humour and Laurel and Hardy's equally anarchist pratfalls. It's the only possible answer to the questions that would have bored Kolatkar silly, the 'which-language-do-you-prefer-Marathi-or-English' question, the 'is-this-autobiographical' question, the 'what-were-your-influences' question, the 'how-do-we-understand-you' question. To all of these he would have had one reply: read the work. Go back to the poems. I can't help you.

I'm supposed to be a critic, but I can't help you when it comes to explaining why *Jejuri* became, for many generations of Indians, the iconic set of modern poems. Perhaps I can do this another way, by tracing my memories of the ways in which I read *Jejuri*. The first time was within the bland pages of my English textbook, which was called something like 'A Radiant Reader of English Poetry' and introduced us, daringly, to Ramanujan and Ezekiel and Kolatkar while balancing them with Alfred Noyes's preposterous 'The Highwayman' and Walter Scott's 'Lochinvar'.

As we turned the pages, drowsing through 'Lord Ullin's Daughter' and chanting wearily 'Lightly, o lightly we bear her along', we came up against Kolatkar's images of sunlight as a sawn-off shotgun with a shock that I can still feel today, so many decades later.

In college, someone had a battered cyclostyled copy of *Jejuri*, the print smudging blackly across the lines, Kolatkar's words obscured by chai stains and flyspecks. Those were brushed off each time so that we could read the poems, but they always came back, so that we always read Kolatkar through a living prism of India.

Squashed samosas merged into type when we were well off; sweat stains splotched those pages in summer. Four years later, I'd graduated to a samizdat copy of *Jejuri*—it remained persistently either out of print, or when it did emerge briefly into print, it was out of the reach of my meagre funds.

This was wrapped within the folds of a calendar that featured a manically grinning Ma Durga whose face had the exaggerated pout of filmstar Sridevi, and whose body was draped in the kind of sari Mandakini would later make famous under a waterfall. Given Kolatkar's views on religion, this seemed appropriate.

Jejuri is to be published within respectable covers this year, and the two books of poetry released a bare month before Kolatkar died bear no resemblance to the crumpled and life-stained palimpsests in which I met his poetry first.

I don't know whether I can handle the newness, the respectability; but then again, as I learned first from Arun Kolatkar, iconoclast, recluse, thinker, poet, it's not the book that matters but the words.

(Written in 2004, after Arun Kolatkar's death on 25 September.)

3

Jeet Thayil

The house in which we're meeting is bare, the boxes of books still unpacked, two lonely chairs anchoring the emptiness of the room. Jeet Thayil and his wife will settle in soon, but this empty space is the perfect place to have a conversation about Indian poetry.

Fulcrum is an elegant little poetry magazine published from 'a room in Boston', already seen as one of the most significant of its kind. Jeet Thayil edited *Fulcrum* Number Four, which contains two sections: Poetry and Truth, and Indian Poetry in English. It's an astounding collection—fifty-six poets, from places as far apart as Fiji, New York, Mumbai, Sheffield, Coorg, Berkeley, Bangalore, all, as Thayil says, connected only by language, English.

Some familiar names are here, from Nissim Ezekiel, Adil Jussawalla, Arun Kolatkar, Eunice de Souza, Dom Moraes to Kamala Das, Ranjit Hoskote and Dilip Chitre. There are poets who aren't as well known in India as they should be, from Aimee Nezhukumatathil to Mukta Sambrani and R. Parthasarathy. And there are a handful of 'lost poets, the ones we forgot about': Gopal Honnalgere, Srinivas Rayaprol, Lawrence Bantelman.

'I think one very fine way to tell the development of a society is how it treats its poets, its gay people, and its women,' says Jeet. 'And in those three areas, we really are backward. I believe that two generations from today, there may be value placed on all of this. Young people today read poetry, they buy books, they read poetry on the Internet. The Internet has taken poetry out of that academic conversation, which has to happen if poetry's going to live. Say "poetry" and there were a lot of people who were turned off already, who had forgotten that a poetry reading is just a man or a woman speaking to you. Poetry needs to resonate with you if it's going to live. It's human speech, and it's the most beautiful speech, it's elevated in a way we can't have in our normal lives; it contains the best of us.'

What Jeet is trying to do with Indian poetry in English is an archaeologist's job: to recover what was lost, to take scattered shards and isolated schools of poets and fit them together in a pattern. It was *Fulcrum*'s editor, Philip Nikolayev, who first broached the idea of a special issue of Indian poetry. It took Jeet nine months of concentrated work to put it together, and a revised version of this anthology, with sensitive portraits of several poets by photographer Madhu Kapparath, will be published by Penguin India later this year in *60 Indian Poets: 1952–2007*. It's one of the most ambitious, and most significant, anthologies of Indian poetry to emerge in recent times.

'I don't know why Indian poetry has been so clannish, so fragmented,' says Jeet. Previous poetry anthologies have collected remarkable work, but have often, in his opinion, been bogged down by the need to categorize. 'We've seen slivers of Indian poetry, tiny parts of the whole—women poets, the younger poets, post-Independence poets, diaspora poets; different "versions" of Indian poetry. It's so fragmented, so clannish, and it's only when you put it all together that you realize Indian poetry is an enormous thing. It can compare with the best in the world—with Latin American poetry, with European poetry.'

Amit Chaudhuri commented, after reading *Fulcrum*, that India's poets were actually producing better work than India's fiction writers; an observation that Pankaj Mishra had made almost a year ago. 'Interesting that two novelists should say that the poetry is better than the fiction,' Jeet says. In the introduction, he looks at the problems that poets face in India: 'Unlike Indian novelists, poets receive no advances; their books are usually out of print; even the best known of them have trouble finding publishers and are virtually unknown outside India . . . That they continue to produce original work is nothing short of remarkable.'

When he began work, Jeet had the usual suspects on his list. He found a great many more, courtesy the legendary Adil Jussawala. 'In Adil's apartment in Mumbai, the manuscripts, the photocopies and the books have displaced the human beings. Adil gave me a couple of feet worth of books—it took me months to go through it. And there were all these guys whose work had been forgotten. Like Lawrence Bantelman, who wrote five books, went to Canada and vanished. It's like a Rimbaud story, nobody knows whether he's alive or dead.'

Both anthologies pay homage to the dead—as Jeet points out, we lost nine poets between 1993 and 2004: A.K. Ramanujan, Srinivas Rayaprol, G.S. Sharat Chandra, Agha Shahid Ali, Gopal Honnalgere, Reetika Vazairani, Nissim Ezekiel, Dom Moraes and Arun Kolatkar. In 'Dirge', Vijay Nambisan writes: 'The poets die like flies . . . How well they wrote, those friends now fettered, how the Indo-Anglian tongue/Allowed them to be lovely-lettered, their lives lived when the world was young . . .'

That reference to the 'Indo-Anglian tongue' reminds us both that the debate over English is never going to go away. Jeet sees no reason why poets who write in English should be seen as somehow less Indian or less authentic than their counterparts, but he acknowledges that the argument refuses to die. I like Arundhati Subramaniam's tart perspective in 'To the Welsh Critic Who Doesn't Find Me Identifiably Indian':

This business about language,
how much of it is mine,
how much yours,
. . . how much from the salon,
how much from the slum,
how I say verisimilitude,
how I say Brihadaranyaka,
how I say vaazhapazham —
it's all yours to measure, the pathology of my breath . . .

For Jeet, the return to India has coincided with one of the most productive phases of his life. He spent his early years in Hong Kong, and became a poet in his twenties after coming to Bombay to do a BA. Dom, Nissim, Adil, Eunice and a dozen other poets eventually became friends and colleagues, but it was a rough apprenticeship. There was no space for poetry; he remembers that period as a time of isolation. He published a few collections of poetry over the next two decades, did an MFA in America, shifted to New York, and came back to Delhi after 9/11 to find his feet in a city newly hospitable, experimenting with tenuous new energies and conversations.

In addition to the anthology, Jeet has completed work on a book of new poems, his first collection after *English: Poems*, is putting together a special issue for the *Journal of Postcolonial Writing*, and has finished a work of non-fiction. 'It's called *An Alien of Extraordinary Ability*,' he says of the last, 'which was the category under which I was approved for a green card; it's for writers, professors, filmmakers. The book is about a man who comes back to India after many years away, newly sober, and he sees the country and himself as if for the first time.' (*Alien* ... was never published, though some passages from this book worked their way in slow mutation into Thayil's fiction.)

He was, he says, an alcoholic (as were many of the Bombay poets) and an addict for almost two decades: 'I spent most of that time sitting in bars, getting very drunk, talking about writers and writing. And never writing. It was a colossal waste. In two years I've done more than I did in twenty years. I feel very fortunate that I got a second chance.' These days, he says as we make our farewells, the only addictions he has are poetry, and coffee. 'Coffee's much easier to get than heroin.'

(Note: Jeet Thayil published *These Errors Are Correct*, a collection of new poems, in 2008, after the sudden and tragic death of his wife, Shakti Bhatt, from a brief illness. In 2011, he published a novel, *Narcopolis*, a Bombay-noir classic that was shortlisted for the Booker; and an opera, *Babur in London*, performed in England in 2011 and 2012.)

4

Agha Shahid Ali
(1949–2001)

Agha Shahid Ali was the only person on earth who could actually say, 'Calloo, callay, oh frabjous day' and make this sound completely normal.

He said it to a passing waiter at the India International Centre (IIC), with an air of grave solemnity. Then he explained how to pronounce the word chortle: 'Chortle, with a long "o", and some reverberation on the "r". Massage the "ch": chooooorrrtle, chhhhorrrrrrrrtttle. Like the charawk of an egg-laying hen.'

The waiter, unused to guests making egg-laying sounds, peered at Ali under his brows and left, his back radiating disapproval.

Kashmir's best-loved and most quoted contemporary poet had his arms out like hen wings: 'Chortle from your diaphragm! Imagine you're a hen! Charawk!'

You couldn't meet the man for more than three minutes without returning with a wealth of anecdotes, and recipes—Shahid loved to cook, and could recite the ingredients of a good roghan josh with the same flair he would give to a Ghalib ghazal. You couldn't spend three hours with him without being added, with grand openheartedness, to the swelling ranks of his friends. Rukun Advani remembers him as an exotic among the dull array of Delhi University professors, a bird of extremely flamboyant feather and prodigious reading habits.

Kamila Shamsie recalls the bon mots that Shahid scattered with Wildean aplomb wherever he went. Old friends remember the warmth that Shahid brought with him. Kashmiri newspapers remember him with sadness, for the passing of this passionate chronicler of their bloodstained history: his words have become a talisman. 'My memory gets in the way of your history,' he wrote, speaking not just for Kashmiris, but for all those in occupied lands and all sorts of war zones—the real and those of the psyche as well.

When he spoke of exile, he didn't stop with this century; his mind went back to Ovid, poet of the *Metamorphoses*, the first exile. He was not an exile, he said of his years away from Kashmir—in America, in Delhi—but an expatriate, able to return to the sights, the sounds, the sensibilities and the memories that he mined so carefully for his poems. The care with which he separated the two states came from a deep understanding of the difference between those who could go back, and those who would never buy a ticket for home, either because they were not allowed to, or because 'home' had been erased by history.

He brushed away questions of identity, playing the label game with me as he'd played it with so many interviewers: 'I, Agha Shahid Ali, could be a Muslim-American poet, an Indian-American poet, a Kashmiri-American poet, an Asian-American poet, and what country does poetry belong to? What does it say on poetry's passport?'

His view of history was similarly vast; Jezebel, Ishmael, Rumi, Lal Ded, Melville, Begum Akhtar—he claimed the world, and was at home in it, wherever he might have been. He stored the memories others might have discarded, or refused to explore because they were too painful; his mother's illness and death in America became a way for him to return, through loss, to early happiness, never forgetting that the path back was through unbearable grief. At one point, the post offices in Kashmir ran out of postage stamps, and Shahid collected that image too, bags and bags of unopened mail piled up on the floor, letters written with urgency, carrying news or love or hope that would never be delivered.

Everyone has their favourite Shahid moment. Mine happened when, during the course of a half-hour interview that transmuted into a six-hour conversation, it became blindingly obvious that: 1) Agha Shahid Ali did not believe in false modesty, 2) with his skills, modesty wasn't an option.

We were discussing his poetical progress: akin to a mountaineer's determined ascent of the toughest peaks, no blind follower of free verse, Agha had written ghazals in English, attempted sestinas as well as sonnets, and, to crown it all, had written a canzone.

This is a deceptively light and graceful piece of verse, founded on a rhyme and scansion scheme dreamt up by a sadist in a bad mood. 'No one's done it for YEARS!' Shahid exulted. 'It's supposed to be too DIFFICULT! They all said it couldn't be DONE!'

And then this man in his late forties, clad in an impeccable kurta-pajama, danced a triumphant jig around the room, singing in melodious Henry Higgins fashion, 'But I did it, I did it; I did it, I did!'

In an age when most writers mimicked either the mannerisms of seasoned diplomats or exuded the bratty sulkiness of pop stars, Shahid was an original, his nearest possible rival Oscar Wilde. The flamboyance, the voluptuous savouring of words, the ready wit—all of these helped create a persona for him that almost, though not quite, obscured his work. The poetry was too compelling to be ignored, in its clarity, its beauty and its anguish, as he chronicled the descent of his homeland, Kashmir, into endless years of war and occupation, among other subjects.

Those who made the journey from the poems to the man often floundered ('Agha Shahid Ali is a strangely cheerful man . . .' said one interviewer, flummoxed by this writer of deeply thoughtful verse who coined comic epigram after epigram); to make the journey in reverse was oddly reassuring.

Of his writings, only *The Country Without a Post Office*, originally published by Ravi Dayal, was available in India for many years, though now *The Collected Poems* can be easily found in most bookshops. This is one of the most acute, most haunting and most passionate love songs to Kashmir ever written. *Rooms Are Never Finished* was nominated for this year's National Book Award in the US.

It includes 'Lenox Hill', a screed of mourning for his mother who died of a brain tumour in 1996 ('. . . they asked me, So how's the writing/I answered, My mother/Is my poem'), and for her beloved Kashmir where she was carried after her death by her family. By the time the NBA ceremony was held, in October 2001, Shahid was dying, also of a brain tumour. He had made his preparations, written his death poems, read them out to his friends in the US.

I heard of his death on a Saturday night, in the middle of a party in Delhi. Lines from one of his poems cut for a moment through the buzz of people enjoying themselves:

Stone, grass, children turned old:
The dead have no ghosts.

I knew Shahid only slightly: four unforgettable meetings and a few phone conversations aren't enough to explain the intensity of the grief that came over me. Several of the people in the room knew him better; we didn't say much about it, just turned the party into something resembling an Irish wake.

Shahid, who was so vividly alive and to whom being maudlin was a deadly sin, would have appreciated that.

★

It took almost four years for Agha Shahid Ali's first collection of poems to make its way to India, where it was finally published in 2001. Ali's country, in *The Country Without a Post Office*, has no borders, no official sanction, no national anthem. In *The Blessed Word: A Prologue*, he traces Kashmir's lineage of grief and mourning back to the time of Habba Khatun, sees in its present ravaged state the trials Osip Mandelstam wrote about when his country went through its darkest times.

Few contemporary poets can claim as much mastery over form

as Ali. Ghazals and sonnets are handled with equal deftness, and Ali writes prose poems and blank verse with the ease that comes only to those who have mastered the rules of formal poetry before venturing away from them.

Most of the poems here lead inexorably back to Kashmir: its history, its paisley patterns steeped in blood, its legacy of grief. Ali's images are unwavering, mirrors held up to reality: 'a shadow chased by searchlights is running/away to find its body . . .', 'The houses were swept about like leaves/for burning . . .', 'Death flies in, thin bureaucrat, from the plains—a one-way passenger, again . . .'

Underpinning the elegies is a hard appraisal of the stories behind the headlines. The most frightening element of the violence that seeps into most of these poems is its impersonality. Sample *Death Row*: 'Someone else in this world has been mentioning you,/ gathering news, itemising your lives/for a file you'll never see.' There are comparisons to bloodbaths in other parts of the world—Sarajevo, Armenia ('O Kashmir, Armenia once vanished'), ancient Greece—as if to emphasize the continuity and remorselessness of the process whereby people and their histories are obliterated.

In 2009, eight years after Shahid's death, activists and journalists began to write about the unmarked graves, the mass graveyards, of Kashmir. Basharat Peer wrote about meeting sand-diggers who found body parts in the river Jhelum, about the mass graves in villages near the Line of Control that concealed thousands of the disappeared.

And before the fact-finding teams, there was Shahid's poetry, his dispatches sent from the war zone that was Kashmir in the 1990s. 'The city from where no news can come/is now so visible in its curfewed night/that the worst is precise,' he wrote, giving Peer a title for his own memoir of Kashmir, as though the two authors were fellow soldiers sharing the same battlephrases. He wrote of the shadows running away on Zero Bridge, the boys tortured in the interrogation cells of Gupkar Road, the friend whose ghost whispers to him, 'Each night, put Kashmir in your dreams.'

Along with the paisleys and the chinars, he set down the stories from the country without a post office, of son after son taken away, never to return, of the bodies tortured, dismembered, dumped in mass graves, from where they mutely tell their stories, so many years after Shahid and others first started writing about them.

(Based on reviews and interviews written and conducted between 1999 and 2001.)

5

Kamala Das

Belong, cried the categorizers. Don't sit
On walls or peep in through our lace-draped windows.
Be Amy, or be Kamala. Or better
Still, be Madhavikutty. It is time to
Choose a name, a role ...

— *An Introduction*, Kamala Das

A name, a role, a religion, a language: all her life, Kamala Das questioned and rejected belonging even as she longed for it. By the time of her death this weekend, seventy-five and still settling into an identity, Kamala Das stood for certain things in the public imagination: she was the short-story writer, the woman who wrote of sexuality with a freedom unthinkable for the times, and then retreated into purdah, an apostate turned convert who rejected Krishna for Islam.

Few of this generation's women writers know her as more than a name—sometimes a caricature—and to some extent, Kamala Das left behind a mixed legacy, too much rubbish thrown in with the good stuff. Those who read in English knew her chiefly as a poet, and she could be a very acute one; but she was also overly prolific, and many of her poems suffer from a lack of revision. She was far more interested in capturing the perfect emotion than the perfect line.

Those who read in Malayalam knew her as a short-story writer whose work reflected the frustrations of a generation of women who were just beginning to question marriage and the domestic life, just beginning to embrace their own sexuality and need for freedom. Many knew her only by her autobiography, published as *My Story*, which was an often intense, often rambling account of her loves, her writing, her need for something larger than the world of tradition and the hearth.

> . . . No, not for me the beguiling promise of
> domestic bliss, the goodnight kiss, the weekly
> letter that begins with the word dearest,
> Not for me the hollowness of marital vows and
> the loneliness of a double bed, where someone
> lies dreaming of another mate, a woman perhaps
> lustier than his own . . .
> — Annamalai Poems

Kamala Das grew up in a house where literature and writing was the order of the day—her great-uncle was a writer, her mother, Nalapatt Balamani Amma, was a respected poet, and her father was the managing editor of *Matrubhumi*. She wrote as a child, but only began to write professionally after marriage and motherhood. Her views were shocking in that time, her frankness about female desire revelatory and unsettling.

> Gift him all,
> Gift him what makes you woman, the scent of
> Long hair, the musk of sweat between the breasts,
> The warm shock of menstrual blood, and all your
> Endless female hungers . . .
> —*The Looking Glass*

Today, it's hard to fully understand the impact these lines would have had for a previous generation. Writers like Catherine Millet (*The Sexual Life of Catherine M*) and Charlotte Roche (*Wetlands*) now examine their sexual history in detailed laundry lists that leave nothing, from hemorrhoids to orgies as meticulously planned as a nineteenth-century tea party, to the imagination. But for women—and men—trapped in a multitude of roles that stressed the centrality of the family, Kamala Das's passionate evocation of desire, her demand that women be given lives, and rooms, of their own, was revolutionary.

In her sixties, Kamala Das discovered a need for a different kind of submission, to faith. It was a choice that turned in another direction from the freedoms she had so often longed for and fought for. Her conversion to Islam created yet another identity for her; as Suraiyya, she abjured many of the things that had defined her as a writer. Hindus, especially the liberal fold, were shocked at this late-life change of faith. Nor did it please those who had studied Islam in depth and felt that Kamala Das/Suraiyya had woefully misunderstood the faith.

Kamala Das had become, she said in an interview, a 'puritan in all senses'; she was seeking a kind of safety after the years of rebellion. In the process, she lost the ability to define herself, except in the most fluid terms—she remained, till the end, a seeker who never quite knew what she was looking for.

(Based on pieces written in 2004 and 2009.)

THREE

Writers at Work

1

Allan Sealy, in Dehradun

Like most fans of his work, I assume I know Allan Sealy: through the five previous books, through the readings he's done over the years, the occasional journalistic writings that my generation of students used to discuss late into the night, from the interviews and book signings. Allan has his fair share of the usual paraphernalia of a writer's life, especially when that writer comes from a generation so often analysed and written about: the same generation as Amitav Ghosh, Shashi Tharoor and company. His peers in college were Ghosh, Mukul Kesavan and Rukun Advani—all four have made their mark on literature, Ghosh and Sealy as novelists, Kesavan as an academic and writer, Advani as an independent publisher.

The Trotternama, Sealy's first novel, is a mock epic that replaces the grand historical figures of the old 'namahs' with Justin Aloysius, the Great Trotter, officer and inventor who lives on the sprawling grounds of Sans Souci in Naklau. Like one of its predecessors, G.V. Desani's *All About H Hatterr*, *The Trotternama* is both elusive and immortal—reports of its death are usually proved to be exaggerated, though it's only a handful of readers in each generation who respond to the slightly manic history of the Great Trotter and his seven generations of family.

Running through its exuberance is a sadder and now almost-buried history—the story of the decline of the Anglo-Indian community, the carefully culled biographies scattered through the book no match for oblivion. 'I wish to show you how History is made,' a character says. 'Understand first, good adept, that there are no sides to it . . . Front and back there be, certainly, which the vulgar call past and future . . . But sides, no.'

First published in 1988, *The Trotternama* stands at a crossroads. For the next two decades, Indian publishing (if not all Indian writers in English) would be in the grip of the marketplace, which exerts a kind of dictatorship of success on writing today. *The Trotternama* was also the last true successor to *Hatterr* and *Midnight's Children*—with a few scattered exceptions, the Indian novel in English took a much more conventional and far less experimental narrative direction in the 1990s.

Sealy has always written against the grain of the marketplace, giving up early on commercial success, looking instead for the freedom to experiment—in a recent novel, *Red*, he includes poems, for instance, mingling with the prose. Landscape is crucial to his books; just as a writer like Annie Proulx sculpts the raw material of a place like Wyoming into her stories and novels, Sealy works best with places like Dehradun, making occasional forays into Delhi ('a good lover,' he says of the city, 'but a bad wife').

From Yukon To Yucatan was an early example of what he could do in other genres—Sealy turned a sharp eye on America, allowing himself to see the US as an exotic, unknown country, in just the way most travel writing outside of Europe and America explains the unfamiliar. His novels overlap without ever returning to the same terrain; *The Everest Hotel*, set in Dehradun, explored political and personal fault lines, betrayal and friendship; *Red* comes back to a fictionalized Dun, but is an interrogation of art and creativity. Nestled in between the two was *The Brainfever Bird*, an unusual love story that brought a Russian expat together with an Indian artist, in Delhi, a city defined by puppets, theatre and the relentless pulling of strings.

It's only now, breathing in the crisp air of this afternoon in Dehradun, standing in the garden of his house—'look for blue gates and trees, lots of trees'—that it strikes me: I have never seen Allan Sealy in his own element. This man moves with exuberance around the garden as he shows off the trees he planted ten years ago. ('Brazilian coral bean [scarlet], Mexican silk cotton [pink and yellow], Chinese golden shower [dread dominatrix]', as his narrator names them slyly in *Red*).

He talks of broadband connections—will they deliver him from the agony of crawling speeds on the Internet, the tyranny of Dilawar Singh, the local linesman? And of his hatred of phones: we spend six serene minutes eating an excellent lunch cooked by Allan and his wife—steamed vegetables, baked fish, strawberries and jaggery and cream—ignoring the shrill summons of the baleful instrument on the side table.

We exchange poetry, a Borges collection for Craig Raine, and Allan discusses his early infatuation with painting, his wary infatuation with Delhi, his lasting love for Dehradun, which appears in *Red* lightly camouflaged as Dariya Dun. The difference between the quiet man I've seen in Delhi, the one who says he would like to return to Doon because his garden is coming up and that's much more important than longwinded seminar questions, and this confident, open writer is startling.

His other books are explained in chronological order as a journey (*From Yukon to Yucatan*), a chronicle (the vast and capacious *The Trotternama*), a fable (*Hero*), a calendar (*Everest Hotel*) and an illusion (*The Brainfever Bird*).

But *Red* carries no colon, no explanation. It starts with Aline, a woman we meet in a museum who sees the world through colour, and ends with Zach, a musician who understands the world as sound. Their stories are connected by N, the narrator, a writer who lives in the foothills of the Himalayas. Presiding over their lives is Matisse ('he's the patron saint of my book'), whose The Red Room and The Painter's Family tower over the novel. The alphabet offers the reader a kind of guide, taking us from A for A line, to Z for Zaccheus, Zeebytes.com, Zipphone, Z-zzz and Zom. Artists rule the book: Aline paints, Zach serves his music, N writes, and a gang of Blackshorts in the Dariya

Dun valley, unable to enter the world of museums or music ateliers, make a fine art of thieving and creating truck paintings.

'In *The Brainfever Bird*, I tried to do something that probably doesn't come naturally to me: narrative! It's a terrible confession, in a conventional sense, because a novelist is supposed to tell stories,' says Allan. 'But I don't think that's a novelist's sole or even primary duty. With *Red*, I just gave in to my notion that you should go off: I've always done that, from *The Trotternama* onwards.' Each chapter of *Red* plays on a different letter of the alphabet. 'It keeps you on the straight and narrow, but it also allows you to branch off. You should be able to jump in at any point. I love that bitty approach.'

The inspiration for *Red* is right behind me, in the glorious, singing, bright red paint that covers the shelves of a tiny pantry. Allan explains how the drawing room used to open into a doorless bathroom: his mother had intended to use the space as a schoolroom for small children, and the absence of the door was deliberate. The bathroom gained a door, the kitchen a small pantry, and we acquired a new Allan Sealy novel—all through happenstance.

'I was painting this—the shelves, the alcove,' says Allan, reaching for his copy of *Red* to explain. 'It's in the poem, it's in the poem, that's where it is.' And he reads from the poem on page 248: 'Red came to me this way, no lie/ With the astounding rightness of a black swan's beak . . .' He went off to Hurla hardware, the shop I had passed earlier on the road, and found a litre of Signal Red.

One red they carried in acrylic and only one
not my dodgy haemoglobin red mercurochrome or port
not scarlet crimson not poppy not opticalmouse red not glorypea
nothing on the fancy shade card but
stopgo red.

It turned out to be a close cousin of the red Matisse was famous for. At the time he wrote *Red*, Sealy had visited The Hermitage, spending hours in front of *The Red Room* and *The Painter's Family*, carrying back as a souvenir the cups in Petersburg blue from which we're drinking freshly brewed coffee. 'There are more Matisses probably under that roof than in the rest of the world put together,' he says.

Sealy saw a parallel between what had happened in Matisse's family life and his own—the surface peace interrupted by quiet schisms, the family dealing with the artist's disappearance into a world where no one else can follow. He was fascinated by Matisse's apparent conformity, the turbulence lurking under the beauty of those colours. 'He's such a revolutionary painter; he wears a tie, he's bourgeois, and he's a revolutionary, and then you begin to wonder: maybe revolutionaries do wear ties.'

'I love colour,' says Allan. It's the only superfluous statement he'll make; that love shows all through the house, in the aqua of his study, the monkish yellow of the tiles in the kitchen, the red cafetiere on the table, the weatherworn brick of the garden wall complemented by the brilliant green of the creepers. 'If you write about what you love, you're likely to be able to pull it off, provided you have certain basic skills.'

The conversation turns to practical matters. Like book sales: 'If you're a writer who doesn't sell, the smallest blip of a sale makes you ecstatic.' Sealy is uncompromising: 'Part of me thinks, what's the point of writing if you're only going to write for twelve bright readers. But with every book, maybe one per cent you think of the reader, ninety nine you're thinking of yourself, what you want to say.' Of the publishing industry today: 'Thank god for the way it's set up, successful writers bail out the unsuccessful ones who're willing to do what they want even if they lose their readers. A hundred years ago, there would have been no room for someone like me.' And the name on the cover of *Red*: Irwin Allan Sealy, the full name instead of the initial 'I' for the first time. 'I've been told it's not Indian enough, that the kind of English reader who would look for 'Indian writing' would put my books down. So this is my response. Fuck you. This is who I am, it's also my father's name, it's also a tribute to him.'

He continues: 'It took me till my thirties to give myself permission to see myself as a writer. You're measuring yourself against the best; it takes time to be able to say to yourself, I could do that—I could do better than that. Even in your twenties, you know that life is short, you know that you're never going to read everything you want to read. So you're always sifting. You're trying to get at the very best from the very beginning. If you're actually looking at yourself as a writer, you're looking at all the possible books you could ever write, even if you don't live to write them.'

I ask about his characters, the way they have of popping up from one book to another. Eugene Trotter from *The Trotternama* makes a brief appearance in *Red*; so does Bisht from *The Everest Hotel*. He grins. 'It's nice to keep in touch with the guys—or girls—from the past. When they look at you, it's an accusing look: it says, you have abandoned me. Bringing them back is a way of saying, I have not.'

I can almost see them; Trotter, and his father, serving nimbu-pani at a Daryaganj hotel in *The Brainfever Bird*, Bisht, now at home in the *thana* of Dehradun, other ghosts from Sealy's pages. In this house, where Sealy is so very clearly at home, they've taken possession of quiet nooks and corners. 'I'm very happy,' he says. 'I don't know why. It's a kind of lunacy.' He has plans for the house; more colours to be brought in, walls to be bashed in to make room for windows. More trees planned, to hide his neighbours' houses from view: 'It's nice to just blot out that house, THAT house, that one: Tree! Tree! Tree!' He has taken possession: 'In a way, what you're taking possession of is not the place but yourself, and that's a source of strength.'

The sadness that usually descends on him once a book is finished is in abeyance; he's been thinking of other projects. A novel about a family of engineers, some sane, some crazy. A serious history of Dehradun and the Valley, perhaps a travelogue. A long poem, marking a shift towards poetry, towards condensation. *Red* is the first book he's written on the computer, instead of in longhand, and Sealy thinks that perhaps the medium encourages compression, just as the pen encourages longwinded, Trollope-length narratives, Dickensian digressions.

The novel opens unusually, with a reproduction of Matisse's *The Painter's Family*—the painting is something of an introduction to *Red*.

It is not a happy painting. The painter is absent, represented only by a bust of himself ('Serf'); the wife, in a corner, and the boys are in the background. The central figure is of Matisse's daughter—her mother was his mistress, not his wife—who exudes a nervous, violent energy. Families are complicated, hydra-headed creatures, Matisse seems to be saying; do you really want to look deeply into the nature of the beast?

All this information is cribbed directly from *Red,* and it serves as an indication of the strengths and weaknesses of this formidable and thoroughly entertaining book.

Red is an abecedary: a book arranged in the form of an alphabet. You start with Aline—a woman so in love with Matisse that she will rip his canvases apart (only she knows if it's a genuine Matisse or a clever reproduction that's being dismembered) in order to see how he reached his colours—and move to Zach, a musician for whom the world in all its colours, is audible, a shifting soundscape. Almost exactly in between is the Narrator, who lives in a town called—this will sound familiar—Dariya Dun: 'In the middle station of life, middle class, middling build ... A foothills man, neither plainsman nor Montagnard.'

Aline and Zach meet at The Hermitage, one worshipping at the feet of Matisse—bourgeois painter, but a revolutionary in a tie all the same; one ready to genuflect at the altar of Aline. The chance encounter leads them to Dariya Dun, where N is a friend of Zach's. Here, like live wires finally corralled in the same space, they make connections, shoot off sparks, create electricity and danger.

The Dun is in transition, the quiet valley transformed by better electricity connections, cybercafes that now allow the wonder of paintings downloaded pixel by pixel, in sleazy, worn-out booths where the previous occupant has been surfing porn. Zach and Aline are not the only art-lovers in town: there is a gang of Blackshorts, small-time thieves who worship a snake goddess and take the rites of crime every bit as seriously as art connoisseurs take line and colour. They're led by Gilgitan, an artist twice over—a master criminal, and an amateur but instinctively talented painter of trucks, signs and tiles.

The Narrator grapples with his own problems—a meeting with a daughter he hasn't seen for years, who brings the same energy and disruption into his life as Matisse's illegitimate daughter must have brought into his. Zach moves in steady rhythm between the music that absorbs him to the exclusion of all else and the women who capture him completely, if only for a brief moment in between compositions. Aline, foreigner to the Dun, to the unspoken barriers of caste and class, is the one who makes the most direct connections. She sees little difference in essence between the sophisticated musician who travels the world and Gilgitan, the raw, untaught painter who romances a pig-girl (in one of the few unconvincing sections of *Red*) and falls in love with a paintbox.

Sealy tackles huge questions here: how do you recognize good art from bad; what makes us canonize Art with a capital A and dismiss other kinds of art in lower case; can an artist, a dealer in visions from elsewhere, inhabit the real world? *Red* is daunting, but it is also one of Sealy's richest, most comfortably experimental books yet.

He romps through the alphabet, never forgetting the other meaning of abecedary—a primer, the first principle or rudiment of anything— but allowing himself the freedom to include the following: his own poems, a brief explication of the uses of spray paint in lovemaking, imaginary books (*The Nagatarangini*, *The Annals of the Black Codpiece Society*), elaborate games with fonts, misleading definitions.

It's a novel which may frighten off readers unwilling to follow the labyrinth that leads from Matisse to the deadly repercussions of the Blackshorts' thefts, but for those willing to stay the course, this might be Sealy's finest work. It's a pity *Red* is available only in old-fashioned book form: in an ideal, hypertext-friendly world, this is the kind of book you'd want only two keyboard commands for: Press Enter, Play Game.

'The process of writing a book gets you to a higher, greater intensity than almost anything I can think of,' he had said earlier. 'Your world for the duration of that book, the writing of it, is truly other. There's no way of describing it to anybody, even anybody you live with. It's a good feeling, the equivalent of the chemical high. Writers are addicted to that other world in the way that a drunk is to his booze.'

Now, as we say our farewells, I ask if he's moved beyond the need to question himself. Irwin Allan Sealy laughs. 'A writer has constant self-doubt. There is only that interplay between total despair and complete self-confidence. There's nothing else. Really. There's nothing else. Probably both at the same time.' And then he goes back to more important things: the trees need pruning, watering, the civet cats are illegally occupying the verandah chairs, his garden needs attention.

(Based on profiles and reviews from 2006. In 2014, I. Allan Sealy published his seventh book, The Small Wild Goose Pagoda: An Almanack.*)*

2

Kiran Nagarkar

It's two days after Kiran Nagarkar received the Sahitya Akademi Award for his third novel, *Cuckold*, told from the point of view of Mirabai's husband, and it hasn't changed his life one bit. We're headed to the Spice Route at the Imperial, in deference to the writer's preference for Thai food and an allergy to lentils that knocks most Indian restaurants off the list.

No heads turn as we walk in, but that's not surprising. Nagarkar isn't the kind of writer who makes it to Page 3 in Delhi, or to the Bombay version, and it doesn't really bother him. The Sahitya Akademi award came in four years after he wrote *Cuckold*, seven years after the Bombay-based author wrote *Ravan and Eddie* and some three decades after he began writing in the first place. That's a long, long time to wait for recognition; long enough for Nagarkar to admit that the pleasure it gives him is alleviated by a sense of slight bitterness at being unjustly ignored.

He wants a table where 'we can talk in peace'; not necessarily an easy order to fill at the Spice Route, which is always populated by the chattering classes in one degree or another. But the waiters are understanding; they find us a table off to a side in the central courtyard, where we enjoy the brief illusion of being under a Chettinad roof. It's something to do with the acoustics, perhaps, but the table seems to be located in a dead spot: even Nagarkar's voice, strained into relative hoarseness after a cold and two unaccustomed days of speech-making, can be heard here.

It doesn't take us much time to order. He is a main-course kind of guy, so the soups and salads go out of the window. We settle on the chicken done Sri Lankan style, a Thai lamb curry, Thai stir-fried vegetables and steamed rice. As we wait for the food to arrive, Nagarkar toys with the hot towel the Spice Route offers to all its guests.

He grew up, he'll tell me later, in a world where hot towels were unthinkable fripperies. His father was a clerk in the railways, the eldest earning member of a large family. Nagarkar was brought up to earn his own living; he has never hankered after the huge advances and giant royalty cheques that accompany contemporary fame, just ruminated on the recognition that never came to him. 'Not that money would have been despised, you understand,' he says with a gleam in his eye. 'But it was never necessary.'

In the days of the Emergency, Nagarkar did find recognition of sorts, at the hands of the censor board. He'd written a play called *Bedtime Story*, that used the stories of characters in the *Mahabharata*—Draupadi, Eklavya, Karna—to make a comment on what was happening in India at the time. 'I can afford to tamper with an epic like the *Mahabharata*— it's in your bloodstream, in my bloodstream,' he says of the form he'd chosen. The censor board read the play and suggested seventy-eight cuts. 'Only the cover was left.' M.P. Rege went along with him to plead the case of the play. They argued for half a day. 'I think they just wanted to wrap it up by then, so they agreed to twenty to twenty-five cuts.'

But the intervention of the censor board had already branded the play as dangerous. Dr Sriram Lagoo, also a friend of Nagarkar's, called every experimental theatre group he could find in Bombay. There were about 120; four agreed to perform the play. 'It was still jinxed,' he says wryly. 'It went into rehearsal and production so many times, and always something happened.' *Bedtime Story* was finally performed— but it's always been a hot potato for theatre groups. (It was published in 2015; instead of being dated, it had acquired a new relevance and a more intense meaning in this decade of highly polarised politics.)

The food arrives promptly; Nagarkar's a ruminative eater, giving each separate mouthful the attention it deserves, so that the meal begins to take on the elements of a religious ceremony. The chicken and the stir-fried vegetables are excellent, but the Thai lamb curry leaves a lot to be desired. Neither of us could care less, though. The conversation is what we're savouring.

Nagarkar is a man twice repudiated. Once by the English media, that faintly applauded both *Cuckold* and the novel that preceded it, *Ravan and Eddie* and otherwise forgot him; and once by the Marathi literary world. 'A question that keeps coming back at me is, why have you abandoned Marathi?'

At surface levels, it's understandable. He began his writing career in Marathi; even his first novel, *Seven Sixes are Forty-Three* was translated into English some years after it had first come out in Marathi. 'In truth, I had only four years of taught Marathi. I come from a Westernized family—we were part of the Prarthana Samaj. I have an obsessiveness about Sri Krishna that I haven't understood—in my play, in *Cuckold*, it seems that Sri Krishna has always intruded upon me. But I call him "Sri Krishna", "Lord Krishna" because of my background: for most Maharashtrians, he would be just "Krishna". The real question should have been, why did I move from English to Marathi?'

Is it necessary, I ask, for a writer to always have to choose? Why wouldn't it be possible in a country that has so many tongues for a writer to be bilingual in his work, as we so often are in our everyday speech? In return, Nagarkar tells me a story, his voice rising above the growing hubbub of noise as the restaurant fills up. It's about the time he hawked his second novel to the review sections of all the Marathi newspapers, asking them to slam it, to be as critical as they wanted, but just to review it. The response was a stony silence. Kiran Nagarkar, who had crossed over into the alien territory of English, would not be reviewed.

As we help ourselves to more chicken and steamed rice, he tells other, funnier stories. Of the woman who'd come to interview him, who began with a rant: 'There's a limit to how sensational one can try to be. You write a trashy book, and you even had the indecency to call it *Cuckold*, defacing the memory of Mirabai's husband.'

Of the ad agency where he earned his bread and butter for twenty-four years. Of his brief role as a paedophile priest in Dev Benegal's *Split Wide Open*: 'A friend told me after he saw the film, you're just like that in real life. I think that's rather a dubious compliment!' Of another, critically acclaimed filmmaker who does 'serious' cinema: 'You know, the kind of work you would want to run away from if he didn't have a reputation that forced you to stay and watch it through.'

As we ask for a coconut caramel custard for Nagarkar, a Darjeeling tea for me, he suddenly switches gear. 'My own self-deprecation does not reflect the criminal self-assurance I also have—even an arrogance,' he says slowly. 'I'm harsh on myself, yes. There are Marathi writers who say, why do you still write? No one cares, you might as well stop. But there is something inside. A conviction—no, the knowledge—that I am a good writer. I have something to say. And my only agenda is to tell a story.'

He hasn't written anything for the past six or seven years—the toll you pay when your audience walks out of the hall before you even get started. And yet, Nagarkar is ungrudging of the success that other writers have achieved, able to discuss Rushdie with a professor's dispassionate meticulousness, Amitav Ghosh with unsparing approval. His engagement with literature and books is visible at every turn, as the conversation moves from the similarities between the *Mahabharata* and Dostoevsky's works to the question of the architecture of a novel ('a very visual metaphor for me').

As we move out from the pleasantly dark interiors of the Spice Route into the dusty glare of Delhi, he has one last certainty to share with me. If he had to do it all over again, face the heartbreak and the neglect, the criticism and the cavilling, or be given a life filled with all sorts of blessings but empty of writing, Kiran Nagarkar would take the heartbreak. No questions asked.

(Based on interviews and reviews from 2005-06. The Extras, the sequel to Ravan and Eddie, *was published in 2012;* Bedtime Story *was published in 2015, twenty-seven years after he wrote the play. In 2015, the final novel in the* Ravan and Eddie *trilogy,* Ravan and Eddie: Rest in Peace, *was published.)*

3

Manjula Padmanabhan

There is a small hen sparrow exercising her unfledged wings on Manjula Padmanabhan's lawn. The sparrow arrived in the writer's life in traumatic circumstances; since then, she's been nursed back to health, had her cage expanded, been taken on holiday, and rejoices in the name of Catsmeat.

If you can imagine the mind of someone who says she has no maternal urges, who has spent the last weeks nevertheless attending to the needs of a small bird, and who will cackle as she tells you that the bird's dubbed feline fodder, you're getting closer to understanding Padmanabhan.

She's keen to see what Agni, the fusion place at the Park Hotel in Connaught Place, is like, so that's where we head after saying our farewells to Catsmeat (also known, in deference to more sensitive friends, as Birdie Num-Num).

Agni can make you feel deeply schizophrenic: by night, it's a crowded bar; by day it pretends it's a sleepy coffee shop. It's a good place to take an author and illustrator who can execute shifts between professions, genres and styles with the best of them.

At fifty-one, Padmanabhan has one of the most interesting CVs in the world of Indian literature in English: it includes plays (*Harvest,*

Lights Out, The Gujarat Monologues), a comic strip (*Suki*), a travel memoir (*Getting There*), two collections of short stories (*Hot Death, Cold Soup* and the recently released *Kleptomania*) and the first in a children's book series (*Mouse Attack*), and that's not even mentioning her work as an illustrator.

We order luridly coloured mocktails as we discuss how she got here when her original plans included (a) being an IFS officer, like her father, and (b) committing suicide at the age of thirty since that was, in the young Padmanabhan's opinion, the point from which most people's lives go irretrievably downhill.

It was only when her father retired in India that Padmanabhan sought an alternative to the Indian Foreign Service (IFS), belatedly realizing that she might not live up to the standards of propriety required of a government officer. She joined the staff of a small magazine called *Parsiana*. It was printed at the same place in Ballard Estate that had hosted Debonair; the office proper was in the Parsi Lying-In Hospital; it was 'a little community magazine, sparky and sweet' with very high standards set by its editor, Jehangir Patel; and Padmanabhan learned in short order to do everything: she illustrated, she wrote, she read page proofs.

'The germinal period is *Parsiana*,' she says, digging into mini-kulchas with tomato chutney-salsa while trying to explain her multipronged career, 'it explains everything.'

Back in India after a childhood spent everywhere and nowhere, she'd seen herself as irrevocably, unintentionally different. 'I didn't belong back in India, but I didn't belong anywhere else either, and that's a strange place to be, a sad place to be.'

It shows in her work, but typically, as an asset. 'I am not rooted in any tradition. I write about things that don't require a special tradition—they tend to be fundamental. They deal with the body—everyone has one—or very basic emotions, basic motivations. I take what everyone already knows, and then I push it a little bit further.'

Language wasn't one of the areas she worried about. 'I can't even understand what it would be like to not have English. Those of us who are writing in English are not borrowing a language, it is our language—but we are hybrids. I'm aware that being a hybrid, I don't have access to any deep roots, and I don't care. I live in an era where I don't suffer, which is unusual. In any other era, anyone marginal suffered; hybrids were always the first to suffer.'

Perhaps that's where her empathy for the marginal, alien figure comes from: the young girl in 'Betrayal' from *Kleptomania* whose insecurities leave her open to being used; the family in *Harvest* whose poverty makes organlegging a seductive option, the albino mouse in *Mouse Attack*. Padmanabhan met the original albino, a rat, in 1984, on the day Indira Gandhi was shot. She was in a photo studio when she saw a small white shape darting around.

'I said to the man, you have a white rat just behind you. And he said, oh yeah, that's our rat.' Someone had told him he could use the albino rat to scare away ordinary rats.

'It is normal for animal groups to ostracize an albino. That was how *Mouse Attack* arose. I kept thinking about this unfortunate rat—it seemed okay, but it would have been born in a laboratory, and I was wondering, what could its life be?'

When we tuck into gilauti kebabs and Goan prawn curry, both well executed with just a touch of fusion foreignness, I'm thinking that if she'd stuck to the original plan, we'd never have had any of this. No *Harvest*, very few stories, no ambitious children's book series, no Suki, no Padmanabhan. No *Getting There*, in fact, in which she first wrote about the joys of exiting stage left once life gets too boring. 'I had planned when I was seventeen to die at thirty—it seemed that everything started packing up after that, your body, your mind—and I deeply meant it,' she says.

'I think I knew a year before my thirtieth birthday that I wouldn't do it. Suicide had to be not painful, and I had not reached a point of solvency where I could afford an attractive suicide. That was a trivial reason. The true reason was that by thirty, I had a worth that I didn't have when I was seventeen. I did not want to die. At seventeen, I had done nothing with my life; I was nobody; if I died it would make no difference to anyone at all. But at thirty I felt it would. That was a revelation, I'd actually got somewhere, I'd actually achieved something,

I had a reason for staying alive.'

Thinking about checking out was a good thing, Padmanabhan explains kindly, sensing that at thirty (my age at the time of the interview), I'm vulnerable to her special brand of logic.

'It instilled in me a tremendous sense of direction: I wanted to be great and famous and very rich. I wanted to have brilliant affairs and to be a philanthropist. And at thirty, I was nowhere! I had not had any great affairs, I was not rich and I was not happy; the only thing I had at thirty was a sense of value for myself that I had not had at seventeen.'

She mentions, casually, that she remained deeply miserable until she turned forty-two. It's an interesting number: Douglas Adams used it as the answer to the question 'What is the meaning of life?' in his *Hitchhiker's Guide to the Galaxy*. Why was it so important, I ask her; what changed at forty-two?

She takes a beat. 'It was the Onassis Award. Or maybe it was the hysterectomy. I forget which came first.'

Padmanabhan welcomed both. The hysterectomy relieved her of a long-standing discomfort with the essentials of being a woman. (She stopped calling herself a feminist when she realized that she enjoyed very little about being female; she is now married, and has no children by choice.)

She was the first recipient of the cash-rich Onassis Award for her play, *Harvest*; the sudden influx of money changed her life. It freed her from the struggle, often desperate, never enabling, to earn a living. But it also became a marker in more uncomfortable ways.

'In the Indian milieu, you will not be noticed for the creative work you're doing today unless somebody from abroad notices you. And then your own media says, "Aha! You are exciting!" The disillusionment was to realize that six years of Suki had no impact compared to that one news event of *Harvest*. I don't want to be whining but it's a repeating cycle of sadness, that we can't seem to be interested in ourselves for ourselves. There has to be some exterior cachet. It's not like people said about *Harvest*, wow, what a great play. They only ever said, wow, what a lot of money.'

A decade on from *Harvest*, the inescapable economics of publishing still rule her life. Even prize money doesn't last forever.

Dessert arrives; an apple jalebi for me with rabri on the side, chocolate cake for Padmanabhan. It provides a small dose of sweetness in a swell of bitter resignation about today's publishing world. 'They don't publish books as favours to authors. And if the author's work is not supported by readers, sadly, no more work. It's been a bad thing for me that I am unwilling to stump for my own books; it may mean that there won't be more books. Being "famous" is not of any consequence to me now. But I certainly want to be rich because that's the only way I can continue to support my writing.'

There won't be any more books? I'm still reeling at that, even while we're discussing the joys of Myst and Riven, games that the technophile part of Padmanabhan loved being immersed in a few years ago.

'It is the booklover's absolute metaphor—you open a book, you put your hand on that first page and you are in this other world. It is such a fantastic analogy of what happens through literature, through books. It is that which engages you in a book, that immersion.'

Immersion; that's what her work has always provided, that's why I'm a Padmanabhan junkie, hooked on my next fix.

However, life after fifty continues to surprise, as a post-prandial call testifies. Catsmeat now has a companion; an injured pigeon handed over to Manjula Padmanabhan, Medicine Woman, by a friend. It doesn't have a name yet. But it will, it will.

(Based on an interview from 2004. Manjula Padmanabhan published Kleptomania *(2004), a collection of short stories and* Escape *(2008), a dystopian novel about a country with no women except for one. The sequel to* Escape, The Island of Lost Girls, *was published in 2015.)*

4

Khushwant Singh

What do smart sardars and UFOs have in common?
You hear a lot about them but no one's actually met one.

—Politically incorrect joke found on the Internet

I don't know where you'd go to meet a UFO, but the polar opposite
of the conventional sardar joke used to live in Sujan Singh Park.
Make an appointment, dodge a clowder of friendly cats, eyeball
the legendary sign that advises you not to ring doorbell if you don't
have the said appointment, and spend an hour with Khushwant Singh.
Who is—as the old joke has it—still 'a surd among intellectuals, an
intellectual among surds'.

Khushwant Singh, at the age of ninety, has more books behind him
than the number of new author Delhi has birthed in the course of a
year. (Ask him, and he'll respond with his trademark line: 'Any rubbish
I write gets published.') The Library of Congress logged ninety-nine
books about or by Khushwant—and this was in 2002, before he added
more (he's lost count himself). '[This] would inevitably be my last book,
my swansong penned in the evening of my life,' he wrote at the age
of eighty-seven, in the Prologue to his autobiography, *Truth, Love & a
Little Malice*, 'I am fast running out of writer's ink.'

Three years later, he told *Outlook*, 'No one has yet invented a condom for the writer's pen.' His most recent novel, *Burial At Sea*, is simultaneously receiving its last rites from reviewers and making the best-seller charts courtesy his fans. He has finished revising his monumental *History of the Sikhs*, a collection of short stories is due out, he's contemplating another novel—and that's not counting the bits and pieces that feed the awesome Khushwant industry.

His two weekly columns draw postcards by the hundreds and are syndicated in over twelve different Indian languages. I've seen tired army jawans reading it near the Indo-China border: 'Dekh, Sardarji kya keh raha hai.' Years later, on a trip to Kanyakumari, the stall owners on the beach discuss his column in Malayalam. I ask the taxi driver to translate. 'They like the Banta Singh jokes very much.' There is no better homage to Khushwant than to start off a profile on him with the genre of joke he dragged out of the racist closet and made an art form.

The remarkably prolific career of India's best-known and most beloved sardar began with a book that stopped dead after five pages or so. It was called *Sheilla*, because he thought that two 'l's sounded more impressive than one, and he scribbled the title in bold, flowing letters across the front of the notebook. 'You put your name on it,' he says wryly, 'and hoped it would be in all the bookstores.' *Sheilla* never saw the light of day. His second attempt featured a train that arrived in a small village in Punjab during Partition, bearing a terrible cargo. *Train to Pakistan* was first published in 1956; it has never been out of print in India. The village in the novel, Mano Majra, was modelled on Hadali, where Khushwant grew up.

Suketu Mehta, scriptwriter and author, recalls a visit he made to Khushwant's house with director Vidhu Vinod Chopra. 'Khushwant tells us about being stopped at the Dubai airport, where many of the ground staff are Pakistanis. He is the only first class passenger, and comes off the plane first. The Pakistani immigration officer opens his passport, and asks him to wait. Khushwant watches the other passengers leave, anger rising within him. Finally the officer beckons to him. Khushwant says: "So you found only one Sikh to harass?" The officer points to Khushwant's passport. "I noticed you were born in Hadali, Sardarji.

I'm also from Hadali. How could I permit someone from my village to stay in a hotel? You're coming home with me.'"

★

Visitors testify that the standards of hospitality in his household remain Hadali-high—provided you respect his limits. Khushwant maintains an iron schedule. He's up by 5 a.m. and straight to work—'No wasting of time on prayers or anything, my only wasteful hobby is crossword puzzles.' Then he compiles material for his columns ('I slog for them— two a week, and I never miss a deadline'), edits, writes,.strolls around the garden, and entertains a regulated stream of guests until 9 p.m., when he summarily throws everyone out. Bapsi Sidhwa showed up late after she'd sent him the manuscript of *The Crow Eaters*: 'He saw me get out of the taxi and look around confusedly. He clapped his hands to draw my attention and shouted: "You are exactly an hour late. But I forgive you because you have written a first-class book."'

In between, he answers mail. Says Manjula Padmanabhan, 'I am told that he answers everyone, even if it's only with a line on a postcard. I love that story. That tells me more about him than all the tasteless anecdotes that have occasionally trailed his name.' And it's true. He politely turns away authors who want him to read their manuscripts—even so, he has three to peruse at present; gleefully collects the abusive letters ('I challenge you to read this one out loud,' he says of a postcard where the writer packs a wealth of anatomically impossible suggestions); and offers advice, quotations, commentary to the rest.

Sure, the man and the legend are inextricable, even enduring. But what of the work? That's what a writer leaves behind him; that's what will outlast the anecdotes, the warmth, the controversies, the 'dirty old man' tag. Don't knock the 'dirty old man' business; I still remember the fifty-year-old man who announced drunkenly at a party after *Company of Women* came out: 'Khushwant writes for ME! He knows what I am GOING through! He is in the skin of the north Indian MALE!' Suketu Mehta offers, 'As a teenager, I read Khushwant's novels for the dirty bits. [They] were terrific, and very rooted—the rustic Punjabi sex in *Train to Pakistan* must have gotten an entire generation through college. It was a revelation at the time, because the other dirty bits we had access to occured in English gardens and Parisian bordellos; here was sex we could identify with, had a hope of enjoying in our own lifetimes, in our own fields. It was only later that I realized there was real and lasting literary value to the book. But perhaps that's how many of us were first exposed to the great masters, such as Lawrence—through the dirty bits.'

Amit Chaudhuri suggests that with the rise of Indian writing in English, Khushwant Singh, never taken seriously as a political commentator, was reinvented as 'a sort of national literary mandarin. He'd started out as a quite ordinary and unmemorable critic, in the English language, of Punjabi and Urdu writing; now, in his avatar as not only Indian English novelist, but as editor and columnist, his advocacy of Indian writing in English was extreme, and at times absurdly generous. In a dormant literary culture as lacking in generosity as ours was, and is, especially in the Anglophone world, any sign of unprejudiced or unjaundiced receptivity is welcome.'

But Chaudhuri sees in Khushwant's tendency to praise writers in exaggerated terms a symptom of a deeper malaise: 'Singh [in the past] has deemed that Vikram Seth and Arundhati Roy are "Nobel-prize material", as if the Nobel Prize were . . . something you could put on your CV. It's another instance of the (always upwardly mobile or aspirant) familial language with which we've come to speak of culture, books, or writers in India, as we do of our children or our children's prospective spouses—as safe or unsafe investments.'

And Khushwant Singh's absence from two of the better-known anthologies of recent times—Salman Rushdie's controversial *Mirrorwork* and Amit Chaudhuri's own anthology of modern Indian literature—is telling.

Subtract the joke books, the compilations, the flotsam and jetsam, and you're left with far less than you might expect for a writer who's been working for over five decades. (This approach has its risks, as Pankaj Mishra gently points out: 'We are expected to consider our writers as very serious people doing only very serious things. Otherwise it would be easy to see Khushwant Singh as a writer who can do many things well—even things that are probably not worth doing at all, like the joke books.')

The work that Khushwant would most like to be remembered by is his definitive history of the Sikhs—into its sixth edition now. 'I was determined to do that,' he says. He names *Train to Pakistan* as the novel he thinks will continue to last, calls his short stories 'underrated', but singles out *I Shall Not Hear the Nightingale*, his second novel, for comment. 'It's a better book.' He's phlegmatic about *The Company of Women* and *Burial at Sea*: elsewhere, he's said that he never made great literary claims for the former. 'They sell,' is what he says. 'They get panned, but they sell.'

'I toast his individuality,' says Manjula Padmanabhan, 'He is a good middle-of-the-road writer. If there were many more of him, India could justifiably claim a healthy literary world. Sadly, there are so few of him, and so very many beneath him, that he is forced to occupy a higher status than he would if our literary milieu were a little more balanced. He is at least coherent, easy to read, mildly amusing and (oh rare! oh unusual!) literate in the old sense—meaning, he has actually read and enjoyed the classics.'

Bapsi Sidhwa touches a nerve when she suggests that 'writers are seldom candid about who really influenced them—they trot out the usual "accepted" names'. She continues: 'But you can be sure he has influenced South Asian writers . . . Like the man, his writing is clear, perceptive and unpretentious, and like him it is also uninhibited.'

The shortlist for Khushwant is short to the point of abruptness: two novels, three if you count Delhi; the histories; the short stories. At bookshops, I talk to the people who actually sell the products of the Khushwant industry. One says, 'This is the English literature list. The columns will keep selling, so will the joke books. It doesn't matter. You could append his name to a phone book and he will still sell.' (And I'm reminded of the joke about Santa Singh—of the Santa-Banta fame—accosting a librarian and saying, what kind of book is this? Lots of characters, but no plot, no dialogue? Ah, says the librarian. You're the one who checked out our phone directory.)

One of Khushwant's most memorable creations no longer exists: the legendary *Illustrated Weekly*. For Pankaj Mishra, it was 'the first real magazine' he encountered; later, Khushwant's columns 'if you were living in very small and isolated places, as I was, opened a window onto the larger world'. For Manjula Padmanabhan, it was the magazine that 'ALL OF INDIA used to read'. It was a nondescript cocktail-party paper; Khushwant turned it into the journal you couldn't ignore. Nothing was beneath his notice—he was never, says the man who notoriously pleaded Sanjay Gandhi's cause, wrote with such passion on the Golden Temple affair and such clarity on Khalistan, interested in politics, so he wrote about books, nature, gossip. 'I asked questions that touched a chord, even if it was why monkeys had red bottoms,' he says. 'Hadn't you ever wondered? It took a lot of research to find out.' Decades after the demise of the *Weekly*, he remembers each issue, the Kissa Kursi Ka jokes, Dhirendra Brahmachari carrying his white handbag on the cover, every writer he commissioned.

The list of things people remember about Khushwant is as long as the list of canon-worthy books is short. Amit Chaudhuri sat next to him at the closing session of the Indian Literary Festival a few years ago, and noticed that he spent much of the session scribbling in Urdu on a piece of paper in front of him. 'I felt then that just as some writers have wonderful manuscripts they never publish, Singh, in spite of his huge public personality, has chosen to keep the best of himself from us.'

He never talks down to people. He's curious, relentlessly curious. He's candid, sometimes with devastating consequences in a culture used to polite hagiography and the veiled attack. He has, even in his nonagenarian years, the cheerful smuttiness of a schoolboy who never got over being a bosom man ('All men are bosom men'). And as generations of writers and editors will testify, he's generous, even as he's sceptical of greatness ('I have never met great men who don't have feet of clay.')

It's impossible to project Khushwant Singh as just a sales phenomenon; he is no cynical publishing creation. Nor is he, despite the stunning mediocrity of some of his work, a failed writer—just a writer who never had much need to live up to that early promise, whose columns still sing, still reach out in a way our op–ed writers have forgotten how to do. 'If you want to write, you have to be true to yourself,' he says.

Look at him again; the figure in the light-bulb, the whisky drinker who retires at nine, the man who candidly admits to lusting after women in his heart, which, however, belonged completely to his late wife; the quiet historian, the writer whose proudest boast is this: 'I always meet my deadlines.' And the great secret of his success is simple. Underneath the Scotch–and–scholarship hide, behind the mask of mentor or destroyer of reputations, there's the person who, when someone writes to him, always writes back.

I've tired him out; it's time to leave. I ask what lines he'd like to be remembered by, expecting him to choose something from one of his own books. But Khushwant Singh's eyes light up and he quotes Walter Savage Landor's 'Dying Speech of An Old Philosopher':

I strove with none, for none was worth my strife:
Nature was my love, and, next to Nature, Art:
I warm'd both hands at the fire of Life;
It sinks; and I am ready to depart.

(Khushwant Singh died in March 2014, at the age of 99. Among his more significant works were Train To Pakistan *(1956),* I Shall Not Hear the Nightingale *(1959),* A History of the Sikhs *(1966), and* Delhi: A Novel *(1990).)*

5

Arundhati Roy

The lane through which you approach Arundhati Roy's studio, in a moderately affluent New Delhi suburb, is unlovely—its strictly utilitarian aspect as a back alley not softened by the gathering monsoon clouds above. Inside is another matter: Roy's workspace, in shades of ochre with Moorish blue windows, is a warm, welcoming space. 'There's no water,' she says, and just as the lights and fans switch on again, 'but the electricity's back.'

It's a small but essential reminder that even here, in her private space, the concerns of the average Delhi citizen intrude. The affluence generated by the best-selling *The God of Small Things* would have been enough to insulate Roy from all the annoying inconveniences her countrypeople have to put up with. That she stays here is a deliberate choice; her work is here, a point that she will make repeatedly over the next two hours.

Long before I arrived at that back alley, I had been revolving in my mind the two diametrically opposed sets of responses that Arundhati Roy evokes. To many foreigners, the prickliness she sets off in the Indian English-language media is puzzling, illogical, misplaced. To this company—and they include the likes of Amy Tan, Salman Rushdie and many others—Arundhati is a courageous woman not afraid to be the voice of conscience in troubled times.

To many Indians, she is a manipulative poster girl (to use a term she personally cannot stand) who has taken to writing polemical essays because she wants to stay in the limelight without the labour of writing another GOST. She used to live, this band of doubters will point out, in Kautilya Marg—named after a Machiavellian manipulator of medieval times—a distinctly upper-class neighbourhood. Her essays, to them, are shrill rants on subjects that she is not qualified to address. Her recent brush with the Supreme Court—which resulted in an overnight stint in jail—was a martyrdom deliberately sought because she has a Saint Joan complex.

I am here to participate in a conversation; as I will discover, that is Arundhati Roy's explanation of what she has been doing ever since 1997, when GOST came out. Conducting a conversation, between those who have power and those who have been deprived of it; between the hegemony of institutions and the needs of the ordinary citizen; between those who do care, deeply, about the environment they live in, and those who are still mired in apathy.

The rain starts coming down as we begin, drumming softly against the windows. We're discussing the link between her essays and her first, only, Booker-winning novel. 'The roots of so much of what I've written in the essays is in GOST,' she says. One of the passages she's thinking of is the one where her protagonist, Rahel, returns to the river running through Ayamenem, and discovers that it's polluted. Another is the scene set in the police station—drawn from memory, when Arundhati watched her mother, the activist Mary Roy, in a similar situation. In the novel, Rahel watches as the policemen deliberately confront Ammu, her mother, with the fact of her helplessness in the face of their power. 'I'm often asked whether I'm going to write fiction about the Narmada valley [where the controversial building of a dam dispossessed many of their lands and their identities]: it's such a demeaning question. I want to say, it's already done, that's what GOST is about, power and powerlessness.'

As we talk, the room fills up with ghosts and spectres. The ghost of her prescient 1998 essay on the consequences of a nuclear India, 'The End of the Imagination', reminds us that she anticipated the mushroom clouds now hovering over the subcontinent as India and Pakistan face off yet again, both armed and dangerous. 'Just before you came,' she says, 'I took a call from an *NYT* journalist who asked whether I was planning to leave Delhi because of the nuclear threat. I tried to explain that I don't come from the kind of stock that believes you can buy a life. I can't think, "Oh there's going to be a nuclear war, let me go live in Geneva". I can't. Everything that I love and value and hate and fight with is here; if it goes down, I go down. What I do comes out of a sense of love, irritation, anger, it's all just a form of investing in the place.'

Those who read her essays carefully and in sequence may, as reviewer Ian Buruma did, find much to quibble over or differ with. Whatever your differences with Roy's views, few could actually read the collected essays and not emerge with a sense of continuity. She isn't addressing separate issues when she speaks of nuclear bombs, shifts to big dams, continues with a polemic on privatization and the dangers of globalization, and ends by asking America to look at its own foreign policies for an explanation of 9/11.

'All these things—big dams, nuclear bombs, globalization—are about power and powerlessness. Why is one opposed to big dams? It's not the irrigation yields. Fundamentally, one is opposed to the centralization of authority and of resources. With nuclear bombs, it's the same problem. How is the state of the world going to be decided by this person who can press the button? It's undemocratic.' She will say, a little later, that she finds the accusations that she moves from subject to subject strange. 'It's not different subjects; they're all the same subjects.'

When Roy makes a plea, it's simple: don't look at me, look at what I've written. Her eyes are luminous, insistent, as she continues: 'All these people who get nostril-quivery about me: why doesn't she wear a khadi sari and pretend she's an Adivasi [tribal], you know. We have been brought up to believe that the only people who can ask questions have to be Gandhi, wear loincloths, spin, act self-righteous.

If you're seen to be having a good time and still ask political questions, it's a big problem.'

India is more comfortable with activists like Mahasweta Devi, the revered Bengali writer whose writings and life have revolved, for the past twenty years, around her struggle to allow India's tribals to live lives they want to lead, rather than the government-prescribed alternatives.

Arundhati Roy, with her wealth, her blue jeans, her iconoclasm and her resistance to labels ('writer-activist, like a sofa-cum-bed,' she said in famous disparagement) breaks the established mould. Roy's case would be that there should be room in India—or anywhere—for both Mahasweta Devi and her.

'When I go abroad, everybody wants me to pose as some great radical who's been hunted down by this native banana republic— you know, like I'm Taslima Nasreen. I just say, look, I'm having a conversation with an institution in my society. There's no fatwa against me. This is a conversation, and these are the ways in which a democracy becomes sophisticated,' she says. The rain is coming down hard now, like a friendly drummer joining in with our conversation. All these things (the essays, the fight with the Supreme Court of India) are only done out of a huge affection for this place, however terrible it is. Why on earth would someone like me do this? I could be living in the French Arrondissement, I could be in Cannes every year . . . I could do that if I wanted to.'

If she'd exercised that option, here's what she would have missed. An obscenity case against *The God of Small Things*, pertaining to the relationship between Ammu and Velutha in the novel, which was filed in 1997 in the Kerala courts and went on for several years.

The Supreme Court fracas, where Arundhati Roy was pulled up for comments she made—in response to a petition that the august court threw out, in effect saying that the case against her was unjustifiable, but that her comments on the case threatened the majesty of the court. She paid a token fine of Rs 2,000 and spent one night in Tihar jail—not a terrible penance, in physical terms, but a terrible warning, in terms of the precariousness of her right to personal liberty. A case was filed against her after she wrote an impassioned article in *Outlook* magazine, about the massacres in Gujarat. The petition alleges that she, who condemned the killings of over 800 Muslims, is responsible for 'instigating communal hatred'. As is the practice with these cases, she was required to appear personally at a Baroda police station.

'I've always said that the worst thing that can happen to a writer in India is not a bad review,' says Roy, with some understatement. So why, in the face of trenchant criticism, should she continue? Why not move, as she says she can, to the French Arrondissement? Because this is where she belongs, and because her true audience are the taxi-drivers of Kerala, the Bhils of Madhya Pradesh, the nameless legions who write fan-mail every day. And why not temper the writing?

'I think people have a real problem with feelings,' Roy says, 'I insist that feelings are facts. I insist on them. I absolutely do. And I think people get thrown by that.' Not that she holds facts in contempt. On the contrary: 'It is the facts that outrage me (about the Narmada dam issue). It is those facts that fuel my fury.' (Though she doesn't say this, many feel that the jibes against her are misogynist, and in comments' sections online, the abuse against her is often violently sexist: for a certain kind of Indian male, any Indian woman who speaks her mind as fearlessly as Arundhati does is seen as a threat.)

And—final question—why do her critics froth at the mouth at the very mention of her name? Arundhati Roy smiles. The rain is now hammering insistently on the windows, and she loves the feel of this unseasonal storm. 'The reason they go for me . . .' she says, slipping uncharacteristically into third person, 'one has this huge audience. So they're criticizing exactly what makes one the author of a book that sold six million copies worldwide. The way I write is who I am. And who I am is a writer who's read enormously, in every country.'

I think that this is one of the reasons she's disliked in India: she's willing, in a most unIndian manner, to flaunt her success. But success isn't what defines Roy according to Roy—it's all about what she does and how she does it. 'One of the things I demand of a writer— myself, included—is the space and agility to take statistics, to put them alongside the story of a man from the Narmada valley about how he felt the first time he saw the waters submerge his village.'

The demands of living in Delhi are beginning to intrude, in the shape of phone calls, of people wanting to check those dry water tanks. 'I can use feelings and facts and stories and anything I want in my writing. I can use all of these as ammunition. There are no rules for me. I would not accept any rules. I'm going to do what the hell I want so long as I'm not being manipulative and I'm not lying.'

So there it is, out in the open, the reason India's uncomfortable with Arundhati Roy. We don't like nihilists. We don't like immodest nihilists, even if they have a lot to be immodest about. And most of all, we really, really don't like immodest nihilists who're telling the truth as they see it, from the position of relative power they happen to be in. Arundhati Roy's business is to question; only the powerless in India will appreciate that.

(Based on a 2003 interview. In 2004, Arundhati Roy published The Ordinary Person's Guide To Empire; *in 2010,* Listening To Grasshoppers: Field Notes on Democracy; *in 2011,* Broken Republic: Three Essays, *and in 2013,* The Hanging of Afzal Guru.*)*

6

Vikram Seth

At the Seth family house in Noida, Vikram Seth oscillates between charm and gloom. He hates interviews, but accepts with resigned tolerance that he must 'do publicity' every six years or so. He's resigned when an interview stretches for ten minutes too long, resigned when the photographer makes him change his shirt. 'She's the second photographer who's made me do this.'

Then we discover I've selected the same restaurant where the family's taking him for dinner. Vikram's mother, Leila Seth, protests. You don't argue with a photographer, or with a former Justice of the Supreme Court, so we change plans, heading to Dakshin at the Marriott.

Two Lives, the non-fiction work that's forced Vikram back into the glare of publicity, is the most personal of his books, but also the only one where his own voice is so deliberately reined in.

As a teenager, he lived in England with his Shantih Uncle and Aunt Henny, who became 'surrogate parents'. He knew that Aunt Henny, a German Jew, had lost family to Hitler's concentration camps, and that Shantih Uncle had lost his arm during World War II, but that was all. He was floundering—panicking, he says—after *A Suitable Boy*, a writer in search of a subject, when Leila Seth suggested he interview Shantih Uncle.

Two Lives took almost a decade to write. It's part family memoir, part Holocaust remembrance, part personal history, told with a sensitivity that fluctuates between reticence and, for the very private Seth, a surprising openness. 'I thought of it as a three-stranded book, not two-stranded. But then I didn't want *Two Lives* to become Three Lives.'

Home in that period was London, where he used to bathe in the Serpentine ('I've become a bit of a wimp about winter swimming now') and where, walking across Hyde Park, the image of a man, a musician, came to him and grew into *An Equal Music*.

It's also been Delhi; Dariba Kalan, where his father still has family; Rajaji Marg, where the Seth family occupied a sprawling bungalow in a cheerful tangle of separate but intersecting lives, and now the suburb of Noida.

Aunt Henny taught him that language could be a home, too, as she took him through the intricacies of German, a language he found inimical but eventually settled into with great pleasure.

By the time we get to Dakshin, he's done with talking and is looking forward to his vodka (Absolut Pepper, chased with plain coconut water). We order fried prawns as a starter, meen moiley, gongura mutton and kai stew. 'Kai isshtew, kai shtew,' he says meditatively, trying out the poetical possibilities of vegetable curry on his tongue.

I try to get us back on track.

'About the Holocaust ...'

'Actually,' says Vikram, looking around, 'I like this place a lot.' Dakshin is quietly understated, with an appam station, thalis lined with banana leaves. 'I'm just going to hide the red light,' he says, switching his attention to the tape recorder. 'Put a little katori in front of it ... that does the trick.'

The prawns arrive. He's about to expand on the section in *Two Lives* where he's talked about his working habits, a state in which bills, letters pile up and books are scattered around, where he retreats into a disorder from which only close friends can rescue him. But he's distracted by the Carnatic music. He hums. I wait. He sings in snatches. 'Trying to work out what the raga is.' I give up, sit back, and prepare to enjoy myself.

Over the next hour, he discusses his work ('It took me a long time to call myself a writer'), marriage, where he believes, unlike Tolstoy, that all happy families are not the same. We discuss politics, and how ordinary people like Shantih Uncle and Aunty Henny can have their lives changed by parties whose agendas they wanted to have nothing to do with.

Researching the deaths of Aunt Henny's sister and mother has made him sensitive, not just to the horror of the Holocaust, but to the prevalence of commonplace violence. The map of Delhi is scarred by memories of 1984; we've passed roads where, as he says, not so long ago, Sikh families were killed in that terrible pogrom.

This book has changed him, I realize; what he wants to do with *Two Lives* is to get his readers to look behind the closed doors of family history as well as a larger history.

We're at the coffee stage—*kapi*, he corrects me, pointing to the menu where it's spelled K-A-P-I; the conversation has lightened again. He's unburdened by fame, writers aren't recognized in the same way as sportspersons or film stars, he says, ordering the date toffee without looking at the menu.

'I always look ahead to the pudding, just so that I can put myself in the right frame of mind.' What's next? Perhaps a collection of poetry, or essays, or a novella. Vikram doesn't really know, but for the first time in years, he feels free: 'I'm not panicking.'

As we walk out, the seldom-recognized Vikram Seth is accosted by a gorgeous, gushing fan who wants his autograph. He looks sheepish. 'It happens sometimes,' he says defensively.

Right now, he has more important things on his mind than the next fan, or the next interview, or even the next book: he's going off on a very important mission.

I watch as this respected, well-loved writer, praised by the likes of historian Antony Beevor, steps out into the afternoon in search of a damask tablecloth for his mother. It's a suitable quest.

(Based on a 2005 interview. In 2015, Seth published Summer Requiem, *a collection of poems;* A Suitable Girl *is scheduled for publication in 2016.)*

7

Ruchir Joshi

'There's the book, between Delia Smith and Salman Rushdie,' says Ruchir Joshi, gesturing carelessly at the spine of *The Last Jet Engine Laugh*. For the filmmaker-writer, this represents the end of a journey that began almost nine years ago. He began writing *TLJEL* at thirty-four, detouring every so often to make documentaries, and finished at the age of forty-two. The temporal rewards presented themselves early on, in the form of a £80,000 advance, and now that the book's out, they continue to trickle in. There's a phonecall from Star News asking to speak to 'Mr HarperCollins'—they do, as it happens, want Joshi, but someone has entangled publisher with writer. I'm hanging around in his cheerful but horrendously hot barsati, waiting for Joshi to finish dealing with the stream of callers who attend every promising new debut so that he can be taken out for lunch to the Machan. It was supposed to be somewhere more exotic than the Taj Mansingh coffee shop, but practical considerations intervened: on a day peppered with appointments, the Machan is the perfect halfway house.

It's like walking into a wall of coolth after the torrid temperature outside, and we settle down gratefully at the nearest table, where Joshi orders a Foster's while I settle for a sedate fresh lime soda. He seems oddly calm, for a debut novelist, and I ask whether he belongs to the school of writers who can detach the process of writing from the eventual fate of their work.

'That would be lying: I know I couldn't do certain things—no brownnosing or networking or fixing reviews. But one of my friends once told me about my films:"If you're going to do something different, you can't abdicate responsibility as soon as it's finished". Having got a couple of films out (*Eleven Miles*, which tracked Paban Das Baul, Gaur Khepa and other baul singers, and *Planet Kolkata* among them), perhaps I lack the fragility of a first-timer.'

The barrier between writer and filmmaker is thin; during the last two or three years that *TLJEL* took, Joshi was tossing around a few film projects in his mind. 'There are a couple of half-finished, half-conceptualized films I'd like to do now, including a feature script about driving in the mountains.'

The novel itself, which was called 'Midnight's authentic grandchild' by one reviewer, took quite a while to settle into shape. *TLJEL* spans a hundred years from the days just before Independence to two decades in the immediate future. Within its embrace fall a possible ending to Netaji Bose's story, technological warfare, water riots in Delhi, a love story and several fractured loves, tangential perorations on sex, photographs and sewage systems. By any yardstick, it cannot be accused of being underambitious.

'The truth is: it happened. I'd written *My Father's Tongue*, which could have been the beginning of a Kolkata coming-of-age rock'n-roll, losing-your-virginity novel, except that my friends forbade me to do any such thing. It was not planned to the nth degree. There were rough ideas that needed fleshing out, one of the reasons why it took so long. It was a question of letting the damn thing grow organically, with all the fungus, all the unwanted rot. I know people who chalk out a novel in advance chapter by chapter.' Joshi pauses with a director's sense of timing 'I find it admirable. Like people who can do insurance calculations.'

He's onto his second Foster's, having waved away the waiter with a polite 'We'll order later'; we employ the overflowing bread basket to ward off starvation. Isn't it odd, I ask, that there are so few fictionalized portraits of the men and women who fought for Independence? And was there a particular reason why he decided to pick up on Bose's story—both real and imagined?

'Bose is a prime subject for fiction. He undergoes a journey, travels across Central Asia, Europe, Singapore—he's always knocking at the door, there are sightings even after his death,' says Joshi. 'I was surprised that, as far as I could discover, there had been no fictionalization of Bose. He was at the other end of the spectrum from Gandhi's non-violence; he was at odds with the Congress ahimsa postures.'

That is one of the explanations for the dark hints of contemporary violence that criss-cross the novel. 'If you look at independent India, there's a fetishism of militancy and nationalism. In the end, Bose won: Nehru lost, Gandhi lost. It makes much more sense to remove their portraits and put up garlanded pictures of Bose, or of Indira Gandhi on a tank.'

For those who're wondering whether Joshi's rendering of Netaji's final years is meant to be authoritative, he leaves no room for speculation. 'There's a doubt about the story that Kalikaku tells of Bose's last years,' he says. 'There's a doubt about every single story in the book. That's completely intentional. The stories that our parents told us need to be questioned and so do the stories that we'll pass on. What are the new myths we're manufacturing today? How will our children's children treat those stories?'

He's intent, the wisecracking persona set aside for a moment as he grapples with the retelling of the themes that have shaped his life for almost a decade. The present, he explains, is the main focus of the novel—which is, paradoxically, why he skims over it and focuses on the past and future instead. He may or may not know it, but he's following Chinese literary prescriptions: know the past, to know the present; reflect on the future, to change the present. It seems like a good time to bring up the inevitable question of whether he writes 'cinematically'. 'Okay,' he says, starting on another palm-sized bottle of Foster's, 'I know I flirt with pretentiousness by saying this, but certain scenes in the book are deliberately cinematic, while other scenes are constructs, notions taken from contemporary visual art. It's like a collage or an installation, for instance, where what is not said is as important as what is picked out. There's no reason why a novel shouldn't lean on these sources.' And what if, I query, that makes it a less linear, more difficult read? 'Reading a book is a game, a *jeu d'esprit*, and if the reader is seduced enough by that to enter into the game, that's fine. There should be a difference between reading Sidney Sheldon or Robert Ludlum and reading Ruchir Joshi.'

If that sounds arrogant, too bad; he means it as a simple statement of fact. It hints at an underlying confidence, the sort that made Joshi, about a summer ago, take on Pankaj Mishra's polemics in an article that appeared on www.tehelka.com. I raise the issue tentatively, but he's prepared, and willing, to talk.

'I see Mishra's whole persona, his statements about literature, the coming down hard on things not of his ilk as dovetailing perfectly with the political power game that's playing out around us right now. The concepts of 'apasanskriti', the view that 'Yeh hamara culture ka nahi hai', this Sanskritized argument: these have been flipped over and translated in a curious way into a closing of doors, against regional literature and certain kinds of writing. And it's not open to debate. Pankaj Mishra represented, to me, a front for a certain kind of revivalist view of art that enshrines Naipaul's first three books and little else. You can't swim in the ocean, so you want to recast writing as a shallow children's pond! The bookshops of the mind should be open to all kinds of writing. I was trying to rail against the dictating tendency, to open up the debate.'

Controversy, newspaper columns have suggested, are part of the Joshi style. Why, for instance, did he switch publishers midstream, shifting from IndiaInk to HarperCollins in India? Joshi trots out the stock answer, saying that IndiaInk's Sanjeev Saith was a huge support, these things happen occasionally between author and publisher, it's an internal matter. It's an anodyne response. 'It's true,' he says, not giving an inch. And speaks with eloquence about Saith's unflagging help, especially at the beginning of the writing process.

I ask him whether the lack of neatness, the reluctance to tie up loose ends is deliberate, or just messiness. He's not the least bit put out, telling me how he cleaned up an early section from *TLJEL*, smoothened out the wrinkles, and entered it in *The Independent*'s short-story competition. 'I showed it to a friend, who said, "Ruchir, seamlessness is not what I expect from you; it's not your thing."'

We're on the last Foster's; Joshi displays at least one classic sign of the seasoned writer, an ability to drink steadily and stay completely lucid. He drains the glass and concludes, 'So I write cactusy prose, pushing out in different directions. It's not an easy ride, but a writer isn't Lufthansa; I don't specialize in not giving you turbulence.'

(Based on a 2002 interview. Ruchir Joshi has edited an anthology of erotica, Electric Feather *(2009), and published* Poriborton: An Election Diary *(2011). His documentary films include* 11 Miles: A Diary of Journeys, Memories of Milk City, Tales from Planet Kolkata *and* A Mercedes for Ashish. *His second novel,* The Great Eastern Hotel, *is out in 2016-17.)*

8

Kiran Desai

Kiran Desai's first reaction after winning the Booker was to thank her mother. 'The debt I owe to my mother is so profound that I feel the book is hers as much as mine. It was written in her company and in her wisdom and kindness,' Kiran said at the ceremony in London.

Desai worked on the novel that would become *The Inheritance of Loss* for almost eight years. 'I'm a slow writer,' she explained, 'it takes me time to find my characters, their histories, their voices—I like to let the story unfold.' Anita Desai, who wrote *The Zigzag Way* in the same period, spoke of Kiran working upstairs while she worked downstairs, a comfortable harmony connecting mother and daughter. Anita Desai's Mexico novel came out to good reviews; Kiran struggled with a book that was turning out to be larger than she had expected.

After the Delhi launch of *Inheritance*, Kiran talked of the difficulty of slashing 1,500 pages down to 300, of the days she spent interviewing Bangladeshi busboys, Indian waiters and other immigrants to the US in order to do justice to their stories. Her characters are all outsiders: a retired judge living in Kalimpong, scarred by the loneliness and rejection he experienced as a young man living in England; Biju, the son of the judge's cook, discovering the harsh comedy of life as a continually displaced immigrant in New York's restaurants; orphaned Sai, the judge's grand-daughter, stumbling into a love affair disrupted as the hills go up in flames over questions of identity and belonging.

The Inheritance of Loss was richly layered, written with sensitivity and humour, and for over a year, no one wanted it. Kiran Desai collected rejection letters until Hamish Hamilton finally took it.

The editors who turned her down must have winced when *Inheritance* made it to 2006's controversial Booker Prize shortlist, which omitted writers like Peter Carey, David Mitchell, Andrew O' Hagan and Nadine Gordimer in favour of relative newcomers. After eight years of silence, Kiran Desai woke up to a phone that rang off the hook. Even then, she was seen as a dark horse compared to frontrunner Sarah Waters.

(This interview was conducted in Delhi along with the translator and critic Ira Pande.)

Ira Pande: I'm impressed by how you managed to sustain the feeling for this book over such a long period of time—nine years.

Kiran Desai: We writers get competitive about this—how long did it take Mohsin (Hamid) to write his book? Many years ... Nadeem Aslam took eleven years.

IP: More, I thought, and he shut himself in a room ...

KD: He took eleven years, I took seven. It wasn't hard to sustain the feeling for the book, not hard at all. It was hard to finish, to put a stop to it, to go the other way from writing in every direction—that was easy, the difficult thing was realizing that to make a book, I had to do the opposite process and start throwing out bits. I cut a lot from the book.

Nilanjana Roy: I heard you threw out about eight chapters?

KD: It wasn't even eight chapters, it was 1,500 pages, and 800 pages, and 350 pages of it ...

IP: People have started to complain about the doorstopper book from India, because everyone's writing these enormously fat books. Sometimes I feel it would work better if there was more editorial intervention, because as a writer, few could do what you did—chuck out whole bits on your own.

KD: It is hard, because there are so many angles, you can go on forever, turning something around, going into another character, another angle of the whole thing. You have to realize you can't just go on forever, but there is a trend towards big books all over the world. Look at American books—the new (Thomas) Pynchon, (Dave) Eggers . . .

NR: In a way it was a pity you didn't do this, just to correct the gender imbalance.

KD: It is a gender thing! My mother was saying this, how young men are encouraged to write really, really big books, and women are often made to cut that down, almost as if it is a gender thing, that women write smaller, slimmer books and men write big, ambitious books. And the men are being accused of—what is the phrase?—hysterical realism. Which is funny, that's an amusing gender argument, where men are accused of being hysterical and women are being curbed and careful.

I sometimes think it's just the process of writing. We work on a computer, it's easy to keep everything, to research, add more and more. I bet if computers weren't around, a lot of men would write smaller books. Someone said that with Dave Egger it's really obvious—all those additions and all those footnotes that he can only do because he can play on the computer. But Salman (Rushdie) was saying, I realize we should write shorter books because we get paid the same amount! *(Laughs)*

IP: Can I ask you about *The Inheritance of Loss*? Did the title suggest the book, or did the book suggest the title?

KD: The title came right at the end. I'm still not sure it completely fits. A lot of people didn't like it—I've been told it sounds like a self-help manual, someone said, you should just call it *The Loss of Inheritance*, and that would make much more sense. I was struggling to come up with something because it's a book of so many different parts. I thought of all the typical ones: *The Judge of Kalimpong*—sounds vaguely like colonial literature, *The House of Cho Oyu*, and then this came up.

NR: It struck me how much loneliness and isolation there is in the book. Biju, the cook's son in America, Sai, cut off from a normal childhood, the judge alone in England, where you almost feel sorry for him, despite his harshness later . . . Was that taken from family history?

KD: Not quite that close, but the judge's story was certainly taken from hearing about the experiences of people going to England. There is often an attempt to cover up what actually happens when you go abroad. For all immigrants, the story that you create at the end is the story you can live with and that you like to tell. It's not what actually happened. Immigration is like the act of translation, the possibilities of dishonesty are so big, so immense. It's a place where you can embroider any kind of story, and I think most people do. You also want to go there saying that you haven't come struggling like other immigrants might have, you've come from a position of dignity, it's also an attempt to create your past, I think, in a different way. You have to make up a story about that as well.

The loneliness is immense. You're plucked from everything you know, your entire community, you're telling lies to everybody, immigrants are telling lies to other immigrants. I think people find themselves in really lonely places. When I think of myself, I grew up speaking English and being brought up, in a way, to leave successfully. That's what my father said, sadly, to one of his friends: 'What we did in our generation, we made good immigrants.' He was also brought up to be a good immigrant and he chose not to be one.

NR: You left at fourteen when you were studying at a convent in Delhi. Are there echoes of that school in the convent you described in your book?

KD: Oh god, it was awful. I got a note from one of the nuns, I almost fell off my chair, I was so scared. (*Laughs*) The fear was immediately there. It was so awful, I wonder whether other people's experiences were so bad.

IP: The fact that all of us did go to these Catholic convents also opened up for us the possibility of looking at another identity for ourselves. I remember leading two completely dissimilar lives. I came from a very traditional, conservative family, puja was part of my day, but I also went and did Angelus and Benediction and all the rest. It made me a better Hindu after I was exposed to Catholicism. I began to understand and respect what we had much more. What was your convent experience like?

KD: I think of dislocation. We went first to Kalimpong, briefly, went back to Loreto, briefly, went to England for a year, and went to the states, and at a really bad time—it was thirteen or fourteen, that age for me. But when I look back at that convent education, I hope they're not bringing up children in that same way, because every bit of art is stamped out. Wanting to write, or paint, that side of things.

NR: How did you get that back?

KD: It took a long time. I saw reading as an escape from this world. Writing came later, at a much happier and freer time. It was encouraged, it was considered a legitimate activity. I am really lucky for that brief bit of space.

IP: In India you lived in Delhi and in Kalimpong; which cities do you remember best?

KD: I lived in Chandigarh as well, and Bombay for a while, and then Delhi. I lived in Delhi the longest. And now there's totally new things I love about Delhi, I come back, I go to my father's house, climb up on to the rooftop. And it's lovely. The sun sets by the idgah, and we listen to Abida Parveen singing Khusro. Those are the best, those are the good bits of Delhi for me.

IP: And the bad bits?

KD: The bad bits? For me it was the memories of Loreto Convent, now it's just a completely different relationship with Delhi. I love Bombay, I have very happy memories of Bombay. If you grow up in Bombay, if you spend part of your childhood in Bombay, you get deeply attached to it. It's true of everybody I know who's grown up in that city. And I always envied Bombay writers—they seemed to have that emotional depth of attachment to Bombay that seems to power all their writing forever! And it's a glamorous city, the whole package, the mafia and Bollywood, and crime on that glamorous scale. For a long while, Delhi writers felt slightly bad, we only had monuments.

NR: How about New York? So many of you seem to be colonizing New York now.

KD: There's such a huge number of Indian writers living in New York, and few write about it. Suketu is one of the first to venture into New York, and he really should do it; I think he was fourteen when he went there, so he has childhood memories of growing up. Akhil Sharma may be writing about it, New Jersey . . . so it is shifting.

NR: Are you uncomfortable with labels such as 'diaspora writer', or 'immigrant writer'?

KD: You know, you go down those roads and inevitably end up in a place that's senseless after a bit. I always hope that I'll hear some writer talking about these issues in a really clever way so that I can copy what they say, but nobody has. I haven't heard anyone really manage to undo these knots. You stop talking about literature altogether, and you start talking about class and immigration, and end up with a debate that's about much bigger arguments. You can't escape labels a writer . . .

NR: Inheritance would have been a lot less rich if you hadn't had that split perspective, the New York immigrant underworld on one hand, the crumbling houses of privilege in Kalimpong on the other . . .

KD: It's a completely half-and-half book.

NR: How did you start the process of looking at the immigrant population in New York?

KD: It wasn't hard to find those stories. Those stories are as easily available as they are here. It's the same people on both sides of the world; the woman who cleans your house in India, those stories come into your house every single day. It's the same in New York. The characters are made up of people I know, in bits and pieces—like the Zanzibarian community, I couldn't have made that up. People who worked in a little bakery near where I used to live; all the stories of the rats are really based on what happened. There's always a mixture, journalists always ask you how much is fact and how much fiction, but it's always a mixture.

IP: You've spoken a lot about your mother's presence and her support for you and her general aura, and it is visible. Shashi Deshpande (the writer) said she sometimes felt a sense of déjà vu reading you, that it could be Anita in a younger voice. Quite apart from the mother-daughter relationship that you share, which is obviously very close, were you influenced by her style of writing? Her way of looking at India, because she's also had several dislocations, and she's tread almost the same ground, except that it was in another time and in another way.

KD: I was conscious of that, the realization that what we were living through was something that she had lived through and that her parents had lived through. She grew up in an India that was very different from the India of a lot of the people around her, because she had a German mother and her father was a refugee from Bangladesh and had very little family in India as well. So she grew up in a very strange little community, I think, somewhat dislocated, on her own.

So was my father, because his parents left Gujarat ages ago; my grandfather went on this long journey to England, spent the rest of his life in Allahabad and never saw his relatives. There was hardly any communication with them. And that was a whole process, of breaking what we think of as being so deeply Indian, these bonds of community and family and religion.

On my father's side it was ambition to be part of the ruling class, but it was also part of the idea of a secular India, which was really new. He was breaking all of this and gaining a wider idea of India, he was also losing something very old, that had gone back as far as anyone could remember. It's a process that happened within India as well as within the community of people who had left, who had always been leaving and returning.

NR: Do your mother and you travel a lot together?

KD: Yes, we did, still do . . . When we left India, it was just the two of us. I was the youngest child, so I was taken along. We both went through that whole immigrant thing together. She had spent her entire life in India at that point, and all of a sudden, in her late forties, I think, she had to learn how to teach. She was out of the whole cozy world of being a middle-class Indian woman, and suddenly she had to make a living, learn how to drive in different countries, get her pension, all the rest of it, it must have been very difficult.

IP: Was it visible for you then?

KD: No, it's only now I realize how difficult it must have been. She kept it from me, kept all the worry from me. I certainly must have been influenced by her, her writing . . .

IP: You said somewhere that as you enter that house, your mother's house, you feel as if you're in the presence of a writer.

KD: It is strange to go into her house in New York because she lives very much in and among her books, and sometimes it feels like a house of real exile. A lot of immigrants like the thought of being exiled, because it's so much more romantic, so much more elegant than being an immigrant. A lot of people who are immigrants will call themselves exiles . . .

But the word has a deeper meaning. People who are immigrants do feel that they're exiled in many ways, even if the decision to leave has been their own. I go into her house and it does feel like the house of an exile, sometimes I walk into it and it's like looking at those old Russian photographs of Osip Mandelstam's house. How strange that my mother's house should remind me of, you know, looking at photographs of a Russian poet's house! But it has that atmosphere.

IP: And how do you feel when you come to India and enter your father's house, what kind of change is that?

KD: I'm struck by how much at ease he is, in his own life. I was very conscious when writing this book that I've given up that complete ease. You never have it as an immigrant, when you pretend to fit in and you may even feel comfortable, but that kind of ease in your skin and in your house and in your language is missing.

I think as an immigrant your language is curbed, it becomes much more formal, in terms of communicating you have to hold it to a much more basic grammar in order to get your point across. The eccentricity of language goes, unless you really insist on centering yourself within the Indian community. You can't keep the humour. It's a really sad loss, and I could see a lot of the writers in Jaipur who had come from elsewhere, I saw it very much in Salman Rushdie, an incredible happiness in talking.

IP: I hadn't thought of it this way, but a lot of the immigrant writers lack the ability to be irreverent in the way you can if you live here. We curse India all the time but when the same thing is said by somebody who lives abroad we get very defensive.

KD: This brings back vivid memories of growing up in India and having the foreign relatives arrive. And then after they'd left, we used to laugh at them . . .

NR: Was that what got you into trouble, when people in Nepal and Kalimpong objected to the way they were reflected in your novel?

KD: It was really unexpected, that bit of anger, I hadn't expected it. And it only happened after the Booker, at first there was no bad response at all, only a good response. You try to write about characters in particular; suddenly you realize that you're seen as representing a people. That's always just terrible.

Your whole desire is to talk about what one human being might be going through against all these big forces, against what's happening in the world. You're writing in a world of complete imbalance, you aren't trying to represent an entire people. It was just a muddy time, nobody there really knew what was going on in the early stages of the GNLF struggle.

Barkha Dutt (of NDTV) asked me during the Jaipur Literature Festival, well, what is this mixture of sweet and threatening, I didn't put it together in my head at the time, on stage. But of course that's the whole argument against colonial literature, that you're seeing the 'natives' as being simultaneously sweet and naïve, but also as a threat. And my attempt at that moment was to describe what I saw when I was there.

Part of being Indian, or having a childhood in India, is that there will be a moment in your life when you will see normal life slide into violence, and you will hear the sound of a riot, and you will grow up hearing the sound of people screaming for their lives, and you will see fires burning. And you see all the boys in the market, and they're suddenly out on the streets pulling people out of their cars and setting them on fire, and then it's all over, and then they're back in the market. I don't know how you get your mind around it and your heart around it, you can't.

NR: You were very ruthless in the book, when you pointed out that it's not enough to be innocuous, harmless in the way that a lot of people who lived in and around Cho Oyu were. You said there was culpability, said it very clearly.

KD: That society is one I belong to, those two old Bengali sisters ...

IP: I remember that lovely scene where the two sisters have their garden slowly being colonized by squatters.

KD: That scene was not made up, that scene of having to go and talk to the pradhan, where he said, I have to look after my people and who are you to have this land anyway—that was based on real life. There was sudden awareness then for us. You realize you were living in a complete fantasy, on this hillside where it's madly beautiful, and you think you can have it, but you can't have it. There are other people whose claim on it is much deeper.

NR: Will the Booker eventually free you up a bit?

KD: It's such a strange prize, it has an effect on my life, but a prize doesn't make you feel any different, really, it's just a bizarre thing that's happened. I'm not used to getting any prizes, I didn't get any prizes in Loreto Convent!

IP: But there's both sides to it; thankfully now you can afford to write.

KD: Yes, I can afford to write. It was hard. It was so hard, I didn't mind that it was so hard, I don't think you do mind if you're writing, it doesn't matter if you're poor, but yes, I had no money at all, and I had to make a living and feed myself (starts laughing again) which is sad, but true! I lived in a smaller room, and then a smaller room, and then with more and more room mates, and more and more people, and finally in the end, it was really hard to work.

IP: Thankfully that's behind you now, but the equally frightening thing is that now having got the Booker, your next book is going to be that much harder to write?

KD: In India, it seems more important than anywhere! It's very strange, the whole prize-giving world is very strange. Publishers say it's so useful, it brings attention to books, but it's really scary, the focus is on three books, or four books, the rest get lost.

IP: Is there another book which one could look forward to?

KD: Not yet, I haven't begun yet, even reading is hard for me right now.

NR: It's strange, in terms of your writing career, this is just your second book, so you should be given the tolerance due to a writer who's just starting to find her way.

KD: I feel as if I've got a long way to go. This book was an attempt to be direct and honest about a particular process, but I forgot to play. If you read Italo Calvino or someone like that, you realize that to lose that side of being a writer because it isn't the right political moment is very tragic. I wouldn't want to lose that imaginative ability for the sake of a literary trend.

(Published in the IIC Quarterly, 2007.)

9

Vikram Chandra

Almost eleven years ago, Vikram Chandra came to Delhi to launch his first novel, *Red Earth and Pouring Rain*. I found a quiet, unassuming man eager to escape the confines of the crumbling Lodhi Hotel. He explained apologetically that he had been driven out of his hotel room because it smelled of corpses; he didn't have to explain why he didn't want to meet in the lobby (because it smelled of sewers). We conducted the interview in Lodi Gardens, which smelled of neither, and Chandra proved to be an articulate author with a strong sense of history and drama.

It took almost nine years for *Sacred Games*, his behemoth 900-page third novel, to grow out of the seeds of a short-story featuring a young Mumbai policeman called Inspector Sartaj Singh. In between, Chandra brought out a short-story collection, collaborated on a Bollywood film, *Mission: Kashmir*, and offered a tantalizing chunk of 'the Sardar cop book' in the *New Yorker*. Then he disappeared into academia, and now teaches creative writing at the University of California. His fans wondered whether Sartaj Singh would ever return to the mean streets of Mumbai.

Sartaj did, along with Gaitonde, a don caught between the urgent needs of the spirit and the flesh; Jojo Mascarenhas, a coolly efficient procurer of film starlets and models; and a cast of dozens. And the inspector's explorations of the Mumbai underworld, of petty blackmail and international conspiracies involving nuclear bombs, netted Vikram Chandra a million-dollar advance.

That's why this time around we're meeting for lunch at the House of Ming at the Taj Mansingh, where Chandra is staying. It might not be Delhi's most exciting five-star hotel, but it smells of mandarin-grapefruit aromatherapy incense rather than corpses and Chandra isn't complaining. He orders dimsums, I ask for a light lemon-vegetable soup and we settle into conversation.

The Mumbai he's gone back to in his writing is a city he's left many times, but never left behind. He spent his early years in boarding school, so Mumbai was 'one of the first places that felt like home'. As an undergraduate student, he went to the US: 'But Mumbai functioned as *vatan* (homeland).' In the eighties and the nineties, the Mumbai he knew had begun to change. 'There was always the underworld, but in the days of Haji Mastan, the action happened elsewhere. Then it became more dramatic, and the shootouts and hits came closer to home—geographically as well.' Chandra takes a sip of his Diet Coke. 'In my teen years, I'd come close to one "encounter": we were just driving by and heard automatic weapons firing round the corner.' Years later, researching *Sacred Games*, he talked to a policeman about this early memory. 'The cop said, okay, I can tell you who the shooter was and who the policeman was who killed him, but if you really want to understand what it was about, you should talk to X and Y in Delhi.'

That's how *Sacred Games* found its shape, form—and size. Chandra began meeting people. He met ganglords who had the crisp, businesslike air of corporate mavens, property tycoons who behaved like thugs, 'encounter specialists' who were charming, family men unless you recalled that they shot criminals for a living. He met a 'twenty-three-year-old, pneumatic young thing' on the arm of a middle-aged executive and asked her what she did, expecting to hear that she was an aspiring model. 'I'm a courtesan,' she told Chandra. 'You meet the strangest people in the most unexpected circumstances,' he says, if you're willing to listen to their stories.

'There are grand narratives offered to us that work on our lives in a way we don't see,' he says as our steamed rice, light-but-spicy chicken and lotus root vegetables arrive. 'There's the grand narrative of the nation-state, physically inscribed into the landscape and into people's bodies at the time of Partition.'

He saw the twinned stories of Sartaj the cop and Gaitonde the killer as parts of a vast whole that included Partition, geopolitical struggles, the Great Game, and the very contemporary yearning for the revolution that must destroy the world in order to create a brand-new paradise. Some of his ambiguity—the good guys and the bad guys are not so different from each other, or from us—comes from his early readings of the *Mahabharata*. 'Reading Kurukshetra, I thought, okay now there'll be a happy ending. And when there wasn't, it sent a chill through my heart: so the good guys can die as well?'

That complexity drove his vision for *Sacred Games*, despite the inevitable complaints that the book is too long, too layered. 'I saw an intricate web of events and people, connections of power and desire running across the whole country.' Then he grins. 'When I began, I thought I was doing a local story about two guys down the street who had a feud. A short book.' We look at the bulk of *Sacred Games* and start laughing. 'Yeah, I didn't realize how long it was because I'd written it in separate chapters. In June 2005, I told Melanie'—his wife, also a writer—'let's see how long the damn thing is. It was quite a shock, actually.'

After *Sacred Games*, Vikram Chandra says he's taking 'a very determined' holiday; he thinks he's finally done with Inspector Sartaj Singh: 'There was one time Melanie and I were having an argument—the usual couples' thing—and she said, why . . . can't you be more like Sartaj? Well, he's got himself a girlfriend now, he can go away.'

I tell him as we're finishing with coffee that I don't believe he'll be on vacation too long, that he seems to enjoy writing too much to stop. 'Yeah,' says Vikram. His accent still owes more to Mumbai than to Berkeley. 'Everyone has stories, if you're willing to look for them.'

It's not till I re-run the tape for this interview that I realize how accurate he is. The conversation at the kitty-party table-for-fourteen behind us is captured loud and clear: 'But, of course, he bumped her off! It wasn't the affair *na*, but she was telling his business secrets in bed.' If only Chandra had been at that table, I think, we could have had a great Delhi novel next from Mumbai's novelist of the times.

(Based on a 2007 interview. In 2013, Vikram Chandra's Geek Sublime *won the National Book Critics Circle Award for criticism.)*

10

V.S. Naipaul

Some years ago, Patrick French spent over a month in Delhi conducting meticulous, detailed interviews with seven or eight different people. All of them had witnessed a minor but indelible incident at a literary festival involving V.S. Naipaul. Over hour-long interviews, French cross-checked each account thoroughly, pressing for facts and details, until he had an accurate picture fixed in his head.

The incident was one of many in Naipaul's life that never made it to French's biography, *The World is What It is*, but it was an index, if one was needed, of the lengths to which French was willing to go to in order to ensure that this would be the authoritative, not just authorized, version. '[. . .] the aim of the biographer,' writes French, 'should not be to sit in judgement, but to expose the subject with ruthless clarity to the eye of the reader.'

And this he does. The authorial voice of the biographer is all but absent; instead, through a pastiche of interviews with Naipaul, with the great writer's many admirers and detractors, through a careful examination of the voluminous Naipaul archives, French puts together a book that is destined to outlive both the subject and the biographer.

Naipaul's life can be roughly summarized: the insular, deprived childhood in Trinidad, the urgent need to escape that brought him to the UK, the sense of being different and out of place that drove him to depression and rage, the early years of struggle, interspersed with thin success, and then finally the years of being Sir Vidia, the Nobel Prize winner.

The three motifs of his life are equally clear: the fierceness with which he willed himself into existence as a writer, the search for belonging accompanied by the need to repudiate any place that might welcome him, and the intense honesty of his gaze. Those who read him might—and do—disagree with the accuracy of his judgements and might argue with his opinions, but his way of seeing, an innate inability to look away or to see with blurred vision, fuels his work. His insistence on honesty allowed French's biography to step away from hagiography, to be a searing and often disturbing account of the life of one of the most respected and controversial writers of his time.

As a writer, he blurred the distinction between fiction and non-fiction; in his later years, he attacked the form of the novel with ferocity, though many critics believe that it is his novels—*A House for Mr Biswas*, *The Mystic Masseur*, *A Bend in the River*, *The Enigma of Arrival*—that will last. He reported unflinchingly from the edges of a world in the throes of upheaval and change, rendering South America, Trinidad, India, and a score of other places neither as the West saw them nor as their inhabitants could see them: it was his view that drove his narratives, he was, as French notes, 'always, on nobody's side'.

French remarks, a little later in the biography, 'As people and ideas shifted between countries in a way they had not done at previous points in human history, an author who took the world as his subject was no longer impossible. He could carve out a space for himself as a new sort of writer, claiming to come from a place without history . . .' And so he did, sometimes with detachment, often with passion, often with bitterness.

Perhaps wisely, French refrains from analysing the books—as Naipaul has often said to critics and interviewers, everything of importance is in his work, he has little interest in explaining himself. Instead, the second half of the biography becomes an increasingly personal history, a record of a life at once touching—as Naipaul struggled to find the recognition and financial success that eluded him in the early decades—and monstrous.

His marriage to Pat Hale was by turns intimate and abusive; Pat bore the brunt of Naipaul's temper, his often unreasonable demands and struggled, as he did, with the sexual side of the relationship. Naipaul found release in furtive visits to prostitutes; patient, long-suffering Pat cooked, cleaned, set up house and was his most important reader. 'I should have left,' Naipaul told French. 'I didn't have the brutality.' And yet, his relationship with his mistress, Margaret Gooding, seems just as brutal in a different, darker way.

The climax, so to speak, of his marital life, is laid out by French in cold terms. Naipaul has abandoned Margaret, Pat is dying of cancer and Naipaul is made angry by that impending death. As his first wife declines in hospital, Naipaul proposes to Nadira, a Pakistani journalist who astonished him by asking whether she might kiss him at their first meeting. Pat's funeral is seen by some as a shabby affair, but characterized by Naipaul as 'chaste, Quranic in its purity'. Naipaul returns from the funeral, and sends for food, apples and cheese for him, olives for Nadira who will be arriving the next day. In a rare and much-quoted authorial comment, French writes, '[And so] the funeral green olives did coldly furnish forth the marriage tables.'

It is perhaps this passage that has shocked most readers. And yet, what stands out is Naipaul's candour in his conversations with French, his refusal to make excuses or apologies. He has made few of them throughout his life, either to the many friends and supporters who later found themselves attacked or abandoned, or to his many critics. *The World is What It is* offers a powerful insight into Naipaul's journey as a writer and into the life of the man, and it is a gripping, unforgettable biography: yet it is an excruciating read, a book that challenges and exhausts the reader. French writes with the purity and clinical sharpness of the professional historian, omitting nothing, excusing nothing.

The virtues of *The World is What It is* can be found in Naipaul's own writing: an absolute honesty, a refusal to flinch from the unpleasant, an impassioned insistence on objectivity. French, as a biography, also employs the ruthlessness and dispassionate coldness of his subject. The result is one of the most compelling books of the year, an analysis not just of Naipaul but of a certain kind of mind, of the price of greatness. Some may think it too high, on reading this biography of a towering writer who lacks all capacity for compassion, who has humour, but often lacks humanity, who has over time become less and less relevant, in part because he has so little respect for women as intellectual equals. Sometimes it is best not to know too much about the writers whose works and style you admire, and yet, it is impossible to look away.

(Published in the IIC Journal, 2008. In 2010, V.S. Naipaul published a travelogue, The Masque of Africa.*)*

11

Ved Mehta

Indian writing has little space for the family album. The few portraits of parents, siblings or partners that emerge are like the photographs that hang in our homes: officially posed, formally garlanded. Ved Mehta's *Continents of Exile* series is one of our few, monumental exceptions, a long-playing biography on the screens of our imaginations.

Ved is in Delhi for the re-release of the eleven books that make up the series, written over decades, starting with *Daddyji* and continuing through *Mummyji* and *Mamaji* into the personal terrain of *All For Love* and *The Red Letters*.

Nothing is exempt from Mehta's need to set it all down, not the years of apprenticeship with Mr Shawn—William Shawn, the legendary *New Yorker* editor—not his blindness, not his sessions on the psychiatrist's couch. This has its pitfalls, as Ben Yagoda noted in *About Town*, a history of the *New Yorker*. 'Ved Mehta's endless biographies of the various members of his family almost seemed to dare the reader to say, "This is boring!" and flip ahead to the next article.'

Mehta, one of the great raconteurs in person, knows this; he also knows that *Continents of Exile* cannot be ignored. 'When my three-part essay on Mamaji came out, other *New Yorker* writers asked why Mr

Shawn would run this, at a time when people were dying in Vietnam,'
he says. Shawn had his own reasons for shaping and encouraging
Mehta's personal and painful brand of honesty.

★

'I hate the word "memoir",' says Ved Mehta, after I've used it for the
fifth time. 'I prefer biography, or autobiography.' We're discussing the
Indian reluctance to write in the autobiographical vein. My theory is
that there are too many unspoken taboos on writing about the personal,
the familial. Ved's hands flicker in disagreement, like an unconscious
turning of a page to a different chapter.

'Indians aren't reticent,' he says. 'Maybe we still have a Victorian
morality that won't let us speak our minds. But there's a freedom in the
West you don't have here. Writers there are not afraid of not making
a living. They have the freedom to write about sex. The freedom not
to appear dignified, noble, likeable. What would Henry Miller have
written if he'd wanted to be liked by his middle-class relatives?'

I think of my impatience as an adolescent reading Mehta's 'endless
biographies', wading through these meandering accounts of parents,
relatives, lovers, friends, editors, partners. It was years later before
I realized how deeply embedded Mehta's portraits had become in
my mind, as though his family had become mine, as though I knew
Kiltykins and Daddyji as well as he did. It took years to see how tight,
how taut—Mehta's adjectives, not mine—the narrative was; how much
had been skillfully omitted, how accurate the details were.

Mehta would give the credit to Shawn: 'He was a genius, and he
also had enormous taste, sympathy and humanity. These sound like
abstractions, but they are not.' The preferred adjectives to describe
good writing today are 'necessary' and 'honest'; but as Mehta expands
on Shawn's virtues, they seem like the Holy Trinity of truly timeless
writing, including Mehta's own work. Taste, sympathy, humanity.

★

How reliable is memory anyway? Here are three Ved Mehta stories. The Neemrana festival gathered together some of India's greatest writers—V.S. Naipaul, Vikram Seth, Amitav Ghosh, Khushwant Singh and Ved Mehta among others—and then, for inexplicable reasons, sequestered them in a fort-palace far away from their readers.

The insistent literariness of the Neemrana festival was enlivened by a massive disagreement between the wife of the German ambassador and Naipaul. The author and the ambassador's wife threatened, from opposite corners of the fort, to leave if the other stayed on; the combined diplomacy of Pico Iyer, Vikram Seth, Amitav Ghosh and Nadira Naipaul finally persuaded a still-furious Naipaul to come down to dinner.

Ved Mehta walks in late. For once, his normally acute senses fail to compensate for his blindness, and he sees only Vikram Seth and Dom Moraes, not Naipaul. 'Dom,' says Ved in his clear, carrying voice, 'you'll never guess what that terrible old man has gone and done now.'

'No, no,' says Mehta, though he's smiling. 'That didn't happen.' He has, he explains, often had to deny stories about himself.

The late Dom Moraes and he once made the same trip, and wrote separate accounts. Dom had a wonderful story about Ved Mehta as the guest of a maharana, drawn to the lifelike figure of a stuffed tiger. 'May I pet it?' he asks, and the maharana gives his permission, while Dom signals frantically—but ineffectively, since Mehta can't see him—from the other end of the room. Ved, petting the stuffed animal, is remarking on the realistic feel of its fur when the tiger gets up, yawns and walks away.

'Dom,' says Mehta with some feeling, 'treated me as Quixote treated Sancho Panza. I never rode horses. The maharana never introduced naked ladies into my bedroom. And the stuffed tiger story isn't true.' I have a clear memory of Dom telling the story in his rich timbre, and Mehta and I both agree that some stories, however false, should be true.

The third story concerns Mehta's blindness, which he has often written about, commenting that it is for the blind to imagine the world of the sighted—the sighted rarely feel compelled to do the opposite.

One of Mehta's readers, noting the many references in his writing to 'seeing' and 'scrutiny' or specific colours, particular details, is convinced that Ved Mehta is not really blind. At a book launch, the reader decides to prove his theory.

Ved Mehta is speaking to a group of friends. The reader sneaks up and joins the group; then makes a rapid hand gesture in front of Ved's face. The writer continues with his tale. The reader tries a more obvious gesture; the writer is unmoved. The reader, still convinced that Mehta's faking, starts waving his hands in front of the writer's face, jumping up and down. The writer remains impassive. Defeated, the reader leaves, and tells a friend who's witnessed the incident that he was wrong, that Ved Mehta is, indeed, blind.

'That wasn't Ved Mehta,' says the friend. 'That was V.S. Naipaul.'

This story is true.

★

The conversation has roamed from the short attention span of the modern-day reader to the relative merits of Joyce versus D.H. Lawrence to a dispute over whether it was alcohol or buggery that fuelled the productivity of Truman Capote. ('Buggery,' says Mehta, and that settles the matter.)

There is one final matter to be addressed. 'I never started out wanting to write a million words about my life,' says Ved Mehta, and we both contemplate what it would have been like, in 1972, to look ahead at a vista of writing a biography all the way up to 2003. I cannot imagine it, any more than he could, as a young writer. 'Writing is in itself a way of growing up; the more difficult the challenges you take on, the more you change.'

Continents of Exile is balanced by the other books—travelogues, political accounts, short stories—but perhaps Ved Mehta knows that his biographies will define him. There is an end to a novel, even a trilogy; but an autobiography can only end with an obituary, which we will hope is long delayed. However inadvertently he began the project of writing his life, the million-plus words it's taken to cover his history,

Ved Mehta has hit upon the only possible answer to writer's block. Writing your life as you live it is the perfect way to ensure that you will never run out of material.

(Based on an interview conducted in 2009 and readings between 2004–2012.)

12

Nayantara Sahgal

The residential quarters at the IIC in Delhi are reminiscent of reserved airport lounges: they both signify the temporary privilege conferred on VIPs in transit. It is an odd space to meet Nayantara Sahgal, a writer whose life and works are both umbilically linked to the capital city.

But Vijaya Lakshmi Pandit's daughter is here on a mission: to promote the book that she hopes will both round off Jawaharlal Nehru's letters to his family, and remind a forgetful India of Pandit. It is an index of how far the editing of history has proceeded that Before Freedom includes just five letters from Vijaya Lakshmi Pandit. Many more were written, as is apparent from Nehru's responses, but they cannot be found. 'What came down to me was what was in my mother's possession. I did try to obtain the other half of the correspondence—they may be in some archives, perhaps, or some closed sector of a library,' says Sahgal.

It stings. In the introduction, Sahgal recounts the story of the trip she and her sister made to Allahabad in 1990 after the death of their mother. They visited Anand Bhawan, the house that Vijaya Lakshmi Pandit had shared with her brother Jawaharlal for many years, and Swaraj Bhawan, where she had grown up. The guide made no mention of Vijaya Lakshmi Pandit at all.

'There's a definite attempt to blot her out. It's ironic because she herself had no ambition to be anywhere in history.' Sahgal points out that her mother had retreated to Dehradun, where the writer now makes her home, after resigning from Parliament in 1968. 'What threat could a woman who had literally bodily removed herself from public life, what possible threat could she have constituted?' she asks rhetorically. And answers her own question. 'Indira Gandhi was a very different person from her father. He had a very strong, stable confidence. She was, I feel, a person deeply emotionally insecure.'

Sahgal was herself 'blotted out' during the Emergency. 'It was very hard on those who wrote for a living in those days and were not toeing the line of the dictatorship. The publisher who had contracted for *A Situation in New Delhi*, explained that my family name made it difficult to publish me. I can't be expected to change my name to Suzy Brown, I said, and the book wasn't published until much later.'

Looking back, she sees her books, especially the first six novels, as a chronology of the emerging India. 'There is always politics in the background, balanced by the hopes and fears of that time. If *A Time to Be Happy*, my second novel, showed an India at the peak of idealism, *Rich Like Us*, my sixth novel, was about the decline and decay of that idealism.'

In recent years, the blotting out has been a voluntary process. Sahgal has remained an influential figure in the world of Indian letters, heading the Eurasia jury for the Commonwealth Awards in 1990, and being the chief guest at this year's awards, but she hasn't published a novel since 1988. The pen hasn't dried up: she's written two novels since then but held back from publication. 'I didn't feel comfortable in this climate—the packaging, the advertising, the hype.'

Like many of the writers who wrote in the era B.R. (Before Rushdie, as you may have guessed), Sahgal views the present situation with a jaundiced eye. 'I was writing at a time when perhaps writing was not the kind of horse race that it's become now. Before this phase set in it was a highly individual occupation. Now you have to take the 'readership' into account, the market into account.' The eyes, masked till now with the professional opacity of a feted author who also hails from one of India's first families, flash into imperious life. 'I would never have submitted to that in my day.' Our time is up; the next in a long list of assembly line interviews is waiting.

(In 2014, HarperCollins India published Out of Line: A Personal and Political Biography of Nayantara Sahgal *by the well-known feminist editor and publisher, Ritu Menon.)*

13

Pico Iyer

Close your eyes, waggle a pencil over a map of the world, swoosh downwards. Attach the other end of the pencil to a compass and draw a circle, à la Alu in Amitav Ghosh's *The Circle of Reason*.

The laws of probability dictate that wherever the pencil falls and whatever the circle encompasses, Pico Iyer has been within its circumference. As a writer of travel guides, initially; then as a wandering nomad with homes in four continents; as a global soul, a one-man bridge across cultures; as a public man with the ascetic soul of a monk.

Then you come to a circle in west Asia, and tick off Damascus, Syria—but not Iran. Pico Iyer took John Macmillan and Camilla, the two protagonists of *Abandon*, there, but he stopped outside the borders himself. We have, as we discuss this apparent omission, what Pico calls 'two nations on a plate' before us—prawn appetizers Thai and Kerala style, served exquisitely as always at The Spice Route.

The warmth and charm that Pico exudes is genuine, but it masks the man's persuasive powers, not to mention indomitable will. I arrived at The Imperial determined that, after a surfeit of authorial lunches within its portals, we would lunch anywhere but here. Tables had been tentatively booked at Japanese restaurants, at fine continental restaurants, at Italian restaurants.

Pico looked beseeching and murmured something about really, really wanting to lunch at The Spice Route. I murmured something about sudden death and decapitation at the hands of The Editor. Pico looked even more beseeching. To cut a long story short, we found ourselves . . . not elsewhere, Pico rubbing his hands together in satisfaction as he ordered his favourite prawns. 'I had my little heart set on this,' he remarked. (For long-term readers who're wondering whether The Imperial has me on its payroll, I have two words: cold coffee. Read the final paragraph.)

Abandon is another exploration for a man who's spent most of his adult life hacking through the urban jungles of the big city and debunking the myth of paradise lost and regained by national tourist boards. With eight books under his belt, this is only his second foray into fiction—relatively new terrain, to be quartered, explored and illuminated in characteristic style. The quest for a Sufi manuscript takes us from California, where Pico has spent fourteen years, to India, where he has roots, to Iran, where he was careful never to go.

He didn't want to risk his travel-writer self taking over from the fiction writer. He did want *Abandon* to be, for him as much as for his characters, a flight from the known into the unknown, or, to use a phrase he repeats almost as ritual incantation, from darkness into deeper darkness.

We have eschewed wine in favour of disgustingly healthy fruit juices—watermelon for him, fresh-squeezed orange for me. Aside from the many countries he can claim as home—India, England where he went to boarding school, California and Japan where he lived for many years with his partner, Hiroko Takeuchi—Pico explains that he can also lay claim on several religions.

He was born a Hindu; imbibed the principles of Christianity at school and has been a regular at the (Benedictine) New Camaldoli Hermitage in California for more than a dozen years; spent several years in Japan exploring Buddhism in ways more practical than mystic; and found himself interested in Islam more recently.

One of the obligations of being a Hindu, in his view, is to be able to enter the other, to use imagination in order to understand the apparently alien. He took 'the liberty' of translating the word 'Islam'— usually rendered in English as submission, or surrender—as 'abandon', with its dual meanings. 'In America people focus so relentlessly on this clash of cultures, Islam as the enemy, us versus them,' he says, as we order soups rather than a main course in deference to Delhi's appetite-sapping heat. 'I wanted to move away, to explore the notion that Islam might be inside us and around us.'

It is not a unique perspective—as Pico has pointed out, the Sufi mystic Rumi is the bestselling poet in the US. I mull over the prospect of Pico joining him on the bestselling charts: not with the fiction, but with his own poetry. Of the twenty-odd poems in the book, perhaps six or seven are by Rumi. The rest were composed by Pico himself.

As we drift into a discussion of other writers—Pico balanced about Salman Rushdie, me venturing some small criticism—the lights flicker and go out. Perhaps it's blasphemous to criticize Rushdie, I say, as we descend from darkness into deeper darkness. Aha, chuckles Pico, an electric fatwa.

His Tom Yam and my Laksa arrive, and as the lights come back on, Pico gently dissects America. 'America is the strongest country in the world, and the most concerned with changing the world, and the least concerned with learning about the world.' He is as scathing as a man this instinctively polite can be about George Bush: 'When he came to office, he'd been to fewer countries than my nephew and my niece, aged three and four. He is pronouncing vehemently on the world without having seen it.'

Inevitably, we're back with the question of what travel means to the original global soul. Pico invokes a classic moment: 'When you get to the plane, sometimes you can see your house from the air. It gets smaller and smaller until it's indistinguishable from the other houses, and then you're above the clouds, and you can't see it. One of the things I like about travelling—or about retreating to a monastery—is that suddenly all those things that seem so amazingly important when you're at your desk at home become amazingly trifling.'

Perhaps what keeps him going is a different kind of faith, the trust he places in culture as 'an alternative form of politics, with the imagination actually being able to conceive revolutions better than the politicians can'. Pico's next novel has him donning a female narrative voice. 'With my androgynous name,' he quips, 'I'm quite used to receiving invitations to dinner for Mrs Iyer.' Since he does most of his writing in rural Japan, he confesses to having 'fallen into the terrible habit' of taking movie stars as models for his women characters. Camilla in *Abandon* was modelled on Gwyneth Paltrow; those who prefer their women less wispy, dreamy (and annoying, as we've discussed at length) will be relieved to know that Pico's next heroine will be inspired by Kristin Scott-Thomas, who is neither wispy nor annoying.

Alongside the novel, Pico's been working on another travel book, though 'travel' seems a mean and inadequate label to place on those lucid, inquiring writings. This one took him to some of the poorest countries in the world—Bolivia, Haiti, Yemen, Cambodia—in search of a corrective to the prosperity of late 1990s America.

Of course, this wouldn't be poverty tourism, I comment. He winces, but faces the implied criticism head on. 'So much of what I write is about that huge gap between the privileged and the dispossessed. Perhaps this sounds like comfortable liberal guilt. But if you have a choice between being stuck in your cocoon and going out, I'd much rather go out, experience a keener sense of reality. It's a way of unsettling our unreal lives of comfort.'

Unreal is a good word. It encompasses the silver tea service, the Earl Grey and the jasmine tea, the waiters careful not to point out that we have talked at such length that we now sit in a small pool of light in the darkened shadows of the empty restaurant. The bill arrives, including a mysterious addition for a cold coffee that neither Pico nor I remember ordering. I query it, but the man insists it was consumed in the lobby. The meal and the general air of satisfaction makes me too lazy to argue. Besides, I think as we exit, pursued by solicitous hotel staff, it's the one piece of evidence I have that proves The Imperial is, if anything, secretly trying to get a message across: come back with

Yet Another Author and next time it'll be something really expensive added on to that bill.

Fathers and Sons

There is nothing passive about the act of reading. It may seem mysterious that one writer exerts a powerful undertow on your life while another leaves not even a watermark impress, but there is nothing accidental about the choice a writer makes in his literary friendships.

In a hotel room in La Paz, Bolivia, a writer who has come here seeking a break from his desk begins to write, unstoppably. He writes about a boy in school, steeling himself to carve down the next twelve months into manageable chunks of time, left alone among a host of boys whose fathers have all just 'vanished down the driveway'; the boy's name is Greene.

'Was it only through another that I could begin to get at myself?' asks Iyer. And with this, he opens up a meditation into literary friendship—into the twinned faith and doubt he shared with Greene, into a world of fathers and sons, innocence and guilt. *The Man Within My Head* pays tribute, even in its title, to Greene, whose first book was a novel, *The Man Within*.

Pico Iyer's first book, published in 1984, was a collection of essays on literature called *The Recovery of Innocence: Literary Glimpses of the American Soul*. These essays, now hard to locate, came out seven years before the death of Graham Greene, who had written some of the most bitter lines about innocence in *The Quiet American*: 'Innocence always calls mutely for protection when we would be so much wiser to guard ourselves against it: innocence is like a dumb leper who has lost his bell, wandering the world, meaning no harm.'

Neither Greene nor Iyer ever had that kind of innocence themselves, though they saw it and responded to it, sometimes helplessly, in others. In his travel writing, Iyer travels defiantly as a stranger, a permanent outsider wherever he might be, rather than the all-knowing, omniscient narrator who infests the travel magazines. 'So long as I was loose in the world, unaccompanied, I was never bored or at a loss,' he writes.

Greene, unlike Iyer, was often a terrible traveller; 'at night there are far too many objects flying and crawling', he writes of Freetown, where he found life 'pretty grim'. But the two men had a similar eye for detail. Greene's line in *The Heart of The Matter* could have been borrowed from an Iyer travelogue, for instance: 'On the other side of the road lorries backed and churned in a military transport camp and vultures strolled like domestic turkeys in the regimental refuse.'

And Greene's more flamboyant side does not alienate Iyer. He can discuss Greene's many affairs and his drinking with interest, though he shares neither of these parallel and demanding occupations. Drawn to monasteries himself, Iyer has a broad curiosity that allows him to be taken with Greene's plans to open a brothel in Bissau as a way of gathering espionage information. (Kim Philby, Graham Greene's boss, turned this down; it would not have been economically profitable.)

But the affinity—the very real kinship—between Iyer and Greene has deeper roots. 'If you try to push him into a compartment,' Iyer writes of Greene, 'you'll always get it wrong.' He could be writing about himself; both writers have a complex relationship with faith and religion, for instance, and neither can be easily straitjacketed, either as the Catholic writer or as the monkish novelist. 'You can't read the books in terms of ideologies,' he tells us of Greene. In his own writing, he finds himself walking through Greeneland, landscapes of doubt and betrayal, faith and confusion, the loneliness but also the richness of the human condition mapped down to the least explored corners.

It took ten years for Iyer to write this book, and perhaps more; perhaps the account of this intense relationship really goes back to his childhood, shaped at the kind of British schools that shaped Greene. This might be the closest that Iyer—the most open and yet the most reticent of writers—gets to writing his autobiography, which he does sidelong. Why Greene? Why not another writer? He knows and doesn't know the answer to this, and he shares as much as he can with his wife, Hiroko, and with the silent reader.

'I couldn't quite convey even to her how difficult it was at times to read *The Quiet American*: I'd pick up my worn orange copy with the pages beginning to separate from their binding, and I'd see a brash American reaching out for support, or Fowler calling the man he's more or less condemned to death his 'friend' (perhaps his only friend), or see him trying to petition his wife for a divorce and realizing, at the very end, that, as Teresa of Avila had it, more tears are shed over answered prayers than unanswered, and I couldn't say why it struck me with such force.'

When Iyer writes his essay about Greene, 'Sleeping with the Enemy', for *Time* magazine, his father leaves a message on his answering machine. As the father speaks to his son, he is so moved that he begins to sob. 'It was a shocking thing, to hear a man famous for his fluency and authority lose all words.' Some weeks later, Iyer's father is dead; that 'gasping call about Graham Greene' is the last memory he has of hearing from him.

The ideal father, he reflects, would be an adopted one, a virtual or a chosen father who could offer answers to the questions left behind, the ones that sons (and all children) never get to ask their parents in the end. He has no virtual father, perhaps even no need for one. Instead, Iyer has Graham Greene, the man with whom he shares his secrets, his sins, his most intimate needs. It is a closer relationship, this claimed kinship between a dead writer and a living one, than any other could be.

(Based on interviews and reviews from 2003 and 2012, when The Man Within My Head *was published. In 2014, Pico Iyer's very popular TED talk, 'The Art of Stillness: Adventures in Going Nowhere', was brought out as a book.)*

14

Rohinton Mistry

To ascribe motives to Rohinton Mistry that the author may never have had in mind is a dangerous pastime. Mistry, who has no fondness for the present-day recasting of writer as public figure, TV celebrity and soundbyte-generator rolled into one, rarely gives interviews. He is, however, fairly good at expressing his views on subjects such as Germaine Greer's criticism of *A Fine Balance* and Amit Chaudhuri's dig at Parsis in another review. Chaudhuri escaped the kind of unpleasant literary immortality conferred on Greer, whom Mistry has excoriated within the pages of his most recent novel.

Nevertheless, it was impossible to read *Family Matters* without being reminded repeatedly of the two other novels that preceded it, and I found it hard not to think of Mistry's three novels as a coherent entity. All three books follow the same essential structure, superimposing the tangled lives and concerns of their Parsi protagonists over an ongoing narrative of post-Indira India. All three are set in Bombay; or as in the case of *A Fine Balance*, in an unnamed city that bears such a strong resemblance to Bombay that the point is not worth quibbling about. All delve into the complicated, messy business that humans make of their lives, and all trace the legends, myths and present anxieties of India's dwindling Parsi community. In brief, even though

Mistry may not have intended to write his first three novels this way, they form a Bombay Trilogy. And *Family Matters* can be read in two ways, then; as part of a larger structure, or in isolation.

In terms of style, Mistry is something of a throwback, an oddity in the same century that has spawned writers of the demoniacal energy of Michel Houellebecq and Irvine Welsh, or of the ferocious inventiveness of fellow Canadian, E. Annie Proulx. He lays claim to the sprawling, leisurely canvas that belonged to writers from an earlier century, a widely peopled space where narrative is usually linear, episodes and setpieces carefully planned. Hilary Mantel once compared him to Dickens—adding the caveat that along with Dickens' strengths, he also shared that novelist's penchant for caricature.

The first whiff of disappointment with *Family Matters* strikes with the title itself, with its weak double pun surely wispier than the anodyne *A Fine Balance*. The early part of the narrative, though, places us securely in the heart of Mistry territory, where the internal tensions within the Parsi community and the internal tensions of a particular Parsi clan form overlapping stories. At the heart of *Family Matters* is Nariman, his old age shadowed by Parkinson's disease and the legacy of a disastrously unhappy marriage. He is, Mistry gives us didactically to understand, a casualty of the Parsi insistence on keeping bloodlines pure. Nariman never married Lucy Braganza, his long-standing girlfriend, because of the repercussions that decision would cause in his parents' world. Instead, at forty-two, he entered into a bloodless marriage with a Parsi divorcee. Lucy haunts him, however, a living ghost, and his renunciation will eventually have tragic repercussions all around.

His two step-children, Coomy and Jal, have grown up corsetted by bad memories, one in the grip of a stubborn selfishness, the other prey to an equally dangerous passivity. An accident, one of those commonplaces of old age, lands Nariman in plaster, bedridden, helpless and at the mercy of his children. All three of them, including Roxana, his own child, will react to their father's changed position, from benign, sorrowing patriarch to unwanted burden, in different ways. Coomy's relentless will prevails, forcing Nariman to move into Roxana's cramped house, thereby changing the equations between her, her husband

Yezad, and their two boys, Murad and Jehangir. Coomy will meet her appointed end later, as she brings her house down around her ears with perhaps a shade too much literalism than necessary.

As Nariman exorcises ghosts by night and builds an easy, touching friendship with his grandsons by day, the Bombay that all of them knew is changing. The commonplaces of corruption take their toll on Yezad's world, while a more pernicious virus spreads through the city in the form of the Shiv Sena, the new 'stormtroopers' who battle for the soul of a Bombay transmuting uneasily into Mumbai. Meanwhile, Nariman's stories about the legends behind Zoroastrianism and Yezad's quiet visits to the fire-temple illumine another faith, with an antiquity and expansiveness akin to a kind of Hinduism that now seems to be slipping out of reach.

The indignities of old age are painstakingly delineated, with Mistry outlining the outrages of bedpan and incontinence, determined to spare no one, not Nariman, not Roxana and certainly not the reader, both the humiliations and the unexpected graces that this sort of helplessness confers. His touch is far less sure in the final and somewhat contrived section, where the continuing narrative of the family is told by Jehangir, and where Yezad has—improbably—succumbed to the same viral strain of fanaticism that caused the original tragedy in his father-in-law's life.

★

This is also a continuation of Mistry's exploration of the city he left so many years ago, to reside in a country from where he writes mingling the sharpened memory of the NRI with bouts of reacquaintance with the old place. And he is clear that he needs a different way of writing, a path that leads away from straight recording and magic realism alike.

For critics too dumb to get it, Mistry puts his thoughts in the mind of a key character. 'Sometimes   Yezad felt [that] ... Punjabi migrants of a certain age were like Indian novelists writing about that period, whether in realist novels of corpse-filled trains or in the magic-realist midnight muddles, all repeating the same catalogue of horrors about slaughter and burning, rape and mutilation, foetuses torn out of wombs, genitals stuffed in the mouths of the castrated.' It is a familiar catalogue of horrors to us, reading *Family Matters* with its depiction of the Hindutva brigade at embryo stage, in the aftermath of the 2002 bloodbaths in Gujarat.

Mistry's question will remain just as relevant to future generations of authors, who seek to tell the stories behind the headlines in ways that owe nothing either to a too-insistent realism or to a magic realism that might be equally stultifying. But his version of the Shiv Sena's growing hold over a Bombay where even the Jai Hind Book Mart must change its name to the Jai Hind Mumbai Book Mart, where those who dissent will be silenced, perhaps permanently, is uneasily conceived and sketched.

These sections of the novel lean heavily on Mistry's minor characters, and as was frequently the case with his two previous novels, they cannot always take the weight. Vilas, the letter writer whose function is to remind Yezad, and the reader, of the minor symphony of joys and sorrows that make up human lives, is one-dimensional, a pale shadow of the wall-painter in *Such a Long Journey*. Mr Kapur, with his eccentricities and his dreams of taking on the Shiv Sena as an independent candidate who stands for a Bombay where unity and brotherhood hold sway, is a weaker version of Avinash, the radical student leader who becomes a casualty of the Emergency in *A Fine Balance*. This is true of most of Mistry's cast of walk-on players here—the Matka Queen, for instance, is a portrait in eccentricity that we saw before in the form of Miss Kutpitia, queen of black magic, in *Such a Long Journey*.

The resonances between the three novels are not always negative, though. What makes the case for seeing them as a trilogy stronger is the sense of a continuous sweep of history. The Bombay of *Such a Long Journey* is in the twin grip of war and the new, cynical corruption epitomized by the Nagarwala case, which was the real-life inspiration for the fictional trials of Gustad Noble's friend, Major Bilimoria. It retains an aura of hope and cautious optimism, though, that has darkened by the time Emergency settles over the city in which *A Fine Balance* is set. *A Fine Balance*, indeed, was Mistry's impassioned if occasionally over-the-top riposte to those who said of Emergency that the trains ran on time.

When it was nominated for the Booker shortlist, Germaine Greer launched an astonishing, and off-target, attack on *A Fine Balance*. 'I hate this book,' she said, speaking on a BBC radio show, 'I absolutely hate it. I just don't recognize this dismal, dreary city. It's a Canadian novel about India. What could be more terrible?' Greer's remarks betrayed her own relatively shallow understanding of the city—she based her impressions of Bombay on the few months she'd spent teaching at a local college. By citing Mistry's shift to Canada, Greer was in effect erasing the childhood and adolescence he'd spent in Bombay. *A Fine Balance* was not unproblematic, but the worst of Mistry's struggles in that novel came from a predicament familiar to Indian writers: the risk of caricature involved when you translate from a language such as Bhojpuri into English.

And the film version of the book went through a peculiarly Indian rite of passage in 1999, when the censor board asked for sixteen cuts, including the sentence: '1971—Indira Gandhi is the prime minister of India.' *The Guardian* reported that Mistry wrote a long, typically blunt letter to the censor board: 'What is the point of censorship in India? We live in a country where life can be seen in the raw in the streets itself.'

It is a pity that the passage in which Mistry simultaneously attacks Greer and reviews *A Fine Balance* as it should, in his mind, have been reviewed is not one of his best. 'Let me give you an example,' said Vilas. 'A while back, I read a novel about the Emergency. A big book, full of horrors, real as life. But also full of life, and the laughter and dignity of ordinary people. One hundred per cent honest—made me laugh and cry as I read it. But some reviewers said no, no, things were not that bad. Especially foreign critics ... One poor woman whose name I can't remember made such a hash of it, she had to be a bit *pagal*, defending Indira, defending the Sanjay sterilization scheme, defending the entire Emergency—you felt sorry for her even though she was a big professor at some university in England ...' The words are given to a minor character, but the sense that even Vilas in his cameo role finds it hard to get his mouth around them is hard to shake off.

The Bombay in which *Family Matters* is set is demonstrably more discouraging, fuller of menace. Throwaway references to the Shiv Sena and their swaggering, cocky assumption of power allow Mistry to build up gradually but inexorably to the brutal murder of Mr Kapur. But the sense that he desperately tries to convey, of a way of living now under a threat as external as the threat of extinction of the Parsis is internal, comes across more as polemic than as plausible. The anecdotes appear to be culled at secondhand, from newspaper reports or TV segments, and then recast awkwardly in fictional form.

What Mistry is trying to do is difficult, but not impossible. N.S. Madhavan did it, in a chilling and seminal 1997 short story called 'Mumbai'. At the start of the story, the protagonist, Aziz, lives in a Bombay where his reference points are the Air India maharaja, Chowpatty beach and the dabbawalas. By the end, Aziz's middle-class respectability and every other assumption of security on which his life was built has been torn apart by the simple procedure of applying for a ration card. His name, like the name of his interlocutor, Pramila Gokhale ('Maharashtrian. Hindu. Chitpawan Brahmin.') is his 'history and geography'; he cannot prove that his birthplace exists, that he is no infiltrator from across the border, that he has a right to live in the land of his birth. By the end of 'Mumbai', Aziz has been irrevocably changed. 'As he was about to . . . open the window, he felt that the other side would be stacked with innumerable human faces with loveless eyes, as on a peacock's tail. Gripped by an uncontrollable fear, Aziz crept under the bed, and, with his face pressed to the floor, lay motionless, like a stillborn child.'

Mistry has nearly 487 pages in which to do what Madhavan did in about seven. But none of his painstaking attempts to capture the sense of entire communities being held to ransom and the world-view of so many being held under siege manage to communicate the same sense of menace, of irrevocable erasure.

Instead, *Family Matters* succeeds at the level of its title, as a reflection on the incalculable hearts of those whom we thought we knew best, and their ability to surprise us, for good or otherwise. As to the rest, Mistry must content himself with the knowledge that he hasn't shirked the first duty of a writer, which is to hold up to the light all that disturbs him and challenges what he knows to be his verities.

Mistry has named names, as he did controversially with Indira Gandhi twice over (the film version of *Such a Long Journey* was held up by the Indian Censor Board for more than a year, because of its unflattering references to Mrs G); he has registered his protest. It would have been an occasion for celebration if he had also managed to transmute his protest into great literature, but *Family Matters*, satisfying in its humanity and its wise tenderness, remains a big book more by virtue of length than anything else.

(Then in 2010, Mumbai University controversially dropped *Such a Long Journey* from its syllabus after complaints from the Shiv Sena that the book had used 'very bad, very insulting words' in connection with Sena leader Bal Thackeray. Mohan Rawale, a Shiv Sena member, said: 'It is our culture that anything with insulting language should be deleted. Writers can't just write anything.' Copies of the book were burnt at the gates of the university, and Mistry wrote a powerful letter of protest. He had the widespread support of writers and citizens across India. This is from a column I wrote at the time.)

★

'That you say you are offended, insults me mortally. And if you insult one Rat mortally, you offend all Rats gravely. And a grave offence to all Rats is a funeral crime, a crime punishable by—'
—Salman Rushdie, Luka and the Fire of Life

In the city of Mumbai, once upon a time, there lived many storytellers. Some came from the slums, and wrote angry, anguished, beautiful poetry about their lives. Some collected memories of Mumbai with loving care, and set down tales that featured the stories of the real Marathi Manoos, the ones who were Hindu but also Anglo-Indian or had names like Sinai and Pereira.

Some wrote of Firozsha Baag, chronicling the dying world of the Parsis, of ordinary men like Gustad Noble, stumbling from the tribulations of his quiet life into a larger conspiracy involving the corruption of the state, the venality and violence of its political parties. It must be remembered that at this time, Mumbai was also known as Bombay, and Bombay was a city that welcomed *kahanis*, opening its arms to stories and to storytellers. Some of the best found an ocean of seas of stories here: a young man who worked in advertising called Salman Rushdie, two men who knew the slums intimately, Kiran Nagarkar and Namdeo Dhasal, a banker, Rohinton Mistry, who returned to literature in Toronto, remembering and etching the Bombay he had loved so much.

Salman Rushdie spent years in darkness, at the hands of a villain much like the Khattam-Shud he wrote about in *Haroun and the Sea of Stories*. There were many other Khattam-Shuds in India, men who preferred 'chup' to 'gup', and since Rushdie had been unwise enough to write about religion, Islam and the Quran in a book called *Satanic Verses*, they placed his book under a seal of the blackest silence for twenty-three years.

Many argued that religion should not be beyond question, and that the point of a novel was that it was made up, and that perhaps those who didn't want to read Rushdie's ideas might want to stop buying and burning copies of the book and just tell all their friends not to read it. But a ban hung like a shroud over *Satanic Verses*, and in a very strange coincidence, few great novels about controversial religious matters have come out of India in the last twenty-three years. This is, of course, just a coincidence, brought about by the P2C2E described in *Haroun and the Sea of Stories*—a Process Too Complicated To Explain.

Meanwhile, Mumbai was changing too, and becoming a city of Rats, fearsome creatures with whiskers that sniffed out the merest hint of offence, and great sharp teeth called censorship laws, and the thing about Rats is that they were very good about calling up bands of agreeably violent fellow Rats at need. The Rats felt strongly about the Marathi Manoos, a mythical and apparently endangered species that was threatened in Mumbai by anything that was neither pure

Maharashtrian nor a Rat. The Rats felt strongly about anything that was against the spirit of their ancient culture, which is to say anything that criticized Rattery in general and Ratty politics in particular. The Rats felt very, very strongly about books that were freely available, in bookshops or in local universities, that caused offence to Rattishness.

The second thing about Rats is that they are very slow readers. Someone needs to bring a King Rat, or a Crown Prince Rat, a book worthy of burning before he will turn its pages, and the vision of Rats is such that they can only see what offends them. And so, twenty years after Mistry first set down the tale of Gustad Noble, and after it had been not just acclaimed by critics, but loved by non-Rats everywhere, a young Rat read the book. And he was shocked to discover that it offended his sensibilities, by casting aspersions on Rattish behaviour (such as corruption and mob violence and other forms of Rattery), and that it offended particular political parties. It happened to be his political party, but he explained that all Political Parties, like Rats, needed to stand together against anything that might be Offensive, such as books that made people question the conduct of Political Parties known for their tendency to rule by thuggery. (Or Thuggeries, since there were three of them, a big Thuggery, a medium Thug and a little Thuggerish.)

It caused the Rats the greatest offence of all to discover that *Such a Long Journey* was being taught in Mumbai University—which, however, had a fellow Rat at its helm. It was the easiest thing in the world to organize a book-burning session followed by a book-banning session, and the niceties observed, the Rats went back to their holes.

They left us with a question, as Rohinton Mistry becomes the latest in a long line of authors to experience Rat censure and censorship. As Bombay becomes Mumbai—and therefore morphs more and more into Rattistan—will the Rats chase all of its storytellers out of the city? Perhaps they'll be allowed to stay, if they promise to write only blank-paged books in Rattish, a language that has just three words: 'Don't cause offence.'

★

But these events had a happier conclusion; in 2014, Rohinton Mistry
came to India to receive a lifetime achievement award at the *Times of
India's* literary festival. 'A lifetime achievement award is a funny sort
of thing, like a death or a funeral,' said Mistry, opening his acceptance
speech. 'When an author gets one, it reminds me of his or her books.
It is also the beginning of the end.' Then he spoke of growing up in
Bombay, shared his memories of the city's jazz singers and crooners,
and to the audience's delight, sang '*Don't fence me in*', old Bing Crosby
numbers and from *Mother India*, the song '*Na main bhagwan hoon, na
main shaitan hoon*'.

*(Based on reviews and columns written in 2002 and 2010. In 2008, Rohinton
Mistry published* The Scream, *a forty-eight-page story, in a limited edition,
with illustrations by Tony Urquhar.)*

FOUR

Booklove

1

Physical

The Wrecking Ball

It was when we heard about Argha, who was the caretaker and gardener at my grandmother's house, selling the books that we finally accepted the house in Kolkata was dying. The house was of a type once common in Kolkata, now increasingly rare, the few specimens left either already crumbling, already neglected, or looking strangely out of place—forlorn bungalows dwarfed and flanked by multistoried buildings.

But when we grew up, it was the apartment buildings that were rare, especially in South Kolkata. The bhadralok lived in houses like the one on Rowland Road: gracious, sprawling, one-or-two-storeyed bungalows in red or white or cream brick, the louvred window shutters painted in green or blue.

No one in our tiny corner of Kolkata was crass enough to discuss family money (and this sneering at substance was part of the reason why Bengalis ran through family money so easily), but it was easy to see who had it and who didn't. The ones who still had trust funds and deposits and prosperous folders of share certificates had their houses painted every year, the silver polished every week, the red or black stone floors swept and swabbed to a high gloss, the Irish linen or Bengal Home tablecloths washed, starched and returned in pristine condition by the family dhobi. For burra khanas, the plate and china would come out from pantries, the chandeliers or the candelabra would be dusted, the old portraits would receive another coat of varnish, the latticeworked iron door and window grills repainted—even the gravel on the driveway would be shampooed.

The ones who had long since lost their trust funds still kept up appearances: it was considered polite to carefully not notice or comment on the peeling paint on the walls, the widening cracks from roof to floor, the dust on those impractical, beautiful shutters, the dirt darkening the brocade curtains that fell from ceiling, the frayed uniform of Abdul Bearer who was also now *khansama* and cook and *masalchi* and *mali* rolled into one, the diminishing of the silver plate in the grim old mahogany cabinets as creamers and gravy boats and salvers were sold off one by one.

Back in the 1970s, the house in Kolkata was the only fixed point for us, the children of this generation. My father was a government servant; two of my uncles were in the air force; all of us cousins were used to shifting from one government colony to another, one air force base to another, one city to another. For my mother, her sisters and her brother and their assorted offspring, the red-bricked bungalow in Kolkata with the green-shuttered windows and the vast garden at the back was an unassailable point of stillness and rest in lives where everything else was in a constant state of flux.

We were just the children; we weren't supposed to know about the ups and downs of family fortunes, about the generational migration out of Kolkata, about those perennial villains of the piece, Taxes and Rates. The odd bits of gossip that came our way as the first signs of a dying state economy and the waning fortunes of a thousand apparently unassailable families took their toll on those gracious, rapidly emptying and increasingly silent houses and were interpreted in our particular fashion. When we heard that the X's family home was a perfect white elephant, we wanted to see the elephant in question: it seemed in character for a house that had hosted goats, cows and a mongoose in the past to turn now to elephant-keeping.

One by one, all those white elephants vanished, along with the wind-up gramophone players on which the strains of the Andrews sisters or Harry Lauder or Ustad Allauddin Khan or Hemanta could be heard.

It was on a sweltering day in June that walking down a road whose old-fashioned cobblestoned pavements I'd known all my life, I noticed the gap between two houses. The bungalow that used to stand in that space had seemed to be every bit as permanent as all our homes. I had played on its long, cool verandahs every year of my childhood, raided the book cupboards fitted under the stairs, had afternoon tea in the informal drawing room and dinner in the formal drawing room. The wrought-iron grills that had decorated the front porch lay like uprooted teeth in a dentist's office; the foundation stone was all that was left, and a long, snaking line of workers, sweating in that merciless heat, would soon remove that, too. The houses on either side looked exposed, vulnerable; for the first time I saw the cracks running up the façade of one, the banyan tree roots that had taken firm possession of the wall of the other, the dark patches of damp and rot like sweat stains that pockmarked both.

I must have been twelve or thirteen, and for the first time, it occurred to me that the uncertainties of life in Delhi or Bombay (or Bhuj, where my cousins attended a rudimentary school at the air force base) where your house was a shifting point on a grid that expanded or contracted almost arbitrarily, might have infected the changeless, sealed world of Kolkata.

Decay was not frightening, or alien; we had all grown up knowing houses that had rotted from the inside out or outside in, we had seen the linen and the hangings fray at the edges just as the lives of the inhabitants unravelled, thread by thread. Pianos lost their keys, houses lost their music when there was no longer someone to place a hurricane lantern, the flame turned low, inside the Steinway to keep the strings warm in winter, dry in the monsoons. As the next generation left the city—the skeletal, graceful arc of the Howrah Bridge always behind us, never ahead—in search of better jobs, brighter opportunities, first one bedroom and then another, one wing and then an entire floor, were locked up or leased out. But the houses that I knew dwindled into shabbiness or revived temporarily under a new coat of paint, responding like terminal patients to all-too-brief injections of prosperity: they rarely disappeared.

Over the next few years, as the landscape of the Kolkata I knew and had grown up with transformed, what made the new order particularly cruel was the pace of change. The construction crews in Delhi and Bombay worked with swift, brutal precision: old houses went under the hammer, new apartment buildings came up, a neighbourhood could be built, eradicated or reconstructed in the space of months.

The lassitude and lethargy of Kolkata drew out the breaking down of one of those ancient bungalows with their strong foundations and their stone pillars to impossible lengths. The new buildings came up over a space of several seasons, not overnight. The slow, crawling pace at which these transitions happened gave everyone time they didn't want and space they didn't need in which they might assimilate what had happened to houses that had been occupied by three, four, five generations before facing the wrecking ball.

We watched the houses on Rowland Road go, one after another. The new buildings towered over the few bungalows left; no garden had a hedge or a wall high enough to ward off the gazes of curious new tenants on the fourth or fifth floor. And the number of apartments that could be crammed into spaces which a previous generation had considered insufficient for a large family made any form of protest unseemly. Bungalows and mansions in a city as teeming with people as Kolkata were a luxury; just by living in them you were automatically stamped an enemy of the people.

What the houses appeared to stand for was wealth, power, security, a kind of selfishness; the real histories of these houses could be harder to read. It could lie in the dark smudge on the ochre outside wall where a plaque had hung carrying the name of a Muslim doctor whose family had to leave their homes, their possessions and their identities behind during the Partition riots. It could lie in the monetarily worthless sketch of a typical rural Bengal scene that had been done by a great-grandfather who kept this over his desk so that he might never forget, in the rushing tides of the city, the village that he had come from.

It could rest silently on the bookshelves, as our family's history did to some extent.

★

These were floor-to-ceiling bookracks; to pull a book down from the highest shelves, you needed either a ladder or the custom-built cane like an inverted walking stick whose comma-shaped end hooked tidily around the tome you wanted. There were books that even the most intrepid grandchildren had never attempted to read, because they were written in languages that were inaccessible to us: Persian, Sanskrit, Arabic, Aramaic and Farsi, the languages a great-grandfather had learned, loved and cherished all his life. There were the legal books my grandfather, a lawyer and a judge, had amassed. These, too, we avoided. And there were the rest, the usual mishmash of volumes of *Punch* and *The Decline and Fall* jumbled in with ancient travelogues, Georgette Heyers and gothic novels, encyclopaedias and dictionaries of every stamp, the obligatory sets of Tagore, Saratchandra and other contemporary Bengali authors, and cookbooks that went from Bengali cuisine to Escoffier, Miss Beaton and Flora Annie Steele.

No one knew exactly when Argha had started pilfering the books, but by the time we found out, the library had been sadly diminished. Only the front rows remained, and even there, he had skilfully spread out books to hide the gaps. If all of us had been living in Kolkata, he would have found the theft impossible; his raids were testimony to the emptying out of the house, the migration of families.

In typically Bengali fashion, it wasn't the theft that hit us hard—it was the fact that Argha had sold the books to kabadiwallahs, not to bookshops or book dealers. To lose our books to other readers, even if they were non-familial readers, was a bearable loss; to have those books converted into packing material or paper bags seemed untenable. Or so we said, and it was much easier anyway to mourn books than it was to mourn the passing of a house, or a way of life, or an era.

In Kolkata, we took the presence of books for granted: every one of my friends, whether they lived in immaculate bungalows or crumbling cubbyholes, seemed to furnish their homes in paperback and hardback. Bookcases and libraries were part of the furniture, so much so that it never occurred to me to ask why we read the books, whether everyone who owned those books actually read them at all, and why we read the particular books we did. It was only when I came back to Delhi after my school years in Kolkata were over that I began to wonder whether those venerable, mahogany bookcases hadn't become the enlightened intellectual's equivalent of the small gods in the puja rooms that seemed ubiquitous in the capital's homes.

And my reaction to some of Delhi's houses was that of a true believer confronted with evidence of appalling apostasy. There were houses that had everything from Italian marble to Belgian crystal, French furniture and Kerala sculpture, but lacked two things: books and music. There were respectable, prim middle-class homes done up in imitation Ikea that boasted the wide-screen TV set, where books had never crossed the threshold and were not missed. It didn't matter where these houses were located in Delhi's complex social hierarchy: they all seemed faintly obscene to my censorious eyes, those living rooms rendered stark and unpleasantly naked by the absence of bookcases, of rows of 78 rpm records or carefully hand-recorded cassettes.

What I was looking for seemed to be elusive in both of the cities that belonged to me, that I had claimed as my own. Kolkata enshrined its books all too often, and the worth of those books was often measured in their inaccessibility to those who might want to actually read them. And Delhi often replaced books with music, shayari, and references to an oral literature from a vibrant, living culture whose underpinnings I wasn't equipped to even see, let alone judge.

It was a stray visit to Sham Lal's house, as a very junior cog in the wheel at a tremendously respected literary magazine, that helped me find my moorings. Stacks of new books, some still in their wrappers, waited to be read. His bookcases in the drawing room appeared to be constructed out of literature, the books so thickly layered that they took on the roles of dividers, book-ends and bricks rolled into one.

The rooms breathed in a way I hadn't seen very often in either Kolkata or Delhi; the silent compact they made with their owner was that they were there not to be displayed but to be read. Their pages would not stick together because the books were there to be riffled through; they would not fall prey to silverfish because they would be taken out of those shelves, read, and put away again. They would be dusted not as a domestic chore, but because any of these volumes might be needed for reference or pleasure at any given moment in time. The books would be lent out, discussed, argued over, read with pleasure and attention: they would not be allowed to die.

Delhi's bookcases began opening up to me at the same time as I developed an obsession with charting the death of Kolkata's libraries. The readers I met in Delhi had tastes that were far wider than my own; they travelled a lot more, they were generous with their opinions, their books and their bibliographies. The conversations I began to have about books and reading and authors, in this city of ancient monuments and aggressively modern malls, took up from where the conversations in Kolkata had ceased.

I was a fledgling reporter on the arts and books beat for a business newspaper when I married a fellow bibliophile, a man who had, like me, grown up in Kolkata and found home in Delhi. I felt rich when we moved into our first 'married couple' house, dizzy at the amount of space I would only have to share with one other person, after a lifetime of living cheerfully among siblings, itinerant aunts and uncles, cousins, stray guests.

We were gifted a dining table, an almirah for clothes, an ornamental table, and some kitchen cupboards. The first furniture we bought were bookshelves, where we stacked my husband's science-fiction classics and chess manuals, and my eclectic collection of Indian drama and poetry, and world literature and animal stories. Then we spent most of our wedding gift money on books; some weeks later when we realized that books were perhaps not the only essentials, we reluctantly set aside some of the book-money to buy a bed. The bed had inbuilt shelves, and these soon filled up with books, too.

I began to meet writers and editors, and stealthily stalked them under cover of doing interviews for the paper for book recommendations. Macmillan's former editor, Ravi Vyas, returned me to the Russian classics. Krishna Sobti reeled off a list of Delhi writers I should read, and I began buying affordable classics from Rajpal & Sons and Rajkamal Prakashan. For the price of one English-language 300-page hardcover best-seller, I could buy two books by Shivani, one by Kamleshwar, Ved Prakash Sharma's *Vardi Wala Gunda* (a best-selling potboiler loosely based on Rajiv Gandhi's assassination), and a Nirmal Verma novel. The late Patwant Singh gently pointed out the value of archives; often, it was the accounts of architects and the maps of civic planners that would reveal the true history of Delhi, a city that spent the 1980s, 1990s and 2000s endlessly reinventing itself, more even than political or cultural memoirs.

I was too timid to ask K. Satchidanandan, the poet who was one of the stalwarts of the Sahitya Akademi, for recommendations, but he opened up the world of the cheap, affordable, well-produced screenplays and theatre scripts by Mahesh Elkunchwar, Girish Karnad, Vijay Tendulkar and other great playwrights that were sold at the Triveni Kala Sangam cafe. Kolkata had given me a past, grounded me in both the literary history of Bengal and the wider history of eighteenth- and nineteenth-century Indian writing in English, but Delhi gave me another kind of heritage, equally priceless: modern India, in two languages—English and Hindi. It remains a source of sadness that I never learned Urdu or Persian, closing off one massive tributary of the past; perhaps some day I will repair this omission.

★

In my thirties, long after the house on Rowland Road had been demolished to make way for a block of flats, I have developed a habit as unbreakable and annoying as a nervous tic. For my generation, visits to Kolkata are almost ceremonial—the three-month vacations of our childhood days are just memories, it's hard enough to snatch a week or a fortnight out of our impossibly crowded schedules. Scattered across different cities and continents, we make the pilgrimage back not for the house or the city any more, but for my grandmother, a woman who makes the eighties seem like an ebullient, enviable age to inhabit.

'I'm in bed because I did something to my hip,' she said in one of our long, leisurely phone calls. I could imagine her speaking into the bilious green rotary phone, surrounded by stacks of Mills & Boons and the pack of cards with which she played endless rounds of Patience when she was bored.

'Did you fall in the bathroom?' I asked.

'No,' she said demurely. 'I went with some of Mamu's (her son's) friends to see what Rock Around The Clock was like.'

I should have known it was nothing as tame as the usual frailties of advancing age: in her early eighties, Didima used to drive her elderly Fiat with a ferocity that struck fear into the leathery, desiccated hearts of minibus drivers, pursuing those who had the bad fortune to cut her off down Lansdowne past the trams and the tram tracks. The expression on the face of a hardened Kolkata minibus driver who realizes he's being followed, and fluently sworn at in Bengali, by a little old octogenarian lady, is beyond price. Then her eyesight started to falter, and she knocked the traffic policeman's small booth over several times as she swung dashingly around the curve of Rowland and Lansdowne, but she was still aggrieved when the traffic department declined to renew her driving licence later that year.

Rock Around The Clock was then the new disco at the Park.

'Did you like the music?' I asked.

'Oh yes!' my grandmother said. 'They played all the old numbers, '*Blue suede shoes*', '*Love me do*', my kind of music. Then I thought I'd show your generation how to jive—*tomra to naachte paro na*, you don't know what real dancing is—but they really aren't polishing the floors right. Someone should tell them how to do it! We danced our feet off, until I slipped.'

She lives in an apartment built in the block of flats, where the old house used to stand; it's the same place, the same space, but we are now four floors up, and the view has changed. From her bedroom you could see the red-brick house that was twin to our own, now almost the last of its kind left on Rowland Road. It looks so small, so vulnerable, so exposed to the gaze of its neighbours in their five-and-eight storeyed towering blocks of flats; like the head of a balding man, you can see the crowns of the trees, the bare patches of pink cement on the roof.

★

Now, when I'm in Kolkata, there are always two places I visit: the second-hand booksellers on College Street and Free School Street, and the auction houses on Russell Street. I go back to these places the way some of my contemporaries in Delhi subscribe to *The Statesman*: what we're looking for is the obituaries.

My family's books died messily. My grandfather's legal library fared the best, perhaps—his books were distributed among other lawyers and friends in the legal profession, at a time when it seemed that none of his children would follow him into the courtroom. No one had anticipated that my mother would earn her LLB at the age of thirty-nine; for years afterwards, she would open dusty volumes on the intricacies of constitutional law or the law of torts in some lawyer's office and be surprised by her father's seal and stamp on the frontispiece. Some of the children's books were donated to school libraries years before Argha did his raiding. Though my niece and nephew will never see them, it gives me pleasure to think that other children might read them, and greater pleasure to know that *The Little Engine that Could* and *Tuntuni* were not transmuted into paper bags, after all.

As for the rest of the books, the ones that survived the monsoons, the silverfish and Argha's depredations had a harder time outliving the death of the house. My sister, my aunt, my mother and I salvaged a few volumes here and there, just before the symmetry of those open verandahs and those cool inner rooms was shattered by the wrecking crews. The rest of the books were packed carefully into custom-designed crates, dusted with borax and strewn with neem leaves, layered like coddled babies in plastic; despite those precautions, they didn't survive. Histories, geographies, collections of books on Burma and the Indo-Japan war, the collection of biographies and letters put together by one of my ancestors, the first editions, the clothbound classics of Bengali literature decorated with unusually fine calligraphy, huge tomes on painting and architecture—I never read them then, I will never read them now.

In the large echoing spaces of the auction houses, I find families who share something—a look of disbelief, a sense of awkward comedy: can this really be us, selling off Dadua's charcoal drawings and Didibhai's collection of china cats and shepherdesses at a pathetic Rs 1,200 or Rs 800 to the highest bidder? There are soup cups decorated with mushrooms and hand-painted leeks; Murshidabad brass; a rash of Jamini Roys, real and fake; glass, cut-glass, blown glass; dessicated ships in dusty bottles; black-lacquered hurricane lanterns; chandeliers too large for most contemporary ceilings; ancient box cameras and pinwheel cameras that still, miraculously, work; rosewood sideboards and politically incorrect elephant's-foot umbrella stands. The whispered histories of these items are obliterated in the auctioneer's crisp prose: Lot no. 12, assorted glassware and a picnic basket, Lot no. 15, a dancing Nataraja, two Tagore sketches (provenance unavailable), a lady's sewing basket and three scrapbooks. Sometimes there are books, though not often; often, however, there are pianos and harmoniums, their silent ivory keys deepened to golden-yellow with age, and sheet music, brought in by the sackful, sold by the sackful.

*

For the books you must go elsewhere. Standing at the second-hand booksellers on a winter afternoon, I watch as a family brings in the books that haven't been donated or distributed. The mother is calm, matter-of-fact; she haggles over the final price in the same way that she haggles over vegetables and packets of camphor at the Park Circus market. An elderly gentleman—father, uncle, cousin, who knows?— cannot tear himself away; he returns to each pile, nervously sorting through them, separating the cookbooks from the travelogues, trying to alphabetize each small stack. The booksellers watch him wryly. As soon as he leaves, the books will be reorganized, not by genre and author so much as by condition, the rainspotted ones with fragile, crumbling pages tossed aside regardless of content, the ones with pristine bindings and clean pages, which were usually the ones least loved and read in their lifetime, taken to the top of the heap. But they allow him this last, fumbling farewell.

★

The weeks blend into months and years, and I begin to see a pattern. It seems to me that every family selling its books contains at least one collector, one eccentric, one person whose passions were allowed to dominate a small corner of the family library. Butterflies and roses, the art of soap-making and steam engines, histories of the Raj and biographies of Indian women pioneers, treatises on lovemaking or flower arrangements, miniature paintings or modern art: every human passion seems to find a final destination here, on these pavements, to be weighed, assessed and priced. One family brings in a collection of books devoted only to the Himalayas; one family brings in a library of long-forgotten hunting, shikar and wildlife tomes. They hover, they haggle, they smooth pages absentmindedly; the booksellers will perform the last rites, the truly final ones, only after they leave, in much the same way that attendants at a crematorium begin their true work only after the mourners leave.

I want to tell them what I know: that you cannot bring the house or the people you have loved back once they're gone, that every childhood must end, and that no carefully preserved collection of dolls or child's cooking utensils or books will return you to that time.

I want to tell them about the Great Eastern Hotel. A friend, Ruchir Joshi, whose next book is set around that legendary establishment, browsed its archives and came back with photographs. Papers and diaries, letters and telegrams, dance cards and handwritten place settings line the corridors; you have to walk over the yellowing, blackening pages of history in order to locate the little that's left. Paper mildews

and tears; books rot or, as with many of the manuscripts in Kolkata's
National Library, desiccate until nothing is left, until a page will literally
crumble at a touch. In some corridors of Kolkata's libraries, the private
and the public ones, so many books have dried out that to browse the
stacks is to set off small explosions of dust: you don't read the words,
you inhale them.

But I stay silent. We saved the strangest things from our house. A
winding, wrought-iron staircase, unmoored without anything to
hold up, followed my sister reproachfully from one rented house to
another. Somewhere, on a cassette played so often that the tape is now
unspooling, is a recording of one of the last times my grandmother
and my uncle played the piano in the old house. The notes sound
different in that large drawing room, as they move from '*Take five*' to
Rabindrasangeet to '*Don't fence me in*' and '*The lambeth walk*'. We saved
iron grilles from the windows, and huge glass Mason jars; and yes, we
saved a few books.

I suppose everyone needs the small grace of hope. Everyone needs
the rituals of dispossession as much as we need the rites of possession.
We need to docket the china and give it away, to number the paintings
and affix handwritten labels containing their history on the backs
of the frame, we need to give the family books away to libraries, to
friends. Even when you sell entire collections testifying to the curious
passions of the past to a bookseller, what you hope is that something
of these books, these passions, and the people who housed them for
a time will endure.

As for me, I don't know what I hope to find here, in the booksellers'
caverns that smell of dust and mould, in the auction houses that smell
of despair and loss. I have turned my back on so many things: on the
house I grew up in, on Howrah Bridge, on Kolkata. There is nothing
to regret: all of us now have new homes, new cities, new friends, new
books threatening to grow into new libraries. But somewhere in these
two places, the auction house and the secondhand bookseller, in the
histories of the people who come here with their possessions and leave
with small but precious cheques, is something I wouldn't be able to
find anywhere else. I have no exact word for the feeling that brings

me back to the auction houses: a comfort derived not from nostalgia, but from a growing acceptance that the past is over. As families come and go, as the crumbling piles of books are evicted from their homes, weighed and sold to strangers, I feel a reassuring sense of kinship with those invisible readers from the past. On the rusty iron scales, the booksellers place the old books in one metal pan, and along with the heavy stone weights, the memories of readers and their collective booklove swings the balance down on the other side.

(Published in Seminar, *2006, as 'Rituals of Dispossession'.)*

2

Booklove: The Pavement Booksellers

This man would have preferred not to be named. He was once one of the brightest writers of his generation, but that was before certain cosmic signs convinced him that three different world governments were beaming interfering radio signals into his brain.

He lived in a barsati, a two-room island moored in an ocean of a roof. It was my job to coax a column out of him every month for the magazine I worked for at the time. The columns were always brilliant, crisply written, eminently sane, but getting them out of the writer depended on two factors. One was the family of crows whom he had befriended. Some days, he'd shake his head sadly and announce, 'They've been cawing today. Bad caws. Ominous. I can't do it.' And that would be that, I'd just have to return when the crows said it was safe for him to go ahead.

The second was whether he'd bought books that week. The writer preferred to do his book buying from Delhi's pavement bookstalls, both for reasons of economy and because he thought they offered him a more eclectic range. In weeks when he'd brought back a good haul, he was ebullient; he offered tea, conversation, biscuits—and columns. 'But where do you keep the books?' I asked once, looking around the flat. Its furnishings included snake skeletons, dried herbs, mannequins, an impressive collection of knives, but only two bookcases, and those overcrowded. I had begun believing that some of his talk of book purchases belonged to the same realm as the KGB radio station that beamed Russian versions of '*Achy breaky heart*' into his head at 4 a.m.

'Move to that side of the sofa,' he said, pointing. He yanked the Kashmiri rug off the side I'd been sitting on, and there it was: a sofa constructed of the spoils of his book-buying expeditions. There was a geological feel to them. The lower strata consisted of early buys, the results of relatively uninformed trawls through Delhi's Sunday book bazaar in Daryaganj—paperback Steinbecks, second and third rung nineteenth-century British Indian authors, odd tomes on ayurveda and herbal lore. The second strata indicated a shifting of sensibilities: rare and hard-to-find books on the railways, travelogues of fascinating aspect, anthropological works, half-forgotten histories and literary curiosities you would see now only in the catalogues of some Indian libraries.

The topmost layer was more current, exposing the writer's growing fascination with technologies old and new and with the minutiae of life in British India. As we sifted through the pile, the writer's voice sane and cool as he explained the relevance of each find, the 'sofa' diminished until there was no space to sit but the floor.

I had been trawling the pavements of Delhi for years in the grip of a hopeless fascination with books and reading. College professors, librarians and bibliophile friends had often been my companions, but this writer, teetering on and sometimes going over the crumbling edge of depression, was opening up a world I had never seen before. Most book lovers in Delhi, he explained, sneered at the pavement booksellers of Connaught Place, the ones whose stock seemed to consist entirely of roadside tourist attractions—backpacker's guides, the latest best-sellers, a few Indian stalwarts (*A Suitable Boy*, *Kama Sutra*). But the thing to do was to rummage through the stacks at the back; that was where you often found out-of-print science fiction classics—works by Alfred Bester, Philip K. Dick's more obscure novels, old copies of those classic science-fiction magazines, *Locus* and even *Astounding*, sometimes graphic novels.

Today you can buy the entire *Sandman* saga in Delhi's bookshops or Joe Sacco's *Palestine*, while Art Spiegelman's *Maus* is practically mainstream; Fact & Fiction in Vasant Vihar used to stock a decent science-fiction selection before it closed down in 2015, and most bookshops will, at the very least, have science-fiction anthologies and authors like Ursula K. Le Guin, Roger Zelazny and company. But this was in a decade of book parsimony, when any science-fiction past the ABCs—Asimov, Bradbury, Clarke—was a precious, rare find. I listened to every word the writer had to say; he was offering me a road map to booklover's heaven.

The Daryaganj booksellers, he continued, acquired most of their stock from Simla's legendary secondhand bookshops, which in turn had successfully raided most of the old British Indian libraries. So what you got was waterstained Alistair MacLean, third-rate pulp fiction, useless tomes on how to make soap. It was still possible to cherrypick, to find unusual books on heraldic devices or old locomotives. A generation later, browsing on rare book websites, I would recognize some of the books among the writer's collection, selling for exorbitant prices on eBay and other auction sites—not that he would ever have sold his books, not the ones he read and re-read, at any rate.

But the most interesting books, he said, were the ones that the Daryaganj sellers had bought off the old private Delhi libraries, books and manuscripts that had emerged from the dusty trunks and disregarded bookcases that littered houses in Old Delhi's twisting lanes. I remembered what he'd said, that throwaway aside just before he'd shovelled the books back into place and reconstructed his sofa, this year, when a national mission for the recovery of manuscripts sent researchers fanning out across India. In Delhi alone, they collected rare books, long-lost manuscripts, badly preserved histories, tattered but restorable treatises and ancient dictionaries by the sackful from just that one area.

★

My friend's maps allowed me to explore worlds of reading, but it did more than that: as the writer's directions led me down one mean street after another, as his instructions sent me exploring pavements and books I had never encountered before, I finally claimed Delhi as my own city. It was a claim I had resisted; my adolescence had been spent in Kolkata, my reading habits had been formed by that city in the 1980s. When pocket money was plentiful, I did my shopping in the grand manner, buying Tolkien's *Lord of the Rings* in three juicy handsome volumes at Bookworm. When, as was more often the case, my pockets were to let, my friends and I weighed the relative merits of kathi kabab rolls versus books. We usually sawed off somewhere in between—a jhal muri instead of a more expensive roll, plus College Street, where cynical booksellers weighed us with their expert eyes, found us wanting, but genially tossed a few odds and ends our way.

Rajuda knew us best. One of my friends would be sent to the Ayn Rand-Richard Bach-Linda Goodman corner. There was one who wasn't allowed to buy any Jibanananda until his reading soul had been fortified on an eclectic diet of modern Bengali short stories and Wislawa Symborska's poetry. And Rajuda got me right between the eyes, scoring a perfect bull's eye, when we met for the first time. I was looking for Trollope or some such novelist; he shook his head and said, '*Markej podecho? Borjez podecho?*' I had read Marquez but not Borges. '*Aajkaler* generation!' he said, dismissing my entire generation of raw readers, and started me off on a lifelong affair with Jorge Luis Borges, Julio Cortazar and company, through the medium of Latin American short stories.

These were our addas, these crowded narrow pavement stalls, these cubbyhole shrines to books with their soot-blackened walls and their knowledgeable, cut-throat proprietors. On College Street and on Free School Street, there were clear divides separating the 'technicals' from the 'paapular' from the 'aantel', a word that could mean 'intellectual' or 'pseudo-intellectual', depending on vocal emphasis.

The technicals catered to IIT and medical students and also did a thriving line in recycled textbooks—their counterparts in Delhi infested Kamla Nagar near the university to the point where other varieties of pavement books were hard to find. The 'paapular' were infinitely flexible: they sold pirated versions of every best-seller, local, foreign, self-help, bodice-ripping, crime fiction that you could summon to mind. In Kolkata, 'paapular' books also included locally translated versions of James Hadley Chase (where Miss Blandish became Blandish Memsahib) and later, Bangla versions of John Grisham, J.K. Rowling, Dean Koontz. One stall advertised 'Wodehouser daarun golpo' ('Wodehouse's excellent stories') in large flowing Bangla calligraphy, Blandings Castle transferred to Bardhaman, Aunt Dahlia rendered as Dolly Mashima. In Delhi, 'paapular' covered the seedy world of Hindi 'Pondies'—originally printed at Pondicherry Press—where, where Bhabhijis bartered unthinkable favours to collect a suitable dowry, and action thrillers, where Inspector Vinod fended off villains by the score and rested from his labours in the laps of busty but chaste young women.

Bookshops were cathedrals, hymns to the ordered world of literature, where genre fiction and classics never shared the same space. Pavement bookstalls were satsangs, full-scale melas where every god you worshipped, from Nabokov all the way down to Danielle Steele, was available—you just had to find the right high priest.

In bookshops these days I meet old friends, we make arrangements to catch the latest film festival together, we discuss the *NYT* best-seller list and the shift of editors at the *Paris Review* or *Granta* and the newest IWE wunderkind. It's a lovely way to buy books, but sometimes my feet tap out a different rhythm, and I find myself rummaging through the mangy lot of books at PVR Priya, arguing with the man at the JNU bookstall over the merits of Javier Marias versus Flaubert, eavesdropping on the teenagers sharing two cups of smoky chai between eight people.

These shabby, dilapidated stalls are where I first met back issues of *The London Review of Books* and where, nostalgic for Kolkata, I bought copies of *Desh* by the score. Under the flickering light of hissing petromax lanterns, I found Bulgakov and Baldwin and Gordimer, Alice Munro and *Alice in Wonderland*. These are the places where, under patched tarpaulins, my generation bought Beatles albums and Madhubani paintings along with their books. The pavement bookstalls recorded a different kind of history: the flood of Russian children's books, folk tales and Lenin and Marx biographies at the peak of Indo-Soviet friendship, the wave of piracy testifying to the blandness of the new best-seller, the shift as backpacker tomes targeted first Russian, then American and Japanese and now Israeli tourists.

★

My friend, the writer, lost his battle against the demons living in his mind; they took over in the manner of illegal but persistent squatters. He disappeared from the circle of friends—editors and fellow writers— who had tried to help him in one way or another, slipping out of our lives little by little. The years passed and we had scant news of him, and then less, and then none, and finally there was only a stark, belated, heartbreaking update from a member of his family.

He had deliberately sought quarrels, vicious fights where this essentially gentle soul, who knew all the squirrels, crows and mynahs on his terrace by their character traits, took care to speak only the most unforgiveable, searing words, with the closest of his friends. With those of us who were not so close, he had an easier time of it. You stop returning phone calls. You don't open the door when people knock. You stay off email. The city's brisk pace, their busy lives, their own struggles to become writers after the years of being readers: you can slip from the grasp of the people who admire you and who worry about you so easily, not falling through the cracks so much as receding from view, until finally, some two years after the deed, we heard that his demons had won.

I remembered a long summer afternoon, on a day when his mind had been gentle on him, and the personal radio station that had tormented him had been muted for a few days. He had made innumerable cups of tea, and talked about the books he had loved with the kind of intensity that other writers reserved for reminiscences of the lovers who had marked them. 'What I can't stand about life is the living of it,' he said at one point, and then he returned to an analysis of Herodotus versus Antony Beevor as military historians.

I think of him when I browse pavement bookstalls in any city. For me, the appeal of these books are the appeal of nostalgia: my childhood is here. Laid out in shabby covers, in colourful tempting heaps, on the pavements of one or the other of my cities, one copy of adolescence, available for a bargain price. I go through the piles, their dirt-stained, foxed covers, and an argument we often had comes back to haunt me. Could books and reading save your life?

No, I had said; it was the love of living and the search for experiences that we could not have ourself that might save our lives, but being a reader in itself was insufficient. Yes, said my friend the writer who had never been able to finish writing his brilliant, original novel; a book had magic, the page had power, words were not what they seemed. When there were so many more books to discover, he said, which true reader would ever want to kill himself?

(Written between 2003 and 2013.)

3

The Baba Yaga in the Back Garden

The monsoons came early to Goa; I was leaving the beach when the sea went a flat grey and the clouds roiled up, and then I got off the bus and walked the last few kilometres drenched in the first rains, the paddy fields bending emerald, the coconut trees swaying almost all the way down to the road back to the house we were renting for a blessed year away from Delhi. At home, the rain is like another presence, a creature who raps at the windows and rattles the tiles, and over the next few weeks, I will understand why people love Goa—the frangipani trees grow in front of my astonished eyes, the birds of paradise bloom and shoot up overnight, as though the garden was a magical garden, planted with magical seeds, like something out of the old fairy tales.

I have been trying to write in a house with blank whitewashed walls and a high, sloping roof made of burnt orange Mangalore tiles. This is the only house I have lived in that has no books or bookshelves in it. I meant to bring them from Delhi to Goa, but then the writing started, shakily and clumsily, and the books stayed in their cartons in the other city. Nor did I put up paintings or posters, though I had meant to do that too.

The bare walls strip me of the history and memory that is contained in three decades of collected books. This is not a bad thing.

Freddy has to be evicted every afternoon; he is a young, excitable frog in a beautiful shade of red, and he blushes crimson when he is chased out of the bathroom, out of the bedroom, chivvied out of the corners of the dining room onto the Jaisalmer golden yellow steps that lead down into the garden. Today, when I open the creaking wooden doors, struggling with the heavy black bolts, and make the usual ushering gesture in his direction, Freddy shrinks back into his corner, blending in with the extravagantly patterned crimson-and-black floor tiles. It is raining so hard, like something out of a broodier, more ancient fairy tale, that I give up and let him stay.

I start writing, line by line, and the story snakes away from me, so that it has to be wrestled back onto the page each time; it is a good story but a muscular one, hard to manage or control, and like a rider out on her first gallop, I don't yet have the skills needed to steer it. It will be an outtake in the end, but one of the mercies of writing is that you don't know until you're done what will stay and what will die, thrashing and writhing, bogged down in the mud of your beginner's inadequacies.

The blankness of the walls in this large, welcoming, half-empty house is therapeutic in a way working out of a library or someone else's home could not emulate. The books at home have defined me as a journalist for many years now. I am the person who is interested in gender, and food, and travel, beautiful design, women's histories, the secret lives of animals, in imaginary places and imaginary cities, etc etc etc.

But here all of that can fall away, and other things can emerge. I am wrestling with the snake's tail, trying to hold the end of the story flat on the page, but it rises up again and again, unwilling to be fixed in position. The middle of the story is the wrong shape, which is why the end is not working. I should go back and fix this, but there is that lack of skill: you cannot hope to change a car tyre with a painter's brushes, or use a garden spade to sand down a wooden cabinet, but that is what I have been trying to do all day.

When I look up, there is only the rain and the neighbour's many cats peering in curiously, their paws cautious as they pay me furtive visits, and the darkness of the garden. Twilight falls and the blood-red floor of the verandah goes black in the shadows. The empty walls give me nothing that will tell me who I already am, and slowly, I begin to reach for another, unguessable, hidden writer self.

Then there is a miracle. I am standing at the door, listening to the rain, wondering abstractedly why night has dropped down so fast, not realizing that seven hours have passed since I sat down at the dining table to write for five minutes. The falling night made me get up, to switch on the lights; the garden is alive with soft scurrying sounds and the whirring of small insect violin-players, and the ants who live between the champa trees and a corner of the kitchen have marched in for the night in their neatly punctuated lines.

When I turn back to the dining table, the pages I have been wrestling with rise up and shake, violently, fluttering like baleful, enchanted leaves. One sheet of paper shoots off the table. One lands at my feet.

One launches itself straight upwards, into the air, and behind it is the red flash of Freddy. He is probably bored after a day spent sitting quietly in the corner, and he wants to go out, but I am in his way, and he is growing frantic because having leapt on the table, he is lost in the thicket of papers. No matter how high he jumps, one of the sheets jumps with him. It is stuck to his frantic backside, and I have to reach into the air and twitch it off the frog in mid-air. Freddy hops out into the night, a flash of red caught in the pool of light, beautiful against the yellow stone, and then he is gone.

In the kitchen, the ants have left a wordless message for me: the poi, fresh-baked that morning by the village bakery next door, and the home-made mackerel pate I had intended to have for dinner, have been picked clean, which is exactly what I deserve for leaving good food out on the counter so carelessly. There are only seven reproachful crumbs left on the plate, but skipping one meal, or two, in the middle of the plenitude of Goa, is no hardship.

I go to bed hungry but replete, the way you are when a day's writing has been done. It is like being a novice gardener. Humility comes with the territory; the bulbs you plant so haphazardly may never sprout, the branches you prune so clumsily may wither and die, you pull up the good shoots by the roots along with the weeds. But it is still a grand way to spend a day.

At three in the morning, the windows slam and I hear the unmistakeable sound of roof tiles shattering. It seems to me that there is a scraping at the eaves, and in my sleep, I think muzzily, 'I am alone in this house, and I don't know many people in this village.' There is a moon so full that it shines right through the clouds blanketing its surface, bright and hard and merciless, illuminating the black, moss-and-creeper covered garden walls, the spiky branches of the coconut palms in the unlived-in house next door.

I hear the scraping at the eaves again, and then a shadow races across the surface of the moon, so fast that I barely have time to catch my breath before the scraping, khir-khir-khir, begins again. Lying in bed, listening to the rain hammer down hard, I reach out and touch one of the bedposts for comfort, noting that a spider has built a fresh web in a corner high up near the stained glass windows.

Outside the window, the shadow looms closer and closer, and forms into a curious craft, large, as ominous as a submarine, but shaped like a bucket, a pestle.

I know the pilot. I haven't seen her since my childhood, but every wrinkle on her formidably competent hands, the power she radiates, that calm, unblinkered, terrifying gaze, the crone's streaming white hair, flying like a battle flag in this storm identifies the Baba Yaga.

The winds pick up, tearing at the gap in the roof made by the broken tile, widening it; water pours in and I hear its distant splash on the kitchen floor. The lights are out, the power lines down, but moonlight bathes me and the Yaga in a bright, hard, pearly glow.

She crooks a finger, curling it in my direction. Her eyes are hooded, and I cannot see the expression on her face. But I get up, casting aside the sheets, and walk towards the window, hesitating for only a second before she steers her craft down. It is easier to get into the pestle than I had thought it might be, like stepping into a compact river boat.

Her dry hand steadies mine, she turns once to make sure that I have settled, and then we rise high up into the night skies, flying so fast that I am dizzy with fear and exhilaration. Her white hair streams out like a banner, and I clutch on to the sides of the pestle, watching my home in Bastora drop further and further away, shrink as we go higher and higher, all the way up to the moon and beyond. There is nothing about this that does not feel absolutely, frighteningly real, from the rough grain of the wood that the pestle is carved from, to the cool searing touch of moonlight, very close up, on your face.

The winds whip past us, leaving my cheekbones frozen and raw, and I grip harder as the Yaga flies over the rivers, above the storm clouds, hovers at the edge of the sea, and then, faster than I could have imagined, she has looped her craft around and we are flying back, down, diving deep into the heart of the clouds, emerging with heartstopping suddenness at the edge of the roof of the sprawling Bastora house. The pestle is made of an old dark wood that thrums as we fly downwards, towards my bedroom window. The Yaga turns, slowly, and I see that she has raised one bony finger to her beautiful mouth.

Together, we look in through the window, the Yaga and me, the rains soaking her hair and my clothes through.

I am looking at myself. I am fast asleep on the bed, undisturbed by the storm, though I stir uneasily from time to time whenever the roof tiles rattle.

The Yaga is watching me. If I show unease or fear, she will let me step out of her pestle, and go home to join my sleeping twin on the bed.

I meet her eyes, and the moonlight falls sharp and cool on our faces. I gesture to the moon and the clouds: up, please, can we go up again?

We can.

The next morning, there is nothing of the Yaga, not even a white hair left on the old wooden windowsill, but there is a wide gap in the kitchen roof that has to be patched while Freddy hops around, offering froggy advice.

The story from yesterday is beyond fixing. But in the few months I've spent in Goa, something in me has yielded, some idea of writing perfect paragraphs and stories has dissolved forever. One morning the week before, I had stepped into the bakery next door to see that the poi was ruined; the oven had overheated and the brown crust had scorched into black. The poder had been up since four in the morning to heat the oven and get the dough ready, but he offered me and other friends in the village little pillows of pav instead, shovelling the burnt poi into a tin pail. 'Sometimes I feed humans,' he said cheerfully, 'but sometimes it's the turn of the pigs to get lucky!'

I mentally consecrate the ruined story to a passel of pigs and the Yaga's voice whispers to me that nothing is wasted, nothing is meant to be taken so seriously. I type a fresh sentence, and it isn't a complete mess; then I type another, and soon the paragraphs start to march across the screen like well-behaved ant armies again.

Writing is like that. You never know what is going to happen next, and once it does, however strange it might be, you move on to the next thing that is leaking or damaged, in need of fixing or your attention.

★

Growing up in Delhi, our house was one of a cluster of identical, whitewashed, sarkari bungalows perched at the rim of Safdarjung airfield. In the 1970s, Delhi was far from being the megalomaniac megapolis it is these days. Gurgaon's high-rise gated communities were as unimaginable as the idea that you might own a telephone that was not Bakelite, rotary dial and available in black, green and black, or be able to talk to people in other cities whenever you wanted to, without waiting for hours for your Demand or Lightning Trunk Call booking to come through. The sullen concrete slab of the Akbar Hotel, built in 1965, and the geometric spheres of Pragati Maidan, built in 1972, were about as dazzlingly experimental as the city's architecture would get for a long while.

It was a sleepy, friendly city before the Emergency years, not yet swaggering, not yet surly, and in many of its government and timidly burgeoning private colonies, not yet dangerous. In high summer, when the noon sun felt scalding to the skin and the roads shimmered with mirages, families spread bedsheets out on the lawns at night and watered the grass so that we could cool down from a day spent inside concrete houses.

The lack of air-conditioning was a given in most parts of the city, driving people outdoors, and contributing to an atmosphere of relaxed, unsuspicious community. My aunt and her neighbours in Model Town, one of the city's typically optimistically named new colonies would go up to the roofs instead. Summer had a sound to it: the muted airplane-propeller roar of air coolers, lined with real khus, blared in every middle-class home, scenting the heat and dust.

It would have been a sign of decadence—a quality Delhi would embrace joyously, but in a much later era—to leave air coolers switched on in the mornings. As their fans slowed and whirred to a halt, we would hear a different, more urgent blare, the batabatabatabata of pilots in their gliders and fragile stunt planes taking off at Safdarjung Airfield from 7 a.m. and 8 a.m. onwards, lacing the sky with their aerobatics.

I was about seven then, and on the weekends, me and my friends would sometimes get up early to race down to the road that abutted the airfield, just to watch the planes take off and land like giant metallic bulbuls and hoopoes. One of the most daring pilots, the one who flew the lowest over our roofs, divebombing the treetops, was famous: Sanjay Gandhi, the prime minister's notorious son. We were only children, but we knew he had something to do with the Emergency, which spread its rough and inky fingers into everyone's lives. The Emergency was why everyone's parents seemed strained, afraid, and why conversations at the adults' parties had become staccato, taut.

Children have an acute sense for what is not being said, and that was what the miasma of Indira Gandhi's Emergency spread. It was a time when people spoke too carefully, and we, listening from the back verandahs, heard the choked-off words in their strangled, silenced voices.

I was just five or six when the worst excesses of the Emergency years happened. That time is mixed up in my mind with fearsome stories about bulldozers that went crazy and knocked down people's houses for no reason at all, and the vanishing of certain citizens, including people we knew. It felt as though the city had started eating its own and spitting them out at the borders and the edges of what had been familiar, comfortable, unchanging Delhi. One of my father's friends gave me *The School* by Arkady Gaidar. It had been written in 1930, and was an interesting take on Russia through the eyes of schoolboys in the small village of Arzamov. In this passage, the narrator and his friend Fedka are on their way to see a column of Austrian prisoners-of-war. The narrator is wondering what kind of crimes a person has to commit to be a prisoner, and asks Fedka why their teacher at school was arrested unexpectedly, with no reason assigned.

> We ran, Fedka and I, till we came to the ravine. Here my curiosity got the better of me and I asked Fedka: 'No really, Fedka, what was the teacher arrested for? All that talk about being a spy and a highwayman is bosh, isn't it?'
>
> 'Of course it is,' Fedka said, slowing down and looking round cautiously, as if we were in a crowd instead of a field. 'He was arrested for politics, my dear chap.'

A while after this incident, the narrator comes across a book that interests him greatly; its subject is revolutionaries, and nobody in Arzamov speaks of revolutionaries. 'Everything in these stories was the other way round. The heroes there were people the police were after, and the police sleuths, instead of arousing sympathy, provoked only contempt and indignation.' It made sense, as if Gaidar had been Indian instead of Russian.

On the radio broadcasts, those who spoke with the most assurance seemed to be permanently angry. The government issued brisk, cheerful songs that had an undercurrent of menace and nightmare quality to them: 'Kachra hatao!' the government's voice sang briskly, cheerfully, and more houses were demolished, more Delhiwallahs shifted out like garbage to unwelcoming, arid colonies called Wellcome and Sunshine.

I was greedy in my reading then, scanning everything from newspapers to buses for words. So I remember the Emergency as a time of whispered bad news, and exclamation marks: 'The Nation Is On The Move! Emergency For A Stronger More Prosperous Future!' One of the slogans in particular was unsettling and, to my six-year-old self, accusatory: 'You Too Have A Role In The Emergency!' These slogans were painted on auto-rickshaws and buses; they surrounded you every time you stepped out of the house.

Sanjay Gandhi's name was whispered in the markets of Sarojini Nagar; rumours swirled around him, some true, some false. Some speculated that he tore down the homes around Turkman Gate because he wanted to build a revolving restaurant called Sanjay Minar; some said he hated the poor and wanted them blotted out of Delhi. Shopkeepers were sure that it was because of him that officials offered tins of ghee and transistor radios in exchange for The Operation. I thought of him as an ogre, literally, because of simple confusion: they had said in the markets that Sanjay's day at his office began with sterilizations. Unfamiliar with both the processes of birth and of birth control at six, I imagined that Sanjay Gandhi's daily routine involved some arcane form of surgery (and quantities of boiling water). It was not true, but it was not that far from the truth either.

★

But for a child, living in Delhi was freedom in a way that is unimaginable now. Emergency or no Emergency, our house teemed with friends and relatives who wandered in for a meal and stayed, sometimes for days and weeks. My mother has an effortless natural warmth and a gift for making people feel at home; my father loves parties, dancing and gatherings. One parent couldn't help collecting strays; one parent couldn't resist collecting raconteurs. We had a full house, always.

In the afternoons, all the neighbourhood's children were turned out to play, like tumbling puppies, so that we would not get in the way of mothers (there were no stay-at-home fathers, none at all), cooks, household staff and grandparents during the day. We played in each other's gardens, and climbed from the champa and neem trees up on to the garage roofs, and marched along like miniature kings and queens of the back alleys. We stole mulberries off the trees, and were free to roam all the way from the road along Safdarjung Airfield to the perimeter of Chanakya Cinema.

The Chanakya Cinema Complex was a no-go zone. Chanakya screened dreary family films in the evenings and racy films in the mornings, consigning vice in the shape of B.R. Ishaara's *Chetna* and horror—*Aur Kaun?* and other effusions from the Ramsay Brothers—to office-going hours. Yashwant Place was equally off-limits. Because of its proximity to the Russian Embassy, it had sprouted shops in the 1970s called Magazin Dhzoni and Yasha. The shopkeepers still speak Russian (and Arabic); the shops sell furs, leather jackets, will exchange roubles, provide samovars and condoms with the names printed in Russian.

This was not what gave Yashwant Place its sinister reputation: that came from its proximity to the building where Aeroflot had its office, and where India's intelligence services were rumoured to take their suspects for interrogations. It didn't matter whether these rumours were true or false. The malign fog of murmured half-truths lay like a thick fog over the Chanakya Cinema Complex for years, until the family restaurant Nirula's came up, adding its home-made, Indian-style pizzas and burgers to the dubious but tasty momos sold by homesick men from Dharamshala.

We kept to the other side of the neighbourhood, boldly exploring the roads and roofs and treetops. My sister and her friends made a magic geography of the place, to which I added my own favourites. Captain Teach and a pack of pirates hunted each other with cutlasses down the back lanes, near the railway lines. Tuntuni, the story-telling bird from Bengali children's classics, had a neat nest in a large mulberry tree that doubled as the Faraway Tree from Enid Blyton's books. The jackals who howled every night were really the foxes and wolves from Olga Perovskaya's *Kids and Cubs*. Boo Radley's house lay across the airfield, roughly where the current prime minister's home is situated, and the feathery pash stalks concealed Bibhutibhushan's Apu and Durga, running out to see the train go by. In one corner of the sugarcane field (where we were not allowed to go for fear of snakes) if you pushed deep into the stalks, you would see: big broad gnarled chicken feet, a lowering hut with the chimney smoking, a black cat draped across its threshold. Inside the hut, the Baba Yaga lurked. We knew she was there, imported all the way from Russia into our world.

No one dared to go into the sugarcane field to check whether the Yaga was really there. But one day, we pushed in past the dry rustling foliage far enough to see something old, wrinkled and gnarly on the ground. They might have been peepul tree roots. We said they were the chicken feet of the Yaga's hut and fled as fast as we could before the old witch could come out and gobble us up.

★

Meanwhile, I wanted a wolf, but I thought it best to work up to this gradually, given that my mother's hospitality was matched by her temper, which was sometimes frayed by the number of unexpected occupants she was expected to provide for. My sister had asthma, which meant that we couldn't keep animals in the house. But I optimistically smuggled in assorted baby pigeons, kittens in distress, and on one occasion, a lost child who needed rescuing.

This last episode didn't work out very well, because the child was neither lost nor in need of a rescuer (I had been reading too many Enid Blyton stories where children ran around the countryside, doing good in an annoying sort of way), and resented being forcibly rescued. He was a small boy, about three years younger than me. He had been stowed away in the carrot patch in the back garden while my friend Rohit Ranjan and I held a summit meeting about his future.

Our cook, Harilal, found the little fellow before my mother heard his plaintive wails. Harilal and I were good friends, and I took most of my stray animals to him. He helped me hide and feed them, and then he would quietly smuggle the creatures back out, keeping both me and my mother happy. But he was slightly taken aback by our latest acquisition.

'What have you done? Where did you find this fellow?'

'He was lost!'

'I'm not lost! My home is right there, down the road! They made me come with them!'

Rohit Ranjan explained to Harilal, 'He's confused. The trauma of getting lost has addled his brains. We should keep him in the garage.'

The boy burst into tears.

'See?' said Rohit. 'I told you he was confused.'

Harilal, unimpressed with us, asked the boy to stop crying, gave him a toffee, and took him back home.

Foiled, I went back to the house and read *Kids and Cubs* for the seventh time, end to end. But this time, I was on a mission, treating Olga Perovskaya's beautiful stories about the animals her family rescued and looked after in their Alma-Ata home as a shopping list. I crossed deer off the list on the basis that my paternal grandmother had briefly kept one and was jaundiced on the subject: 'Our deer used to head-butt people. And we had to clean up after her. All the time. Worse than a baby!' That reminded me of cows, and cows and I had an inimical relationship. One of them had shown an unnerving amount of interest in me when I was three, and I had not liked being backed into a corner, blowed on and then licked by an over-enthusiastic bovine.

Worse, Perovskaya's Mishka ate paper, and cigarette butts, and then sheets, and dresses, and finally holy pictures. He ate the legs off a picture of St. George and the Dragon: 'His gaze then wandered to The Flood where he greedily consumed both saints and sinners. He merely tore Adam and Eve Driven From Eden off the wall and tossed them to the floor.' I decided a deer wouldn't do.

Then I wanted a tiger cub, just like Vaska in the book, who was afraid of the dark and 'very polite to the dogs'—but Vaska also chewed up brooms 'because he was getting even with all the brooms in the world'. And Perovskaya offered a warning: 'Though he was still very small, he wasn't an ordinary creature, but a tiger, and we would have to seriously consider his likes and dislikes.' Horses sounded nice, but the stallion in *Kids and Cubs* spent a lot of his time running away, and I wasn't sure whether our handkerchief lawn was large enough to accommodate both a horse and my father's friends, who liked to sit out in the evenings.

The story that made me cry the most was about two wolf cubs, Tomchik and Dianka, whom I loved, long distance, from the moment I read about them sitting 'side by side on the threshold of the smithy, looking out into the yard, feeling hurt and lonely'. They would often eat a lot, and if they overate, their bellies would blow up, and they'd have to lie down and crawl about, rubbing their tummies on the grass. I bullied the children next door into lying down and crawling about like wolves for months and months until they were sick of the command: 'Play Dianka and Tomchik.'

I cried when Tomchik was shot by the neighbour, and when Chubary the stallion had to be put down, and when any of Olga Perovskaya's animal friends disappeared or died, and then I would pick up the book, tears streaming down my face, and read it from the beginning all over again.

I had a plan about the wolf adoption. I would persuade my mother to say yes to having a puppy, a kitten or a rabbit, who could all (theoretically) be confined to the back garden so that my sister wouldn't need to be hospitalised with one of her asthma attacks. Then once my mother was used to the idea of a puppy frolicking around the house, it could be cunningly substituted with a wolf-pup, which was after all just a hairier dog. Patiently, I tried to persuade my mother that puppies were excellent companions and that we needed a guard dog: 'For robbers.'

But my mother was atypically tired that year. She had malaria, and then some odd disease where she began to swell up like a pumpkin, her joints so greatly thickened that it was hard for her to drive the old black Ambassador around. That Ambassador had a centaur-like bond with her. WBA 2 responded only to her touch, its engine balking and gears jerking if anyone else tried to drive the car.

Despite her ailments, it wasn't in her nature to be despondent. She worried in fits and starts about her mysterious affliction, and then she would forget all about it and rush around throwing parties or taking the neighbourhood's children off in the big black Ambassador for some excursion or the other.

Then one of my dreams came true, but in a horrible way: an animal did enter the house, a black cobra who wrapped itself around my grandparents' clay water pot. My Thakurda got up at night for a drink of water, and some instinct stopped him from touching the pot. If he'd found a snake in the house today, we would have called the wildlife department and the snake would have been captured and released elsewhere. But in those days, it was the sad fate of snakes to be chased out or killed. I was dreadfully sorry that it had been killed, even if cobras were poisonous; a nest of them lived at the bottom of another friends' garden in the colony, and I thought they were kindly, graceful souls, their black whiplike shapes waving gently at us from a discreet distance.

Thakurda insisted on taking Ma to the doctor the next day for a check-up, because of the shock to her system. It turned out that she didn't have elephantiasis, and that she wasn't dying; the swelling was caused by the incipient arrival of my baby brother. My mother was nearing forty, and had ruled out pregnancy as a possible condition on the grounds that she was too old to get pregnant. I was delighted at the news, and relieved; it seemed to me that it was a lot easier to get my parents to accept a baby brother than it would have been to get them to accept a baby wolf.

My brother smiled a lot more sweetly than I imagined a baby wolf would when he arrived. He also ate a lot less than wolves did, and wrapped the neighbourhood around his tiny fist with his air of being absolutely delighted to see anyone who stopped by his crib. Though, to my slight disappointment, he didn't rub his belly on the grass when he had had too much milk.

★

The Soviet books arrived in gigantic shipments; in 1970s India, thanks to the import laws, books were the one luxury people had. Consumer goods could not be imported into the country freely, which is why Indians of that generation had the most bizarre food fetishes: for Kraft's cheese cubes, or for tinned pineapple, or for slabs of Toblerone. White goods—refrigerators, even steam irons, glassware, ordinary kitchen mixer-blenders—were also not available easily, perhaps because they were seen as corruptions of the West. First citizens would clamour for a fridge, and then who knew what perversions they would demand?

But books, for some reason, could be imported, and the Soviet book ships sailed often to our part of the world, outdoing the missionary ships that came in loaded with Bibles and the Lives of the Saints in lurid colours.

In 2013, when I published *The Wildings*, a saga about cats, cheels and other animals set in Nizamuddin, many interviewers asked about influences.

'Richard Adams' *Watership Down*, Kipling's *Jungle Book*, Olga Perovskaya's *Kids and Cubs*, *The Three Fat Men* by Yuri Olesha,' I'd say.

And the interviews would come out dutifully mentioning Adams and Kipling, but blanking out the Russians. It was not the fault of the interviewers. They had started reading in the 1990s and the 2000s, and they were completely unfamiliar with the Soviet authors. They hadn't grown up singing the cosmonaut song from Victor Dragunsky's *The Adventures of Dennis*: 'On the dusty paths of the distant stars/Our footprints will remain.'

The big distinction between Soviet children's books and Enid Blyton was simple: the former were more real, while Blyton fell into the realm of fantasy. The world of the Five Find-Outers (and dog) or places like Sunnymead Farm were as exotic as Tolkien's orcs and elves, and as remote to our experience. The muffins, scones and ginger beer could have been fairy food in that decade—dwarf bread was as foreign to our experience as the concept of a 'scone' in a country where cakes were either Britannia's sliced monstrosities or were flat, homely objects baked in a tin over a coal oven.

There's a passage in *The Adventures of Dennis* where Dennis' friend lists all the food he likes—fried liver, meatballs, herring, split-pea soup, green peas, boiled meat, caramels, salami, anchovies, salmon, pickled pike, catfish in tomato sauce, sardines, sugar, tea, jam, soda pop, seltzer, borsch, boiled eggs, hard-boiled eggs, and even raw eggs, and halvah. It was a thrilling mixture of familiar, everyday things—meatballs, peas, sugar, tea, eggs, halvah—and foreign objects, from pickled pike to boiled meat and borsch. It sums up the lure of the Russian books for me—so everyday, like the trials and obstacles the children go through, but with just enough of the unfamiliar to spice the reading.

When I asked friends—many of them now writers and publishers—for their memories of Soviet books, it was like opening the floodgates. If you lose a political and trading connection with a country, as India did with Russia, you also lose part of your personal memory. At the hundreds of literature festivals sprouting like dank mushrooms across the country, there are no panels on *The Three Fat Men* and their influence on our political nightmares, Bulgakov or Arkady Gaidar's impact on our writing styles, no self-important papers on The Influence of the Soviet School on Indian Writers of X Generation. And yet, we remember it well.

Annie Zaidi—playwright, poet and novelist now—wrote to say: 'One thing that distinguished the Russian books from other kiddie books I saw was that they were more real, more everyday. I had never seen a book where the illness and pain of a small child was at the heart of it, its raison d'etre. Silly stories about daddy's childhood being an escape, and the father's helplessness in the face of pain—this was very rare. It still is. Too many kids' stories are about superheroic qualities or adventures, which is a sort of fantasy too. And now, even the fairytales are sanitized to remove all traces of real pain.'

Meenakshi Reddy Madhavan, now a novelist and celebrated blogger, remembered Galina Demykina's *The Lost Girl and the Scallywag*, about a girl who discovers she can walk into a painting made by her grandfather. Salil Tripathi, human rights consultant and non-fiction author, was given a birthday gift at the age of ten—a set of Tolstoy's complete stories translated into Gujarati. The editor Sonal Shah's grandfather brought back books from China—the illustrated children's version of *Journey to the West*, books like *Dreams of Red Mansions* and Mao's poetry. 'There were also picture books for smaller kids that were basically the communist party propaganda version of the "Good Indian Boy" charts,' she wrote.

Benjamin Zachariah, now a scholar and academic, remembered the man who used to sell Soviet books door to door 'I was in Presidency College, in my second year, when the Soviet Union came to an end.' Arunava Sinha, the translator and writer, recalled the book ships quite clearly, and Indrajit Hazra, writer and journalist, directed the nostalgic to a Soviet books showroom near Hedua, close to College Street in Kolkata with caveats ('not for the fainthearted').

Many remembered the science books—*Physics Can Be Fun*, the Yuri Gagarin autobiography—along with the more frightening books. Documentary filmmaker Bishakha Datta's memories of the menacing shadows-and-spies world of *The Three Fat Men* were as strong as mine. The editor Simar Puneet wrote about Albert Likhanov's *The Maze*, with 'bleak and beautiful illustrations by Yuri Ivanov—the first book that made me feel like a grown-up'.

And then Kavitha Krishnan, gender activist and politician, dug out a page from *Kids and Cubs* online, and wrote: 'But the nice memories are a bit spoiled now learning from Wikipedia that the author spent a long time in a labour camp post-1943.'

I froze in mid-post and stared at the screen, images tumbling through my head—the line drawings of Olga Perovskaya and her sisters, 'four little girls in red hats'—and thought of how badly I'd wanted to meet Perovskaya, to thank her for the magic of *Kids and Cubs*. The Internet gave me meagre details. She had been arrested in March 1943, and sentenced to imprisonment during the Great Purge. The sentence had been commuted to exile at some point, and she had been released in the mid-1950s. Her books had not been published for ten years, though she was eventually rehabilitated.

I could not find out which camp Perovskaya had been sent to, but Anne Applebaum's matter-of-fact descriptions of the Soviet gulags in the 1940s are fearsome. 'The word "GULAG" is an acronym for Glavnoe Upravlenie Lagerei, or Main Camp Administration, the institution which ran the Soviet camps. But over time, the word has also come to signify the system of Soviet slave labour itself, in all its forms and varieties: labour camps, punishment camps, criminal and political camps, women's camps, children's camps, transit camps,' she wrote in an introduction to *The Gulag Museum*.

I think often of Perovskaya's years in the labour camps. She must have broken frozen ground along with the rest of the Russian families caught up in the jaws of the labour camp machinery, walked for hours every day to put in another nine or ten hours of work, survived the bedbugs, the small and distinct kicks, blows and other cruelties of the guards, slept on the bare planks in that freezing cold, eaten meagre soup from those battered tin plates. She died in 1961; she was fifty-nine years old.

★

I lost my fear of the Baba Yaga gradually but surely. It was replaced by something that I was too young to recognize as envy. The Yaga was wise, if curmudgeonly, but it seemed to me that anyone would be short of temper if uninvited princesses and Vasilisas insisted on dropping in without notice. She had her own property in the shape of a mobile hut; her own high-speed, very cool transport.

She was not afraid of displaying her wrath or behaving badly, or eating the odd annoying person, all qualities that I secretly envied because I was so often told that displaying your anger and having tantrums were not ladylike things to do. I did not want to be ladylike at all, but between the nuns at my convent school and a battalion of aunts, it was thrust upon me. The Yaga fascinated me. She had wisdom, which is distinct from intelligence, and she drew her formidable power from sources other than youth, beauty or charm, which made her a quirky role model for a young girl.

She was not like the witches in some of the grimmer Russian fairy tales, which did not soften their violence. I read many of these, including one about a brother and sister pair, Sister Alyonushka and Brother Ivanushka. The brother was changed into a little goat by black magic, and as for the sister: 'One day the Merchant went away from home and all of a sudden a Witch appeared out of nowhere. She stood under Alyonushka's window and begged her ever so sweetly to go and bathe in the river with her. Alyonushka followed the Witch to the river, and when they got there the Witch fell upon Alyonushka and, tying a stone round her neck, threw her into the water and herself took on her shape.' When she realizes that the goat knows her secret—he sings to his drowned sister—she decides to kill him. The goat sings to Alyonushka:

Sister, dear Sister Alyonushka!
Swim out, swim out to me.
Fires are burning high,
Pots are boiling,
Knives are ringing,
And I am going to die.

She sings back to him:

Brother, dear Brother Ivanushka!
A heavy stone lies on my shoulders,
Silken weeds entangle my legs,
Yellow sands press hard on my breast.

I was seven when Sanjay and Geeta Chopra left their home in the tidy military enclave of Dhaula Kuan to go to the All India Radio offices. They were supposed to take part in a Yuv Vani programme, which was to start at 7 p.m. At 8 p.m., their father, Captain Madan Mohan Chopra, switched on the radio and heard an unfamiliar voice, not his daughter's, compering the programme. He left on his Bajaj scooter earlier than usual to pick up his children at 9 p.m. They weren't at the studios; they had never reached.

At different times that evening, two witnesses saw a struggle take place in the back seat of a mustard-coloured Fiat—it looked as though a boy and a girl were fighting with the driver and another person. One of the witnesses, a junior engineer with the DDA, said that he caught a glimpse of the boy's shoulder; it was bloodied. He saw the boy wave his hands, 'beseeching help'.

Two days later, on 28 August 1978, a cowherd, Dhani Ram, followed his cattle across the Ridge and found the dead bodies of a boy and a girl. The bodies were decomposed, and in the medical report, the list of injuries sustained runs a full, and heartrending, page. They had been tied down, tortured, hit by blunt instruments and their murderers, Billa and Ranga, had hacked at them with a kirpan so viciously that their skulls and spines had fractured in several places.

Billa and Ranga were hanged for the murders of Sanjay and Geeta Chopra in 1982. They had kidnapped the children for ransom, and grew frightened when they learned that their father was a naval officer: that was an explanation for the act of murder, but not for the hours of torture those two children had been made to suffer.

I remember how the picture of the murderers on the front pages had smudged and blurred, the carbon spreading on the cheap newsprint to create a second set of phantom nooses around their necks.

The murder of the teenagers was tragic, but not sensational in the way it would be today. There were no 24x7 news channels, no Breaking News headlines, no panels to talk it to death, no outrage cycles on Twitter, and perhaps crucially, Delhi was a smaller place. Their deaths and the bottomless grief of their parents hit home for many families in a way that might no longer be possible. Our neighbour wept, holding her own, younger children close. The news of the injuries were not flashed in photographs that violated the children's last mortal privacy; it spread slowly across the city, becoming a focus for the many, nameless fears that had spawned in the Emergency years.

After August 1978, we could no longer go out and run around in the same way. Mothers called their children home, fearfully, and the habit of travelling only in large groups seeped slowly into our bones, until by the time I was nineteen, it seemed abnormal to go out in Delhi alone or with just one another person. The violence of mobs, or of the state, or the cruelty of rogue politicians, was in many ways, part of the centuries-old history of the city. But the understanding that you could no longer trust strangers who would stop to offer children a lift in their car on a hot day was a new and painful idea to assimilate. It was violative in a far more personal way, and it warped and shaped Delhi's future growth.

But so much else was changing. On a June morning in 1980, two years after the killings of Sanjay and Geeta Chopra, we heard the familiar, brash baratatatatatabatatatata of Sanjay Gandhi's plane. It was a cherry red plane, a Pitt Special stunt model, showy and responsive. My mother was chatting with the neighbour; I had successfully found some excuse to stay at home and read *The Firebird* instead of going to school.

Then the sound of the engines stopped, abruptly, and we all looked up, but there was nothing in the sky.

My memory of Sanjay Gandhi's death is not visual but aural—the absence of a sound, a pause lengthening unbearably. Then we heard the shouts and calls of alarm, cries for help, from people who lived in the houses closer to Safdarjung airfield. Later in the day, the gaunt, elegant woman who had been prime minister came in her car. She was accompanied by very little security, aside from her personal guards. Mrs Gandhi stood briefly on the side of the road, looking out towards the spot where her son's aircraft had fallen from the sky, and the grief on her face was indescribable. None of us, children or adults, approached her; we stood back and some people quietly turned around and walked back to their homes, to let her mourn her dead in peace.

In a few months, the memory of Sanjay Gandhi's death faded; some whispered that it was a conspiracy hatched by faceless men. But in our colony, we felt it was an easily explained accident. He had been reckless in the air. Those who had seen the plane go down said he had been trying one low loop too many, and that the engine had stalled.

Soviet books still flooded the market, but Enid Blyton had been joined by Puffins from the UK—wonderful books like *Stig of the Dump* by Clive King, *The Battle of Bubble and Squeak* by Philippa Pearce, *Watership Down* by Richard Adams, recolonizing our impressionable minds, the West claiming us back from the Ruskis. We didn't really care whether the stacks of Puffins and Radugas or Mirs represented attempts to influence the mind of the Indian child by missionaries, the Soviets, or the Western neocolonial establishment: we just grabbed whatever stories came our way. In my house, Bengali children's books, my grandmother's *panjika*s, Premchand and a chirpy Hindi magazine called *Champak* and quantities of Amar Chitra Kathas formed a tiny phalanx of defence between us and these 'phoren influences', and most of my friends were similarly bilingual, if not trilingual.

By the early 1980s, the children who'd been my closest friends left as their fathers were transferred elsewhere. The new kids who came in liked Archie comics, which I despised, mistrusting their bubblegum boy-girl love stories and the profligate way in which burgers and ice-cream shakes were consumed instinctively.

The new kids wanted to watch *Krishi Darshan* and the new shows on television in the evenings instead of climbing trees or racing around the roofs playing that bit from the *Ramayana* where Hanuman sets fire to Lanka. The new kids didn't care one bit about either Long John Silver or Tibul the acrobat and Dr Gaspar Arneri, and after a while, I left them to their own repetitive Archie-Reggie-Betty-and-Veronica games.

I spent those months in a comfortable nest halfway up the champa tree in our back garden, with the Puffins and the Soviet books balanced on alternate branches, and it was one of the happiest summers of my life.

(Written in 2014-15)

FIVE

Booklovers:
Five of the Best

1

Ravi Dayal

Publisher

The most impressive aspect of Ravi Dayal's drawing room is the stern order that he's imposed on the books that inhabit the house. They do not overflow from their shelves onto the floor; manuscripts remain in their allotted cupboards, instead of doing duty as dust traps in corners. This, for a publisher, is highly unusual (I know one who has achieved equilibrium between books and furniture by doing away with the latter and piling up the former in vaguely sofa-and-table shaped formations).

So when Dayal, one of the most respected independent English language publishers today, looks slightly sheepish, I don't get it. Then he comes out with the dark truth; his books aren't in order, they've merely been redistributed into other houses—his daughter's, into the family home, anywhere that can house them and stave off the rising tide of disorder that dogs bibliomaniacs.

'I discovered why elephants migrate in a forest—they create such a mess, what with leaves, and dung, and broken branches, that they have to go off twenty miles away,' he says by way of explanation. 'That's what publishers do. When the mess becomes too large, they shift offices.'

Not that Ravi Dayal has ever had an office, in the conventional sense,

273

to shift. 'There was a roof over my head,' he says of his Sujan Singh Park flat. 'One was very lucky.' (That particular phrase recurs often: when he speaks of the authors who flocked to him, Amitav Ghosh among them, of still being in business as an independent publisher after so many years, of his years at Oxford University Press.)

He began with no staff; he still has none, except for the assistance of family and friends. His savings, carefully garnered over the twenty-six years he'd spent at OUP, were respectable for a generation accustomed to taxation at 70 per cent of income, but not enough for even a moderately sized operation. 'If I had started off with my limited capital—a lakh and a half, another four lakhs saved in fixed deposits which I thought was a fortune, really—even a five-people office would have foundered in a few months.'

Ravi Dayal was lucky, though, in that the imprint that bore his name offered him ample scope to display his talents. He's always been commissioning editor, copy editor, designer, accountant and on occasion, sales and marketing department rolled into one. The Ravi Dayal imprint created quite an impact when the first books rolled out from its presses—Amitav Ghosh, Ranga Rao and Khushwant Singh (who happens to be Dayal's father-in-law) were among that first batch. Khushwant Singh's *Train to Pakistan*, now hailed as a minor classic, was virtually rescued from paperback extinction. 'People were mildly intrigued,' he says with some understatement. 'This is what one had turned to after years spent among good and godly learning at OUP. I was very lucky. The manuscripts started arriving thick and fast.'

They still do. He reads, on average, two to three manuscripts a day—'I really can't pretend to look at a lot of them for a long time'—and still doesn't consult anyone's opinion other than his own. This allows Ravi Dayal, the imprint, a glorious eclecticism that few other independent publishers can lay claim to. In the recent past, for instance, the house of Ravi Dayal has produced a collection of essays on the fiction of St. Stephen's, a collection of poetry, a book on plants, debut fiction and Amitav Ghosh's *The Glass Palace*. The output is necessarily small, limited both by Dayal's natural fastidiousness with regard to manuscripts and the physical constraints enjoined by a one-man publishing outfit. 'I wanted to be slightly footloose,' he says with the air of a man aiming for the impossible, 'not to be engulfed by work. I'm afraid I am—engulfed, that is.'

Opinions differ about what makes a Ravi Dayal book so special. There is a handcrafted feel about most of his titles, a diligent perfectionism that ensures few if any proofing errors, an attention to detail that is almost extinct these days. There's the quirkiness, too, that accompanies the Ravi Dayal owl logo—you never know what it'll be perching on next, just that whatever it is will be impeccably chosen.

And he holds a rare distinction, in both Indian and Western publishing terms—you'll never hear a Ravi Dayal author complaining that he was inadequately or insensitively edited. The levels of loyalty Ravi Dayal commands can be measured by the example of Amitav Ghosh, who has never shifted publishers—while rights to subsequent editions and international editions are often with other publishers, Ghosh remains essentially a Ravi Dayal author. The only exception was *The Glass Palace*, which was jointly published by Ravi Dayal and Permanent Black. (The latter imprint was floated by Rukun Advani, who spent many years at OUP while Dayal was there—and whose only novel, *Beethoven Among the Cows*, was published by Ravi Dayal.)

The launch of *The Glass Palace* also marked the only occasion when Ravi Dayal, Inc., has actually hosted a book launch. 'Rukun and Anuradha (Roy, co-founder of Permanent Black) did most of the work, it wasn't hosted by me in my solitary incarnation,' Dayal points out gently. While several other publishers today harbour a deep scepticism about the actual value of a book launch, most go along with the diktats of the times. 'Launches are wonderful places for people to meet, but I dislike the set format, the pallid drinks, the stale pakoras. It takes quite a lot of bandobast, besides. I don't have the time for it.' It's a policy that ensures that very few manuscripts from the Page 3 world arrive at Dayal's doorstep, which is little loss to him.

Though most of the books in the house are related to his work, in one way or another, Dayal is an avid reader, discussing the books he's known the way another man might reminisce about old acquaintances. In his college years, the pattern was to read a great deal, but not to buy much—both because of the lack of availability of books and because of limited funds. The books he retained were an eclectic lot—Isaiah Berlin, books on fine art, Lampedusa—and most, he says with a trace of regret, have crumbled under the onslaught of years of dusting and cleaning.

His experiences in Oxford were similar. 'Oxford in those days: the library was very good. One read enormous amounts, but there wasn't enough to buy books. You'd pick up some remaindered thing that was off your subject—Matisse prints, the like. In your room you had three shelves—most people had two books, I had twenty-five. I remember that the ban on *Lady Chatterley's Lover* was relaxed while I was there, so of course everybody went off and bought the book. One's bookshelves were empty without that book.'

The sun looks overbright when we finally move outside, away from the bookshelf-lined rooms and the faint plunk-plunk of a piano still more or less in tune and Dayal's gentle, precise conversation. It's hot and humid, but he intends to take his daily constitutional around the small park in the centre of the colony. Lodi Garden is a stone's throw away, but Ravi Dayal doesn't go there very often these days. I ask why and he breaks into an impish smile that makes him look years younger, almost like the Oxford graduate he once was. 'After forty years of publishing, it's full of rejected manuscripts,' he says, and is off, doing his rounds with brisk enthusiasm.

(Written in 2004. Ravi Dayal died in 2006.)

2

Prof. Meenakshi Mukherjee

Critic

The Prospectus of the nineteenth-century *Mookerjee's Magazine* declared that, 'Our Magazine will be a receptacle of all descriptions of knowledge and literature, Poetry, the Drama, vers de société, Criticism, Prose Fiction, Sketches, Philosophy, Politics and Sociology' and so forth for another two ambitiously inclusive lines.

Prof. Meenakshi Mukherjee, scholar, critic and writer, who died in September 2009 at the age of seventy-two of a sudden heart attack at Hyderabad airport, enjoyed quoting the Prospectus; in some ways, it reflected the contents and broad scope of her own formidable mind. (She gave *vers de société* a wide berth, but was open to the rest.)

Criticism of Indian writing in English suffers from two major problems. Much of it is unintelligible, especially criticism as practised by followers of Gayatri Spivak and Homi Bhabha, and requires the skills of an expert in linguistic forensics to decode. Much of it is invisible, relegated to obscure academic journals or to the thriving but insular seminar circuit. Very little of it is actually influential, or lasting, but Meenakshi Mukherjee's contributions are likely to fall into this category.

She taught at several universities in India, from Patna, Pune and Hyderabad to JNU in Delhi, as well as at the universities of Austin, Chicago, Berkeley, Macquarie, Canberra, and Flinders. At the centre for language studies and literature in JNU, Prof. Mukherjee ushered in a kind of golden age of reason: she encouraged questioning from her students, and expected debate and inquiry from her colleagues.

She wore her scholarship lightly, though it was formidable.

She received the Sahitya Akademi Award in 2003 for her book *The Perishable Empire: Essays On Indian Writing In English*—it marked the only occasion in the history of the Akademi that this award had been given to a critic, not a writer of fiction, literary non-fiction, or a poet. Her other books include *The Twice Born Fiction* (1971), *Re-reading Jane Austen* (1994), *The Perishable Empire* (2000), *Considerations: Twelve Studies of Indian Literature in English* (1977), *Midnight's Children: A Book of Readings* (1999), *Early Novels in India* (2002) and an anthology, *Another India* (edited along with Nissim Ezekiel).

★

Engaged with the world of books and letters to the last, Dr Mukherjee was on her way to Delhi for the launch of *An Indian for all Seasons: The Many Lives of R.C. Dutt*, which was to be her last work. When we heard that she had collapsed at Hyderabad airport, ripples of shock and sadness eddied out from Delhi and Hyderabad to places as far away as Melbourne, Chicago, Dhaka and Purulia—to name just a few locations from which emails mourning her sudden death were received.

There was no sense, in Prof. Mukherjee's presence, of reading literature as dead texts from a distant past. Her years in research, and her long partnership with her equally distinguished husband, the late translator and academic Sujit Mukherjee, gave her a holistic view of Indian writing in English that few other practitioners possessed. Meenakshi Mukherjee could trace the lineage of IWE much further back than Bankimchandra's *Rajmohan's Wife*—considered the first true novel written by an Indian in English. Through her scholarship, she offered a much more interesting history than the accepted one of a novel, imitative of its Western counterparts, that sprang out of nowhere from Bankim's mind.

In her excavation of history, the Indian novel had been emerging in unusual form well before the nineteenth century. The first two books that snagged Meenakshi Mukherjee's attention dated back to 1835 (Kylas Chunder Dutt's *A Journal of Forty Eight Hours of the Year 1945*) and 1845 (Shoshee Chunder Dutt's *The Republic of Orissa*) respectively: both were works of alternate history, imagining an uprising against the British, and a future without English rule.

Years later, when she translated Lokenath Bhattacharya's unusual and sadly forgotten fantastical novel, *The Virgin Fish of Babughat*, she was fascinated by the question of imagination. The Indian expression of it may have been influenced by magic realism, or by the European novel, but it had a different fountainhead, in her opinion. Bhattacharya's novel, for instance, is set in an imaginary prison where the inmates have the 'freedom' to explore sexuality. But it's the guards who decide on the pairings of prisoners, and erotic exploration soon becomes just another fatigue-inducing prison ritual.

The narrator of *The Virgin Fish of Babughat* is bound by different rules—he must commit his thoughts to paper, by order, and he is rendered frantic by the fear of losing language, the necessity of facing blank page after blank page every day. Typically, she didn't just translate *The Virgin Fish of Babughat*—you might say that she excavated and resuscitated it in the 1970s, an operation that she would perform often as a critic, gently and sometimes forcefully reminding us of a history of Indian writing that seems all too perishable. 'We have bad memories as a nation,' she once told a group of her students. 'We prefer to reinvent our histories and erase the inconvenient parts of it rather than to learn from it.' Over the decades, some of us have watched as classics of Indian writing die, and are sometimes rediscovered—G.V. Desani's *All About H Hatterr* is embraced by one generation, forgotten by the next, Arun Kolatkar's *Jejuri* was allowed to drop into obscurity until the *New York Review of Books* brought out a new edition this decade. I have often thought that Meenakshi Mukherjee was right in assuming that the critic's job in India is also to be the keeper of memories.

In one of the last conversations we had, just before Meenakshi Mukherjee was supposed to come to Delhi for the launch of her biography of R.C. Dutt, we discussed the Indian writer's love for fantasy, for the picaresque and for alternate histories—all these exerted a powerful fascination for the early pioneers, before the conventions of the middle-class novel took over.

It's worth mentioning her original essay, 'The Anxiety of Indianness', which provoked an intense exchange between her and the author Vikram Chandra. The debate that she and Chandra had over a decade ago is an old one; it's dogged Indian writing in English ever since Bankimchandra's novel, *Rajmohan's Wife*, came out, and the question of who (and what) puts the Indian in Indian writing in English is very much alive today. Prof. Mukherjee wrote: 'If I were to write a novel in Marathi, I would not be called an Indian writer in Marathi, but simply a Marathi novelist, the epithet Marathi referring only to the language, not carrying the larger burden of culture, doctrine and ethos. No one would write a doctoral dissertation on the Indianness of my novel . . . Our discourse on Indian novels in English tends to get congealed into fairly rigid and opposed positions.'

She went on to make a point that often gets lost today: it's not just the authenticity of the writer in English that is debated and picked apart; the assumption, as she says, is that an indigenous readership was presumably more 'authentic'—a viewpoint that she personally did not subscribe to. The unspoken premise in this war, she continued, is that writing in English and writing in the other Indian languages are antithetical enterprises marked by a commitment to, or betrayal of, certain cultural values. 'To me, the issues are not moral but social, entangled with questions of class and regional mobility. Those who write in English do so because—no matter what language they speak at home—they have literary competence only in English. Contrary to popular belief, not all of them achieve fame abroad and most are read by numerically fewer people than those who read a *bhasha* novel.'

It's sad that one set of writers will remember only the skirmish between the professor and the writer Vikram Chandra, which he documented, memorably, in an essay called 'The Cult of Authenticity'.

Meenakshi Mukherjee had noted the tendency of some Indian writers in English to exoticise India unnecessarily, to produce the modern equivalent of sadhus and maharajas in an attempt to establish their authenticity.

Mukherjee picked on Chandra's collection of short stories, *Love and Longing in Bombay*, as an example of this trend, for his use of words like Dharma, Artha, Kama and Moksha in the titles. In retrospect, she was right about the anxiety of writing India that infected a certain group of writers—and perhaps still does. But she was dead wrong in her selection of offenders—Chandra couldn't be accused of this particular crime. When some of us taxed her with evidence to the contrary, years ago, she was delighted. 'A proper argument!' she said, and settled to it with her trademark relish and acumen. Neither side succeeded in convincing the other, but we, at least, retired with a far broader sense of our literary history once she was done with her examples.

This isn't my favourite Meenakshi Mukherjee memory, though. That would be one shared by generations of students at JNU and the many other universities where she taught: the memory of engaging with 'MM' or Meenakshidi as she opened up our forgotten literature and unexplored past to us via Raja Rao's *Kanthapura*, inviting us to claim Indian English, in all its richness and complexity, for ourselves. She was, like many in her generation, comfortably bilingual; unlike Raja Rao, she had made a home for herself in English as well as Bangla, and in her criticism as well as her teaching, language and spirit went hand in hand.

To borrow from the title of a key anthology edited by her, there was another India out there, and she wanted every reader to make his or her own explorations of that familiar and unknown country.

(Written in 2009, in tribute to Prof. Mukherjee after her sudden death.)

3

Sham Lal

Editor, *Biblio*

For a certain generation of writers, thinkers and intellectuals, Sham Lal was not a man, but an institution. For another, younger and more fashionable set of 'intellectuals', Sham Lal was a half-remembered name, his integrity almost old-fashioned in a time when it was normal to change one's opinions as casually, and as frequently, as you changed your clothes.

Sham Lal, who died at the age of ninety-four, was not to be found on Page 3 or among the rent-a-quote intellectuals who make their names on television shows. He had been the editor of *The Times of India* in an era when the measure of a newspaper lay in the quality of its writing and reportage, rather than the quality of its marketing campaigns. He was one of the founder-editors of *Biblio*, the literary magazine that used to function as an oasis of intelligence in a desert of fatuity, and many of us looked forward to the essays he wrote for *The Telegraph* well into his nineties.

I was a junior dogsbody at *Biblio* when I was taken to Sham Lal's house to meet the editor. Like many other first-time visitors, it seemed to my dazed eyes that the house was constructed of books. Bookshelves reached from floor to ceiling in every room, their contents neatly ordered, spanning several centuries of human thought and creativity. He had original issues of *The Paris Review, Criterion*, and of defunct but once-great Indian literary magazines, vast collections of poetry and drama, and what appeared to be every important work ever published in the fields of history, criticism and the humanities. It was one of the best private libraries I had ever seen, and being there was like being inside a particularly well-stocked, curious and disciplined mind. Sham Lal himself was lying on a couch, reading Isaiah Berlin while columns of books rose up from the floor to spill over the cushions, keeping him company.

He was not a hoarder of knowledge. The book-lined house in Delhi's Gulmohar Park functioned as a superior literary saloon for many years, with some of the greatest and most interesting figures of the age, from Octavio Paz to Bipan Chandra, dropping in to spend time with him.

I am often saddened, and sorry, when I meet younger writers or colleagues in journalism who don't know of Sham Lal, even when I know this amnesia is not their fault. They have missed out on so much. Most of his writing retains its freshness, clarity and incisiveness, and he wore his erudition lightly. His intellectual engagement with the world stemmed from an enormous respect for ideas, beliefs and the language that provided the building blocks for argument: 'At a time when political rag chewing, hack writing, mass media banalities and high pressure sales talk do as much to corrupt the language as industrial wastes to pollute air and water, it is the poet's job to preserve the integrity of the written word.' This may have been the poet's credo, but it was also Sham Lal's own.

I still remember his piece on Kafka and Thomas Mann, which begins: 'For long, I have had the uneasy feeling that the doctrine of karma takes us straight into Franz Kafka's world. For, when most religions which had their birth in this country seek release—whatever the name by which they call it—from the cycle of rebirths, and explain away all that the individual suffers as a consequence of his or her deeds in a previous life about which he or she knows nothing, the story is not very different from what the Czech writer tells in *The Trial*.' Sham

Lal drew his philosophies from the world he was born in, and reached out with equal assurance to the wider world of Beckett and Kafka, Sartre and Berlin. Some writers escaped him: he found Jack Kerouac's world of dharma bums vapid, he noted Ezra Pound's insanity, but not his genius.

There is a term that has fallen into disuse these days, when hyperbole has turned every writer inexorably into a genius producer of masterpieces and every reviewer into a critic of searing insight and intelligence. It used to be honourable to be considered a man of letters—it stood for someone who was deeply engaged with the life of the mind. If you look at the index to *A Hundred Encounters*, a collection of Sham Lal's writing, you gain some sense of the generous breadth of his world. It begins with Adorno and Akhmatova, moves through Baudelaire, the Bible and the Bhagavadgita and traverses via Vishnu, Vidal, Van Gogh and Vyasa to, finally, Andrei Zhadnov. If one generation of thinkers had every reason to remember Sham Lal, the next generation has every reason not to forget him.

(Written in 2007)

4

P. Lal

Writer's Workshop

In the homes of Indian writers of a certain generation, there'll always be the Writer's Workshop shelf, given over to hand-bound books, the cloth borders taken from Orissa saris, the title often hand-calligraphed. You don't find them in bookstores that often these days, but there was a time when Writer's Workshop represented, in effect, the sum total of the aspirations of Indians writing in English.

Prof. P. Lal, the man behind Writer's Workshop, and perhaps the last of the dying breed of 'gentleman publishers', died this weekend at the age of eighty-one in Kolkata, where he had lived and worked most of his life. In the fifty years since he had started Writer's Workshop, Indian publishing had changed beyond recognition. There were now a multitude of publishing houses, literary festivals, book launches—all the infrastructure that was missing when he and a group of friends began Writer's Workshop.

'The reason I went into publishing is simple—nobody was around, in 1958, to publish me. So I published myself. Half a dozen others—friends—also found this expedient attractive. So we formed a group, a nice consanguineous coterie. We wrote prefaces to each other's books, pointing out excellences, and performed similar familial kindnesses in other ways as well. We believed, with Helen Gardner, that criticism should flash the torch, not wield the sceptre,' he wrote of its beginnings.

The 'half-a-dozen others' included Anita Desai, and Sasthibrata Chakravarthi, the author of *My God Died Young* and other minor works that had a brief vogue in the 1970s—but from the start, Writer's Workshop would aim to encourage those who were not destined to become famous, opening its doors to major and minor talent. A.K. Ramanujan, Vikram Seth, Jayanta Mahapatra, Kamala Das, Agha Shahid Ali, Keki Daruwalla, Mani Nair, the enigmatic Lawrence Bantleman (who disappeared in Canada) and a score of Indian poets would find their first moorings within the elegant covers so carefully crafted by P. Lal's endeavour—but so would hundreds of other now-forgotten writers.

On a personal note, I might add that one of their youngest members was my sister, who had written a precocious short story at the age of nine, and who for years was made welcome at their meetings. Chai would be ordered—'and a Coke for Baby'—and while she never took up writing, she remembers the warmth and acceptance P. Lal and his circle handed out to everyone who happened to stray within its borders.

As Indian publishing came of age, the importance and necessity of Writer's Workshop began to diminish. The space that P. Lal and his friends had created in 1958 was crucial—both in terms of establishing a publishing house for writers, and setting down the importance of Indian writing in English.

One of the first controversies that erupted was the attack on Indian poetry in English by Buddhadev Bose, and then by Bose's son-in-law Jyotirmaya Datta. The latter wrote an essay, 'Caged Chaffinches and Polyglot Poets', that P. Lal responded to—with his usual spirited but gentle liveliness—and in many ways, these attacks offered a meeting point for those who were just beginning to write in English, using it as an Indian, not an alien, language.

P. Lal was also a writer, poet and academic, but he will perhaps be best remembered for his magisterial translation of the *Mahabharata*; it's perhaps the most complete rendering of the epic available. It was typical of him that he would hold a weekly reading, every Sunday, open to all, from 1999 onwards, in honour of the grand oral tradition of the epic. So many of us, writers and readers in Kolkata, attended those sessions, discovering a community and a fellowship long before there was the season of book launches.

The impact of Writer's Workshop cannot be measured by its 3,000-odd titles, or by the influence it once wielded as a publishing house. It was, like Clearinghouse in Bombay, a literary movement, fuelled by the agile mind and precise labours of P. Lal. In my copies of the books produced by Writer's Workshop, there was always this, in calligraphy: 'Layout and lettering by P. Lal with a Sheaffer calligraphy pen. Embossed, hand-stitched, hand-pasted and hand-bound by Tulamiah Mohiuddin with handloom sari cloth woven and designed in India, to provide visual beauty and the intimate texture of book-feel.'

Few publishers today, however brilliant their lists of authors, have that kind of passion, P. Lal's celebration of 'book-feel', and his insistence that literature was a large, rambling house, its rooms broad enough to accommodate all, however modest or stellar their individual talents.

(Written in 2010)

5

K.D. Singh

Bookseller

The Book Shop in Jorbagh, Delhi, was a lot like the magical places of fantasy described in the books it carried: larger on the inside than it seemed from the outside. The space it occupied in the lives of city readers was far broader than its compact premises would indicate. You could leave some of Delhi's large chain bookstores with a sense of dissatisfaction, a hunger unassuaged by any of the shiny titles that crowded their shelves, but the indie bookstores did better, from Midland to Motilal Banarsidass or Fact & Fiction and, always, K.D. Singh's Book Shop.

K.D. Singh died last week, of cancer. He was one of the city's finest booksellers for a reason: it wasn't just his love of books that shaped The Book Shop's stock, but the rare combination of talent, experience and an unteachable instinct. He often anticipated the curve, so that it was at The Book Shop that his readers found George R.R. Martin years before the HBO TV series made *Game of Thrones* a household name, or discovered Junot Diaz or Chimamanda Adichie back when they were promising unknowns. But he also had a great selection of translations. The Book Shop had Shrilal Shukla's *Raag Darbari* and

Vaikom Basheer's stories, for example, long after those books had gone out of stock elsewhere.

His customers included most of the city's writers as well as out-of-towners like Ramachandra Guha and Rudrangshu Mukherjee. In turn, Delhi's writers told visiting friends from other countries that they must stop by The Book Shop because its two walls and middle aisle of books contained more surprises than they might imagine. Octavio Paz, Gabriel Garcia Marquez and a dozen others visited, among many others.

The Book Shop opened in 1970 in Jorbagh; by the time its sister shop in Khan Market had shut down in 2006, Delhi had grown from a small town coming up in the shadow of the Walled City to a massive, tentacular metropolis. And yet, for such a large and ambitious city, Delhi has very few good bookshops. This generation of teenagers is exposed chiefly to badly stocked mall bookstores, places where indifferent staff sell kitsch merchandise and best-sellers, like prophylactic inoculations against the love of books.

For authors and readers, the understanding of how crucial bookstores can be in your life runs deep, and the urge to pass on that love of reading is strong. When Larry McMurtry, the author who is also a veteran bookseller, turned sixty-one, he went back to his hometown in Archer County in order to create 'a newly born book town'. Ann Patchett had a smaller-sized dream: when she opened Parnassus Books in 2011 in her hometown, Nashville, it was because she missed the bookstores of her youth. 'Mills could not have been more than 700 sq.ft small, and the people who worked there remembered who you were and what you read, even if you were ten.'

When I read that sentence again last week, it brought back exactly what made K.D. Singh's bookshop so special. He was often ensconced in a corner, listening to jazz, and when I met him at the age of ten, he ferreted out my love for Gerald Durrell in seconds. 'Try this,' he said, handing me James Herriot. It was a perfect recommendation, the first of many through the next thirty-odd years. His wife, Nini Singh, his daughter, equally book-loving staff and Sohan at the door handled business when he was away, but it was a pleasure to see KD in his element, handling readers he knew as competently as total strangers.

I was at the store once when a lady came in, asking for book suggestions. She liked Rumi; KD paused for a second, and suggested Agha Shahid Ali. The next week, I was back browsing (buying books is a ruinous habit) when another person asked for suggestions. 'I love Rumi's poetry,' he said. KD directed the man to Jiddu Krishnamurti: the two customers had browsed books differently, and to him, their minor shifts in taste were as clear as footprints.

Over the years in Delhi, I sometimes missed living in a city with great public libraries, and often wondered what it might be like to live in Tokyo, with its 1,675 bookstores, or Paris, with 1,025 bookshops. But the truth is that all a reader needs over their lifetime is one good bookstore, preferably run by a great bookseller.

When K.D. Singh's cancer set in, we missed him and the book talk terribly. In all these years, he had seldom gossiped about the publishing industry; he preferred to chat about the books themselves. It was easy with him to start discussing authors in one decade and to finish three centuries further back in time. The day after he died, The Book Shop was open for business as usual, a reflection of the values he and his family had brought to the book-selling business.

It will be a while before it sinks in that I can't drop by The Book Shop to ask KD what he thinks of Mai Jia's *Decoded*, or of the new translations of the season. But on my bookshelves are the years of spoils brought home from The Book Shop: about three decades worth of reminders of an extraordinary bookseller, and of a friendship built on the shared love of books and reading.

(Written in May 2014, after K.D. Singh's death.)

SIX

Plagiarism:
Three Unoriginal
Stories

1

V.N. Narayanan

The voice at the end of the line was perfectly calm; the only suggestion of strain in V.N. Narayanan's conversation came from the long gaps, the pauses, the jerk of disconnection as he jumped from one train of thought to another.

In 1999, V.N. Narayanan was a respected senior editor at the *Hindustan Times*. His weekly column, 'Musings', had run on the edit pages for over a decade, and he moved from subject to subject with enviable fluency. Then one of his columns made the news for all the wrong reasons—Narayanan had plagiarized his entire piece from a column by another journalist, Bryan Appleyard.

Writing about the plagiarism in *The Sunday Times*, Appleyard set out what had happened: 'The column appeared in the *Hindustan Times* last month under the headline "For ever in transit". Of its 1,263 words, 1,020 were identical to those in an article of mine published in *The Sunday Times Magazine* in February under the headline "No time like the present". Of its 83 sentences, 72 were mine. Mr Narayanan even spoke of a sign he had seen while walking through Newark airport in the United States. I did the walking; I saw the sign. Apart from a touch of local Indian spin in theme, detail and tone, Narayanan had ripped me off.

'B.N. Uniyal, who broke the story in the *Pioneer*, made quite a meal of his scoop. He had plenty of material. A collection of Narayanan's columns—which are called Musings—had been published under the title *I Muse, Therefore I Am*. In the preface he mocked those who would accuse authors of plagiarism and wrote of taking the ideas and words of others "to innovate something of your own". Uniyal was having none of this. "You have not only lifted entire paragraphs and sentences from Appleyard's article," he wrote, "but have actually stolen all his experiences, his ideas, his reflections, even his person and personality."

'Narayanan was at first too distressed to talk but promised that he was "going to choose an appropriate time to explain my action to all of you". But he took my call at his Delhi home. "Mr Appleyard," he said, "I am being massacred here. I have been 38 years in journalism. I'm out of it now."'

In the weeks and months that followed the plagiarism scandal, I had several conversations with journalists and writers where we talked about our own fears. 'Narayanan may be an extreme case, but his kind of plagiarism is something that all of us who write for a living secretly fear might happen to us,' I wrote at the time. 'Most of us read furiously: books, newspapers, magazines, columns on the Net, blogs. As Anne Fadiman commented when speaking of John Hersey's extensive—and unacknowledged—borrowings from her mother's writings, one of the occupational hazards of being a certain kind of reporter or editor-writer is that you get used to running other people's prose through your typewriter and calling it yours. Another occupational hazard is simply that much-derided plagiarism defence: it was my unconscious wot done it, so sorry. It's been over-used, but cryptomnesia does occur more often than we realize.'

It was about two months after the Appleyard plagiarism scandal broke that Narayanan called me, ostensibly to discuss the column I'd written on the subject. He wanted to answer a question I'd asked, a question that perhaps lay at the heart of the whole business: why, even if he was pressed for time and thought he would steal Appleyard's central conceit, would he not change words, phrases, the recounting of memory? He had made no attempt to cover his tracks—the column was a straight lift, but by changing key details from Ireland to India, Narayanan had also established his intent to steal.

★

My notes on the conversation are first scribbled, in exact shorthand, then the writing slows, then there's a series of question marks, a few stray phrases and my unjournalistic comment: 'What the hell really happened here?' Narayanan talked for over an hour, his voice shaking from time to time as he tried to explain—but continued to shy away from a complete explanation. He never used the words 'plagiarism' or 'theft' or 'stealing'. Instead, he spoke of the ennui of writing for years, of searching for a subject week after week, and I felt a small shiver of hack-writer's sympathy.

Had he ever done this before? Had he ever stolen from another person's writings? Narayanan refused to answer the question directly. He had already stepped down from his post, and his writings would not appear for the next eleven years in any major Indian newspaper, though the magazine *Life Positive* would carry some of his columns. Some journalists, sifting through the mass of columns he'd produced over his thirty-eight years in the business, found suggestions of borderline plagiarism—an idea lifted here, a phrase evocative of someone else's writing there. There appeared not to have been anything as blatant, as obvious, as Narayanan's lift from Appleyard—except for a case in 1992, seven years before the plagiarism scandal broke. Accused of plagiarizing part of a column, Narayanan had blamed his 'photographic memory', and the Press Council had exonerated him.

Over the course of our conversation, Narayanan offered partial, and mutually contradictory, explanations. He had copied and pasted Bryan Appleyard's article, struck by the central idea of visiting airports, intending to do his own piece on the subject. (This didn't explain why he had not, in fact, used his own memories of visiting airports and instead stolen Appleyard's memories of walking through Newark airport.) He was working against a tight deadline—again, an explanation I was instinctively inclined to be sympathetic towards; the writer fears the blank screen, the hardened hack fears the blank space in the newspaper where his or her column should be. And he had, inadvertently, sent in his working notes for the column instead of the piece he had written. (But this didn't explain why he had replaced all of Appleyard's personal references with his own set of Indianised references.)

It was, in many ways, the most strikingly odd conversation I have had as a journalist. There was a sense of shared embarrassment, a sense of being a reluctant listener at a reluctant confessional. Narayanan circled around and around the central issue, unable to confront it, unable not to address it. I see from my notes that I asked him the direct question—had he plagiarized Appleyard, and had he been aware of the enormity of what he was doing—five times, not with accusation, but with compassion.

Perhaps the compassion needs to be explained. Plagiarism is the most heinous sin in a writer's book, for a reason; it's not just the theft of an original idea, but it's the theft of another person's voice, the most intimate and irreplaceable part of a writer's style. Even journalists— workmen-like carpenters rather than artists—have their signatures, their voices, and what Narayanan did to Appleyard was unforgiveable. I understood, instinctively, Appleyard's anger and outrage, even as I understood, a little more dimly, Narayanan's predicament. Most journalists recycle original ideas, or borrow inspiration from a wide variety of sources, or learn to add in just enough of their own opinions and perspective to put their byline on a piece, especially if they're on the news desk. But for most of us, crossing the line between inspiration and plagiarism is unthinkable.

(For years after talking to Narayanan, I became obsessive about my own, minor writing, checking each piece several times to ensure that I hadn't stolen a word from another writer's work. On one occasion, I read my column in print, chilled by the conviction that I had come across those paragraphs before—and I had, in a column on the same subject that I had written several years previous. Autoplagiarism is a dreary confession to make; it smacks of either narcissism or lack of imagination.)

In every response Narayanan made to my question, it seemed clear that the line had begun to blur for him, perhaps years before the actual plagiarism occurred. He spoke about the trickiness of memory—how could anyone of us be sure of what we remembered? He spoke of the curse of having a photographic memory, and of the difficulty of then separating your own thoughts from what you had read. I could, again only dimly, follow this train of thought. Many of my writer friends abstained, like ascetics, from reading literature while they were working on fiction—the fear of contagion, of absorbing another writer's style or mannerisms or turns of phrase was a very real one.

Narayanan spoke of the tyranny of the weekly column, the necessity of serving up ideas, frequently one's own warmed-over ones, like so many meals made up of leftovers over the endless procession of years.

At one point, he asked a question that really does matter: didn't his record count? All those years of original, unplagiarised prose that he could, in sincerity, lay claim to as his own work—had this one (or two, or three instances) instance of plagiarism wiped out all of that? The only possible answer is that yes, it had; just as a thief doesn't get brownie points for all the homes he's left in peace and not violated, all it takes is one instance of plagiarism for the work of decades to be permanently tainted.

The conversation ended on that hanging note. V.N. Narayanan never admitted his guilt, and to this day, I don't really understand why he chose to unburden himself to a very junior journalist and columnist he didn't know. But over the months that passed, I thought less and less about his crime, and more and more of the burden of guilt that he carried. I thought of how slippages happen, in one's moral universe, so gradually that one might not even notice when a line has been crossed. I wondered if his exoneration in 1992 by the Press Council had been good for him, if it hadn't in some way fostered a belief that he could get away with anything. I wondered, having a bad and patchy memory myself, if having a photographic memory could cause such confusion in one's mind that you might mistake a page by another writer for your own work.

And I wondered, if after decades of letting the lines blur, it might not come as a relief to be caught. Like an exhausted mountaineer up on the slopes—from my notes, I see that V.N. Narayanan uses the word 'tired' some twenty-six times, 'exhausted' eleven times—he might have wanted to pick up a stone and throw it down the mountainside, knowing in advance the weight of the avalanche that it would bring down on his head.

2

Kaavya Viswanathan

In 2006, a young writer called Kaavya Viswanathan became famous for all the wrong reasons.

The story broke when *The Harvard Crimson* cited a dozen-odd passages from *How Opal Mehta Got Kissed, Got Wild, and Got a Life* that seemed strikingly similar to passages found in two of author Megan McCafferty's books, *Sloppy Firsts* and *Second Helpings*. McCafferty was an odd choice for a plagiarist: her books came out in the last six years, and she's a fairly well-known author in the teen market.

Here's a sample of what *The Crimson* found, and there was passage after passage like this one:

> From page 213 of McCafferty's first novel: "Marcus then leaned across me to open the passenger-side door. He was invading my personal space, as I had learned in Psych class, and I instinctively sank back into the seat. That just made him move in closer. I was practically one with the leather at this point, and unless I hopped into the backseat, there was nowhere else for me to go."

> From page 175 of Viswanathan's novel: "Sean stood up and stepped toward me, ostensibly to show me the book. He was definitely

invading my personal space, as I had learned in a Human Evolution class last summer, and I instinctively backed up till my legs hit the chair I had been sitting in. That just made him move in closer, until the grommets in the leather embossed the backs of my knees, and he finally tilted the book toward me."

The New York Times said that the similarities were more extensive than even *The Crimson* indicated—they counted twenty-nine passages to the *Crimson*'s dozen. Kaavya's defence was that she did it, but she didn't know she was doing it—the classic unconscious plagiarism plea. She was 'very surprised and upset' to learn about the similarities; she 'wasn't aware of how much' she may have 'internalized Ms McCafferty's words'. There was much scope for irony here: when it was revealed, before the scandal broke, that Kaavya Viswanathan's original debut novel had been massaged into shape by editors as well as something called a 'book packaging company', her editor asserted staunchly that the writing of *Opal* was '1,000 per cent' Kaavya's work. Make that somewhere around 900 per cent.

What made Kaavya's plagiarism, unconscious or not, such a burning issue that the *Malaysian Star*, the *People's Daily of China* and the *New Guinea Gazette* would all consider it front-page news? This was a book from a genre not especially known for its originality—boy meets girl plays out against the battlefield of SAT scores, teen friendships and fashion bloomers.

It's a first novel that was massaged and pummelled into shape— again, long before the plagiarism storm broke, Kaavya's editors were comfortable admitting that *Opal Mehta* needed more work and more 'inputs' than most manuscripts, though they gave her credit for an 'original' idea. Given that one of Megan McCafferty's novels is about a young girl trying to get into Columbia, and that Kaavya Viswanathan's novel is about a young brown girl trying to get into Harvard, the only thing original about *Opal Mehta* lies in the fact that it features an Asian protagonist. In other words, we may not have known how much of *Opal Mehta* had been borrowed, accidentally or not, from another published writer; but we did have a fair idea of the many processes that went into the manufacture of this book, complete with the advance, the hype, the deal.

Kaavya Viswanathan was definitely a plagiarist, but she was also a competent writer—and a product of today's market, a contemporary success story where the key elements are packaging and media managing, and where the book itself is just the content.

This is usually the point at which a reviewer is supposed to snort, paw the ground and tear into the bad, bad marketing machine that treats literature like burgers: all best-sellers have the same basic formula, tweaked a little bit for local palates. And I do understand Amit Chaudhuri's impatience with the Indian literary world for treating books as success stories, yet another mark of the India Shining brand conquering the world, the author as the son-in-law who's done so well.

But for the first time in publishing history, as several commentators have been pointing out recently, it has actually become possible for anyone to be a writer. There is no formula for great literary fiction, which is a bit of a problem; but then the market for literary fiction is a niche market, a boutique market, so the mainstream reader doesn't have to worry her head over that particular issue. It is often seen as a bad thing that more and more novels are being produced—I use that word deliberately—today; that creative writing courses allow anyone with a smidgeon of talent access to a wider market, once they've polished their skills; that any reasonably bright person can hammer out a book in six months and have a decent shot at being published.

The obvious argument against applying the laws of the marketplace to literature is that sales are far more important in publishing terms than quality. If you look at what's been resold to India as the great Indian novel in recent years, if you look at the world's best-seller lists, it's hard to disagree that publishing is no longer about looking at the literary qualities of a book.

But there's another way of looking at this: for the first time in the history of writing and publishing, it is possible for everyone to be, or contemplate being, an author. In the initial stages of this exercise in democracy, books will almost by definition be written for the moment;

a lot of what 'succeeds' will be only average; a lot of books will be written by many for a very few readers.

Narayanan's plagiarism ended his career. Kaavya's borrowings did her book great harm, but her career suffered far less. She studied law at Georgetown, and in May 2010, the online magazine *Gawker* carried the derisive headline: 'Harvard's Most Infamous Plagiarist Is More Successful Than You.' The young student had been accepted for an internship at one of New York's more successful law firms, and appears to have moved on from the scandal. Aside from the massive advance that *Opal* had attracted, it was hard to take the plagiarism very seriously.

Writing about the Kaavya Viswanathan scandal in 2006, I made this admittedly prejudiced observation: 'I cannot care as much about moderately well-written teen stories as I do about fiction that is genuinely original. Genuine acts of plagiarism force us to see things we would rather not see, like the despair and hubris of a talented mind spiralling into its own darkness. In the brand-new world of publishing as it stands today, even plagiarism has become a simulacrum, a pale imitation of the real thing.'

Four years after the Kaavya Viswanathan case broke, another teenager was accused of plagiarism. Helene Hegemann is the seventeen-year-old author of *Axolotl Roadkill*, and her book seemed to incorporate scenes, lines and descriptive passages from the works of several other authors—most notably a German artist called Airen. But Hegemann never denied incorporating work from other authors into her novel; her defence is that attribution is unimportant, because she's remixed the material in a way that makes it her own. She and several commentators in Germany didn't see this as a case of plagiarism so much as a case of lack of attribution: Hegemann said recently that she should have acknowledged her sources.

Hegemann's generation, brought up in the mashup culture, will inevitably challenge the sanctity of authorship. If literature can have several versions and multiple authors, just as a Web page is a constantly updating version of itself, then the yardstick will shift to the quality of the mashup, as you evaluate the author as remix artist. Airen, the author of the stolen work, was reported to be less than indignant about the theft and more concerned with attribution—and perhaps that's where the legal issues will eventually rest.

It's an intriguing and disturbing shift: a generation used to viewing the written word as so much raw material already has trouble understanding the need for attribution. Hegemann understands this better than most of us in the over-thirty generation: this isn't about the death of authorship, but about the death of originality.

These stories, Hegemann's and Viswanathan's, have happy endings. The next one is not like them at all.

3

Indrani Aikath-Gyaltsen

*T*he *New York Times*' 1994 review of *Crane's Morning*, by Indrani Aikath-Gyaltsen, ended with a brief excerpt from the book, a scene between husband and wife who share 'a life of parallel solitudes, acrimony and utter lack of communication'. The excerpt closes with the suicide of the wife, within hearing of the husband: 'He was staring miserably down the stairwell when the shot rang out, metallic and ominous.'

In the 1990s, Indrani Aikath-Gyaltsen had begun making a name for herself as a writer. Her first book had been published by P. Lal's Writer's Workshop, an independent imprint whose main business was the encouragement of unknown writers. But Aikath-Gyaltsen, born into a family of land-owners in Bihar, now ensconced in her second marriage in the often lonely and isolated world of a tea-planter's wife, had larger ambitions. She enlisted Khushwant Singh as her patron; he introduced her to Penguin India's David Davidar, and her first book, *Daughters of the House*, came out to approving reviews. Penguin India signed her up for a ten-book deal; Aikath-Gyaltsen, who often boasted that she could write a book in six months, settled down to work.

Crane's Morning was received with restrained enthusiasm—it was the kind of second novel that confirms an author's reputation without breaking new ground. Reviewers admired the style of the book, though some commented that it had an old-fashioned air about it, and with the distinction of a brief review in the *NYT*, Aikath-Gyaltsen seemed to be ready to take her place in the ranks of India's rising writers. The 1990s was a decade of great and not-always-wise literary ambition—it may have been the first decade when it had become almost as important to be acknowledged as a writer as it was to write well. Khushwant Singh's home in Sujan Singh Park, the approach strewn with a sleepy advance guard of striped cats and kittens, was a shrine for the ambitious: a pilgrimage here to seek his blessings and advice was seen as essential by some, and Singh took an avuncular interest in the careers of his protégés, many of them attractive, determined and sometimes pushy women. Aikath-Gyaltsen shared her writing with him bit by bit, chapter by chapter, as she worked.

The *NYT* review ('Moonlight in a Net') came out in February 1994. In March, a woman in Ontario sent a letter to Aikath-Gyaltsen's publishers. *Crane's Morning*, said the woman, was plagiarized from *The Rosemary Tree*, a 1956 novel by Elizabeth Goudge. The accusation was repeated by a librarian in Concord, New Haven; when they compared the two books, Aikath-Gyaltsen's publishers had to concede that it was true. From its opening paragraph to its closing sentences, there was no question that *Crane's Morning* had been plagiarized.

Aikath-Gyaltsen was not there to respond to the charges. On 3 October 1993, she had written a letter to her mentor, Khushwant Singh. 'I am still in a very bad frame of mind . . . Afraid to live, afraid to die. But you are right. Only I can help myself.' According to the *Washington Post*, she was found unconscious later that day by a niece, lying on the floor, froth coming out of her mouth. She died on 4 October; it was widely suspected, but never proved, that she had tried to poison herself.

✦

In my somewhat ramshackle and rambling library of personal books, I have a copy of *Crane's Morning* and *The Rosemary Tree*. When the plagiarism accusations were first levelled against Gyaltsen, few Indians knew of Elizabeth Goudge, and few in the UK or the US remembered her work. Goudge, who died in 1984, was best remembered as the author of the children's classic *The Little White Horse*; her novels had enjoyed a brief vogue in the 1940s and 1950s, and I dimly remembered seeing copies of *Green Dolphin Country* and *The White Witch* in hill-station libraries. They were the kind of books you'd find in a small Simla or Mussoorie hotel, tucked away behind reminiscences by old India hands and Raj-era cookbooks.

The Delhi Gymkhana Club library, unsurprisingly, yielded a copy of *The Rosemary Tree*. (The DGC library was a treasure house of forgotten authors, one of the last places in Delhi that stocked copies of Aubrey Menen alongside the Mills & Boons and James Hadley Chase.) It had last been borrowed in 1972, and when I asked the librarian if I could buy it from the library, he looked at its water-stained cover, the dust on the spine, and said I could have it for free.

The Rosemary Tree was set in a Devonshire village; *Crane's Morning* was set in the north-east of India. And from the opening sentences, it was clear that the two books were one and the same.

Chapter One, *The Rosemary Tree*, Goudge: 'Harriet at her window watched the gulls with delight. It meant bad weather at sea when they came up-river, and she had known when she woke this morning in the waiting stillness, and had seen the misted sky, that the long spell of fine weather was going to break in a gale.'

Chapter One, *Crane's Morning*, Aikath-Gyaltsen: 'Old Vidya sat at her window and watched the cranes with delight. It meant bad weather on this plateau when they came from the east and she had known, when she woke this morning and had seen the misted sky, that the long spell of fine weather was going to break in a rainstorm.'

I had wanted only to compare the two books, to have an assurance that this was, indeed, plagiarism and not accidental resemblance. Sometimes, without writers meaning to steal, there will be a resonance from one book to another; more gravely, sometimes an otherwise original book will echo a line or a paragraph from another work. Those are borderline cases, troubling but not always plagiarism. As I read both books, though, it was appallingly obvious that this was not a case of 'inspiration'; this was as clear-cut as plagiarism would ever get.

The Indrani Aikath-Gyaltsen case is little more than a literary curiosity, her story a tragic but slight footnote in the history of Indian writing in English. She had not written enough before her death at the age of forty-one, nor was Goudge a remarkable enough writer for the plagiarism to carry epic weight. But the experience of reading those two books, side by side, has never left me. Every paragraph in *Crane's Morning* echoed, faithfully, its predecessor in *The Rosemary Tree*. The plot of one book was transferred with absolute fidelity to the other— Aikath-Gyaltsen omitted, for obvious reasons, a sub-plot involving one character's musings on the Anglican church, but otherwise there was little difference between one book and the other, in terms of structure, theme, characters, dialogue.

When I met Khushwant Singh for a brief, journalist's interview in March 1994, I asked him a very naïve question: could he forgive Aikath-Gyaltsen? He said forgiveness was beyond him, that he felt sorry for her, but he didn't understand why she had done it. For him and for those at Penguin India, the sense of betrayal ran deep—they had been at the receiving end of Aikath-Gyaltsen's conversations about how her book was progressing, writerly discussions about the development of various characters. They had been made party to her deception, for months.

Aikath-Gyaltsen handwrote her books, and this is the image that stayed with me, of a woman opening another writer's novel, and transferring it meticulously onto blank sheets of paper. It was, in its way, a perfect transliteration—it is not easy, as those opening paragraphs indicate—to transfer a Devonshire novel into India, and Aikath-Gyaltsen did a thorough job of changing the landscape. It cannot have escaped her, as she went over Goudge's book paragraph by paragraph, that she was stealing another writer's work, as she changed gulls to cranes and found plausible reasons to explain why a convict called Vikram might quote Tennyson. Primroses become marigolds, bad marriages stay more or less the same, the mansions of an Indian village called Mohurpukur stand in for the country houses of England. As she wrote, she must have known what she was doing.

In the wake of the ugliness of the plagiarism scandal and her early death, many readers went through Goudge's remaining works to see if Aikath-Gyaltsen's first novel, the accomplished and haunting *Daughters of the House*, had also been plagiarized. If it was, too, stolen goods, it did not become apparent then and hasn't in the intervening years. It is entirely possible that *Daughters of the House* was a work of original talent, that Aikath-Gyaltsen, looking outwards to a promising literary career, wrote it herself.

Plagiarism is, in many ways, the most baffling and inexplicable of literary crimes: with the risk of discovery so great and so continuously present, why would anyone be a plagiarist? The usual reasons were proffered in the case of *Crane's Morning*: Aikath-Gyaltsen had writer's block and a deadline hanging over her head, she had the laziness that dogs all writers and she thought she could get away with it, she was desperate for fame and acclaim and didn't want to have to wait till her own talent came back.

But when I think of the months she spent, in her house in the hills, handwriting page after page of a book not her own, it brings up a deep and terrible sadness. It is hard to condemn Indrani Aikath-Gyaltsen, despite the way she betrayed those who had believed in her and trusted her. She must have read the reviews of Goudge's book, the line in the *New York Times* review that praised the writer's 'richly lyrical style full of humour and insight'. She must have known that the praise was not for her sentences, the sentences she had so carefully transcribed but not written herself.

(Based on columns written in 1994, 1999 and 2006.)

SEVEN

Expression

1

Hold Your Tongue

This is what it came down to, the Voice of Enraged India raised against the unspeakable filth of Westernized India: a small group of about twenty to thirty women, one man appointing himself as one of their leaders, clustered in front of the Delhi Art Gallery in Hauz Khas.

They were members of the Durga Vahini, a Hindutva right-wing group, there to protest an exhibition of paintings, 'The Naked and the Nude'. I was there to see the exhibition; over the last two years, one of the small compensatory joys of living in the city had seen the DAG exhibitions, on landscapes, printmaking, modernism, shifting lessons in art history. Their shows—on Chittoprosad, on four centuries of prints—had become a visual memory for me, an alternate history of modern India squabbling with itself, fascinated by influences from Europe, intent on recovering and playing with its own traditions, rich in colour and line, endlessly curious.

Some of us—a friend, Mitali Saran, and me among them—thought we should try to strike up a conversation. It seemed rude to be attending the same show, even if with different aims, and not to talk about why they saw obscenity where we saw art.

'Do you know what paintings they have inside? They are showing paintings of Damini, the rape victim!' one woman told us. 'How can you support this?'

'Damini' was one of the nicknames the papers had given Jyoti Singh, a physiotherapy student who had died of the terrible injuries inflicted on her after being gangraped, in December 2010. Delhi had been out on the streets protesting for months afterwards, demanding an end to the violence that was claiming the lives of woman after woman.

That was a lie, I said. I had seen the paintings, and there were none of the rape victim. They had been told lies, and I asked where they had heard this from.

'Are you from the gallery?' she demanded. No, I said, I was a writer. I was curious about why they wanted to shut the gallery down. If they were assured that there were no paintings of rape victims, could the rest of us be allowed to see the show? Behind me, a woman was whispering to a friend in Hindi. She was saying, I only came out for Damini, because they shouldn't have done this to her, if her paintings are not there, why are we here?

The women at the back of the crowd looked worried. 'Talk to them,' they said, urging us to go the front and speak to some women who appeared to be leading the protests. A policewoman watched us, a senior officer. She assessed the situation and dismissed it, deciding that we were all harmless. The lady who'd said the paintings were of the Delhi rape victim changed her tactics. 'You're a woman,' she said, 'how can you support dirty pictures, where women are drawn naked, to be stared at by everyone? Would you bring your brother to see this? Your father?'

I ventured to suggest that both of them—one an art enthusiast, one a collector of art who would sometimes buy paintings and books in lieu of the household groceries, upsetting my mother—would love the show. 'You would come here with your father?' another woman said incredulously.

My father is one of my best friends, aside from being my parent. He's been there for me through the small hurts and larger crises of my life, taught me how to play golf without accidentally hitting the peacocks on the Delhi greens, embarrassed me by showing up at my book talks or prize-giving ceremonies and telling my friends stories from my misspent youth. We talk and argue every day over films, books, art, life: he introduced me to the works of Toni Morrison, Czeslaw Milosz, Salman Rushdie, Nadine Gordimer, Norman Mailer, Somnath Hore, Picasso, Anjolie Ela Menon, before I turned eighteen. He would love the art on display, I said. There was silence.

I felt it was impolite to continue without introducing myself, but we ran into an unexpected obstacle—the women were uncomfortable about sharing their names. 'Why do you need to know?' one woman asked aggressively. Another whispered her name to me, but said, don't write it, Didi, my family won't like it. Do they know you're here? I asked. Yes, yes, she said. I have permission to go out for all Durga Vahini work and mandir work. Yes, I said, it is a lovely day to be out. We exchanged conspiratorial smiles, and then a friend of hers grabbed her and took her away: why are you talking to that woman, don't you know she's on their side?

The arguments continued. They were easily summarized.

1. The naked figure was not part of Hindu tradition and our great heritage prevented us from dishonouring women this way.

The human body is neither obscene nor ugly, we suggested. Besides, we have a long history of nudity in art, from Gandharva and Chola statues to the Rani ki Vav in Gujarat, Khajuraho, and of course, the modern art on display here. The man stepped in front of the women. 'You are teaching the wrong things,' he said. 'Our Hinduism does not allow it.' I got angry. 'My Hinduism is not your Hinduism,' I said sharply. 'You cannot steal my religion.' Then I felt ashamed of myself, for having lost my temper so easily.

2. It did not matter whether nudes in art had once been part of Hindu tradition. It was not part of our lives now, and this exhibition denigrated women. Men would look at these paintings, and inflamed by lust, go out to rape women

We rebutted this as gently as we could, but the divide between our worldviews was beginning to open up. The women were growing heated, and now they had begun to grab at us, holding our arms, clutching at my waist, so that they could make their arguments. 'You should leave,' the woman police officer said quietly to me. 'They are getting angry.' But we were finally talking. It seemed wrong to leave now.

Two women, younger than the rest, waved away the ideological arguments. Could I understand—could we understand—that they felt ashamed and threatened by the idea of nude paintings? What did I mean, when I said the female body was neither shameful nor to be feared? Was I not upset at the thought of men looking at naked women in the gallery, and then outside? Why, they asked again, did I think bodies were beautiful?

The man cut them off. That was not the point, he said flatly, and they stepped back. The point was that these disgusting, shameful works were being displayed in the open market. It was their duty to stop people from seeing them. But, I said, talking past him to the women, even though I thought there was no shame in the sight of the human body, and I did not think the female body was sinful in itself, I understood that they felt otherwise. We disagreed, and that was all right. So they should tell their families and friends not to see this show. Why stop us, who felt differently, why take away our right to see what we wanted to see?

Some of the women were nodding. But the man said, and two of the women said, you do not represent Hindustan.

Another friend, tired of the arguments, said flatly, neither do you. The women and I shook hands. Thank you for trying to explain, I said, and I meant it. Some more of them held out their hands. The man looked upset—stop shaking hands, he said to them. I shook his hand and said thank you, and he seemed even more upset.

The policewoman told us again to step back. She and I chatted for a while. There would be no violence, she said, not from this lot. They were melting away already because there were no television cameras. There was no point trying to talk, she said briskly, their world and mine—she took in my jeans, my dark glasses, and even though some of the women were similarly clad, in kurtas and trousers, our accents marked us out as different—had nothing in common.

Inside the gallery, it was quiet and calm. Groups of artists, including Ram Rahman and Kanchan Chunder, a few visitors to Hauz Khas who had come in before the barricades closed, and some who'd showed up in support when they heard about the Vishva Hindu Parishad (VHP) protest, were taking in the show. Two policewomen walked around the gallery as well. They liked Raja Ravi Varma's paintings of Krishna and the naked gopis, exclaimed at the beauty of the blues in a Husain abstract, but frowned at the Souzas.

'What a dirty fellow,' one said.

Why, I asked?

'Look at how closely he's looking at the women he's painted,' she said. 'Everything he's looking at, and she doesn't mind.'

How did she know that the woman in the painting didn't mind? I asked, fascinated.

'See her face,' the policewoman said. 'She's enjoying him looking, no?'

The policewoman, I thought, had missed her calling. She would have made a fine art critic.

When we left, the TV cameras and trucks had gone. And so had the protesters. The gallery, one of the very few in recent times that had not caved, where Ashish Anand, Kishore Singh and the rest at Delhi Art Gallery had gently defended the integrity of the work on the walls, the right of the show to exist, was still open for business.

People would walk in and out for the rest of the day. Some would love the Brootas and the Akbar Padamsees, argue about the sculptures and the (low) ratio of male to female nudes. Some would do the simple thing of looking at these bodies, in all their vulnerability, their sensuality, their beauty and their slow ageing. No one who walked in came in looking for offence, looking for reasons to get angry, and perhaps because of that, no one left the exhibition offended, or angered. Those who had taken offence were staying outside the barricades, and though the distance between the barricades and the open doors of the gallery was small, I could not see a way to bridge that gap.

2

Empty Chairs

Like many others in the country, I have chronicled the relentless assault on writers, journalists and free speech in my journalism, and those columns can be found elsewhere. The list of writers who have been silenced, threatened or exiled since Independence by political violence, long and punitive lawsuits or the indifference and cowardice of publishing houses is dismaying in its length: Perumal Murugan, Salman Rushdie, Taslima Nasreen, Rohinton Mistry, Jitendra Bhargava, Mridula Garg, Arundhati Roy, Durai Guna, Wendy Doniger, James Laine, the lecturer T.J. Joseph, A.K. Ramanujan, U.R. Ananthamurthy, Habib Tanvir, D.N. Jha, M.M. Kalburgi, B.R. Ambedkar, P.M. Antony, Vijay Tendulkar, Aubrey Menen, Stanley Wolpert and many more.

These losses were felt deeply, mostly in the narrowing of consensus on what writers should be free to write. Every political party or group was implicated, from the right-wing, to Left and Communist parties across states in south India, while the Congress Party had a shameful track record in attempting to muzzle speech on the Internet. In this, politicians had much in common with religious bigots and fundamentalists: the one idea that united all of them, from the Hindu right-wing to powerful Islamic or Christian fundamentalist pressure groups, was the belief that they had a right to choke off and suppress anything that offended them.

One year, at the Jaipur Literature Festival, four authors—Amitava Kumar, Hari Kunzru, Jeet Thayil and Ruchir Joshi—read from Salman Rushdie's *Satanic Verses* in protest that some fundamentalist groups were threatening violence if he attended the festival. The contrast between the readings and the reaction was illuminating. In both sets of readings, the audience listened with mild interest, a slight frisson going through the crowd when they realized what the book was; but there were no indignant protests, no angry walk-outs. Some laughed at Salman Rushdie's humour, and smiled at Jeet and Ruchir's performative skills.

Outside, the atmosphere was thunderous. The organizers swooped on the authors before the media could get their cameras rolling, and sequestered them in the author's lounge. Over the next few days, the festival would be threatened by vociferous protestors from Islamic fundamentalist groups in Jaipur. The conspiracy theories would blossom and grow, ignoring the fact that all four authors had chosen to read from Rushdie's book in a gesture of solidarity, and anger at the rising intolerance in the country that clamped down like a giant muzzle on anyone in the creative professions. None of the four had done it in order to be controversial, or anticipated that their readings would set off a chain of anger and swirling liberal angst over whether they had stepped across a line or not.

The policeman who came in from the local Jaipur thana was an old hand at defusing volatile situations. He cut through the learned and thoroughly useless debates over whether reading from the *Satanic Verses* was a crime or not with a set of simple questions.

Were the authors reading from a book or from printed sheets of paper?

Printed sheets of paper?

Then no crime had been committed. Technically, it was the import of the book that was banned. Reading from printouts was fine, though under the labyrinthine laws of the land, the cases in minor courts trundled on for another year or two.

On the final day, the festival had acquired the air of a besieged Mughal court, with protestors breaking through the security lines to raise slogans on the lawns. The organizers hoped to bring Rushdie in for an interview through an Internet hook-up, but a meeting with the protestors who were massed in two corners of the lawns brought back bad news. They were not prepared to listen to Rushdie, or let the audience listen to him. In fact, they said, they would consider even the screening of an image of the author's face offensive, and would see that as provocation sufficient to invite violence.

There were thousands of people on the lawns, writers, schoolchildren, locals from Jaipur, visitors from Delhi who came down every year for the festival. Namita Gokhale, Sanjoy Roy, William Dalrymple and Sheuli Sethi, the team who had successfully built the JLF up from a tiny city festival to one of the largest cultural tamashas in the world, came up on stage to announce that they were not able to continue with the planned conversation between Rushdie and the television anchor Barkha Dutt, given the threats. It was an emotional moment and we were all relieved that they stepped off the stage unharmed. It might have been a much uglier story if they had gone ahead with the broadcast; the fear of violence sparking an uncontrollable stampede was very real.

Over the next few years, the JLF's organizers would have to cope with copycat protesters, many of them eager to use the massive media coverage that the festival received to make whatever political points were on their individual agendas. The JLF team had sent an inadvertently weak message across by not defending the authors who read from Rushdie with sufficient strength or clarity. It would take a year or two of frivolous controversies, many of them patently manufactured by groups panting for the cameras to be turned on them, before would-be limelight stealers realized that the festival was not going to give ground to bullies.

There were two things I learned from the incidents of Jaipur in 2012. One was that the gap between what happens in a reader's head and a protestor's mind is vast, and impossible to bridge. One is willing to listen to a story with open curiosity, understanding that books are not meant to be security blankets—anyone who turns to reading solely for comfort, believing that they have a right not to have their core beliefs unsettled, disturbed or challenged is deluded. Protestors scan books (or plays or poems or films or art) the way an MRI goes through a patient's body—looking for signs of deadly disease that must be uprooted with scalpel and chemo if necessary.

The other was a sad lesson: censorship works best not through bans or even through the removal of books from public space, but by placing authors in a circle of isolation and subjecting them to transferred resentment. At the Kolkata Literary Festival a year on, the filmmaker Rahul Bose and I had a conversation with an empty chair: Salman Rushdie had been prevented from attending because of protests from the usual suspects.

Over time, as more and more artists, writers, filmmakers, activists were attacked, the anger and blame shifted from the protestors, because there was nothing that could be done about them—they acted with the blessings of powerful political or religious groups, and they acted with total impunity, aware that authors and artists would not retaliate with violence or censorship attempts in kind.

It was relatively easy to isolate and ultimately exile writers like Taslima Nasreen, or Rushdie, or later, Perumal Murugan. If one side raised the stakes for organizers of events by threatening and sometimes enacting violence, the free speech arguments were soon turned upside down. It would be irresponsible for organizers to invite such incendiary writers and thereby call violence down on the innocent audience. It was even argued—monstrously—by ostensibly liberal voices, that it was irresponsible of writers who had been targeted in such a fashion to want to participate in these events, given the situation in the country. Everyone was held accountable for the violence they had not committed; the authors who read or spoke up in support of their fellowship, the authors who had been unfairly pilloried in the first place, the organizers who risked inviting either of the above. Everyone was held accountable, except for those who threatened violence in the first place.

The vast number of writers available to speak at festivals masks the rising number of empty chairs, the invitations not sent out to authors who are too much trouble or too outspoken, the books not written by a generation that has read the signs clearly: Do Not Commit Nuisance.

But every time an incident like this happened, I went back to the books. Many of us did and continue to do so. When I went back to *Midnight's Children* and *Shame,* I wondered when Indian writers would once again be free to fictionalize and criticize their history the way Rushdie had been back in the 1980s. Every time someone sniped about Rushdie's 'celebrity status', I thought also of the many years that he had put in as the head of PEN, the international body that fought for the rights of writers, and of his sharp, clear, uncompromising arguments in favour of stepping across all kinds of lines.

I read Perumal Murugan's *One Part Woman* and bought everything I could find of his works that were available in translation, marvelling at the way in which the landscape he knew so well became the red earth of fiction. *The Times of India* literary festival invited Rohinton Mistry to come back, four years after the Shiv Sena had burned copies of *Such a Long Journey* in public, and the writer said to an appreciative audience: 'My first thought [on hearing about the ban on *Such a Long Journey*] was, did it take them nineteen years to come across it? I've heard of slow cooking, but slow reading? I heard that the sales of the book went up after that.'

Empty chairs don't stay empty forever. I re-read Rushdie's *Haroun and the Sea of Stories*, and it was a relief to see that the land of Gup triumphed over the land of Chup, that all the Khattamshuds in the world could not silence a Batcheat or a Bolo. What could happen in fiction could happen in reality; the two worlds had a way of leaking into one another.

★

After what felt like a string of columns on the subject of book bans, censorship and why the apparently reasonable right to take offence can become a terrifying bludgeon in the hands of the wrong people, I began to ask groups of people questions about what free speech meant to them. Even in my quiet backwater, the censorship debates had become relentless, exhausting and pointless: it felt as though we were all repeating the same arguments over and over again, to little purpose. What I wanted to know was simple: what would people talk about if they were free to talk about anything? How would this freedom change their lives, if at all? What did they feel they couldn't speak freely about?

The answers came from groups of schoolchildren and a few college students, from festival-goers and occasionally from writers and artists. This was not in any way a scientific study, but over two years of sporadic interviews and conversations, a pattern emerged. It wasn't startling, but it was heart-wrenching.

The memories and experiences people shared when we talked about censorship in those few workshops sometimes had little to do with trauma—often, people just wanted to talk about silences in their closest relationships. The men often wished they could speak to their partners, parents or friends more freely about their insecurities and anxieties, their dreams of pursuing more fulfilling careers, their desire to spend more time with their kids and less time at the office.

The women often wished they could speak more freely about their deepest desires and their frustrations, about the rampant fear that they would lose their identities and become merely someone's mother, wife, daughter, about their lost goals and dreams. That covered only the narrow if mainstream preoccupations of heterosexuals: for anyone who was part of the increasingly visible and vocal Indian LGBT community, the pressures, and the silences, were of a different and often far more oppressive nature.

As a group, we felt least free to speak in our own homes. We didn't feel free to talk to our families about our deepest wants and needs, about our sexual preferences, about our choices of partner or career. We felt most censored about childhood violence or other abuse, about caste-based violence or taunting, about experiencing or witnessing violence in the family, about cycles of addiction and damage, about the anger and pain that arose out of many of these silenced experiences.

As strangers and friends shared their stories, I felt them resonate: each stumbling sharing loosened some of my own bonds.

I had spent some years grappling with my own ghosts; when the nightmares reached a certain stage, I found that my voice would fade, growing softer and softer against my will, sometimes drying up in mid-conversation.

When I finally broke my own silence, about a much older predatory relative, not a grandfather but of that generation, whose ugly and secretive assaults had ripped apart the fabric of my childhood, I was luckier than many: my father and mother supported my decision to speak out. An hour after the *New York Times* posted the article online, the emails started to come in, first just one or two, and then a steady stream of them—thirty-seven by the end of the first day, and people continued to write in all through the week.

And for weeks afterwards, letters and emails came in responding to the article I'd written, from strangers but also from close friends, chiefly from women but also from a few men. The letters said in essence, as an old and valued friend wrote: 'Me too. This happened to me too.' She and I had known each other for years, and never talked about these experiences, never known that we had this, too, in common. And with each email, each phone call, I felt a sense of kinship grow, and I felt many of the tight knots in my own life loosen.

I learned that all of us had healed after we had spoken up and shared our stories; it was not necessary to go public with one's experiences, but it was crucial to share them with someone, a healer, a sibling, friends, support groups. Often these sharings happened over many months and years; you rarely tell your story just once.

Sometimes you don't even have to tell it. My father made a point of calling every day for months after the article came out. We didn't discuss the past, but every time I saw his number on my phone, I understood that he was letting me know he was there, just in case. We discussed books, and swapped stories of the writers we mutually loved; our positions had reversed, and I was now the one recommending great fiction he absolutely had to read, instead of the other way around.

I learned that there is a big difference between knowing the statistics that say you are not alone, and knowing for sure that there are so many others who share something of your past and your memories. I am no longer in the least apologetic about the times when I've reached out for help; those who seek and can get help from either families or professionals heal faster and have a better chance at creating stable lives.

I learned, as we all had, that there was a time to declare your anger and a time to put it behind you; that the scars run deep and might never fade, but that healing is always a possibility. A wise friend and mentor told me once: 'Suffering is not necessary', by which he meant that terrible things happen, but it is not required that we contribute to the weight of the world's sadness. Joy, he hinted, was compulsory, even if it sometimes felt like a country for which you had no visa.

So many of us had encountered unexpected grace along the way: the support of partners, friends, family, but perhaps also other things, a little more empathy, sometimes a little more of an understanding of other injustices, greater than our own troubles.

For months, the letters came in from all across India, a few from elsewhere:

'Me too.' 'Me too.' 'Me too.'

'I was nine.' 'I was seven.' 'I was fourteen.'

'He was my neighbour.' 'My father.' 'My great uncle.'

'I trusted him.' 'He terrified me.' 'I thought I was the bad one, that there was something wrong with me, not him.' 'His wife knew but she said nothing.'

'I'm still on anti-depressants, but life's better now.' 'It's my sixth year in recovery from x addiction.' 'I used to cut myself, but it's been years since I did that.'

'Me too. That was my story, too.'

Many of those who wrote in were already friends; many more became friends, and that was a gift I had not expected.

It was almost a year down the line when I noticed that some things had become imperceptibly easier: speaking in public, speaking to friends, keeping a diary, even writing, as though sharing my experiences had freed me to find the right words in other ways. And slowly, memory unlocked as well: it was finally possible to remember the truly happy parts of my childhood—the long drives with family, the years of reading in trees, the non-stop flow of friends through the house—without the stains of the sadness, guilt and incomprehension that were attached to the assaults. These memories came to the surface quietly, returning my childhood to me in small pieces: a summer afternoon suddenly vivid with the memories of picking mulberries, learning to steer boats in the slender deltas of the Sunderbans, writing straggly stories as an eleven-year-old in imitation of my sister. Predators take a great deal, but over months and years, I claimed more and more territory back.

There's a word I stumbled across when I was reading an old medical dictionary: eschar. It's the term for the thick, dead tissue—often black, necrotic—that forms over wounds. In most cases, eschar sloughs off eventually once fresh skin has grown under the burn or the pressure wound; in some cases, the eschar covers a larger wound, making it dangerously difficult to treat.

As I heard more and more stories, I felt a sense of grace mingled with sadness. So many of us had been fortunate to find support, and we had eventually healed. And every so often, we heard about those who hadn't made it, whose wounds had gone too deep under the skin to heal. If you are trapped in a family, a culture or a community where you cannot speak the truth about your life, you cannot heal from the hurt, the violation, cannot fully ask for the things you will need in order to leave the past behind: memory can go gangrenous. This is true for everyone, not just for those who survived a certain kind of childhood.

★

I have begun to see free speech differently. The writer's responsibility is not to hold up a mirror to society; it is to honour his or her deepest and most true self. Free speech is not an academic abstraction that concerns only intellectuals and artists. At its core, free speech is about how honest we can be with ourselves, how fearless we can be when expressing our most strongly held beliefs and our most deeply felt intuitions about the world we live in. Sometimes, free expression is unpleasant, unsettling, even shocking; some forms of free expression will be abhorrent to many. The agreement we make, by and large, is to tolerate repugnant and disagreeable views—anything that is not directly harmful or untruthful—in exchange for the right to have our own freedom of expression respected.

And this needs to be acknowledged: freedom of expression is always subversive, just as asking questions is always subversive. One of the arguments many free-speech activists, including myself, have made against book bans is logically impeccable: why ban a book when you have the option to refrain from reading it, and to tell your friends (or followers) not to read it as well? The truth is that ideas are dangerously contagious. They travel as rapidly as viruses, and are almost as infectious—and even if they cannot articulate this thought completely, advocates of censorship understand this instinctively.

Free expression assumes that, in the strictest sense of the phrase, nothing is sacred—there is no line, or sanctum, that cannot be crossed, entered. The family, caste and class, social clans and tribes and religions are all seen to be man-made constructs, open to examination and question. The limits of free expression are always under construction, not at all easy to define or police, but the foundation of free expression is the belief that everything is up for scrutiny.

In essence, censorship and the impulse to ban books are acts of fear. Sometimes they are also acts of violence, but more often, people want to suppress ideas that they find uncomfortable or intolerable. These are almost always ideas and arguments that challenge established beliefs or hierarchies, or that draw our attention to the deep cracks beneath the surface of our lives that we'd rather not look at.

The repercussions of suppressing challenging art, books and ideas are major; but I can empathize with the impulse to shut down what makes you uncomfortable or what you disagree with. Freedom is often uncomfortable. Change is even more disquieting. We all have reasons to resist change, and those of us who argue in favour of free speech would probably make more persuasive arguments if we kept this in mind.

The argument for free speech is seldom made as often or as strongly as the argument against censorship. For most people, even most readers and some writers, free speech remains an abstraction, a high-minded principle that has little application to their own lives. If you can prevent a riot by banning a book or shutting down an art exhibition, most Indians would rather ban the book or the art.

The problem with the argument that books (or art, or films) cause riots is that there hasn't been a single case of spontaneous indignation from the masses over the last six decades—not a single instance where crowds have gathered on their own to denounce erring artists and writers. Every instance of violence, threatened or actual, has been orchestrated by political parties or religious groups. If we were more given to applying logic, we might well conclude that a more effective way of preventing riots would be to ban political parties and religious groups, instead of banning books.

This is usually the point at which public debate on censorship stops, with both sides accusing the other of intolerance and rigid thinking. But there is a seldom-asked question that may be of some use. Who has the freedom to speak or express themselves with complete confidence and ease in contemporary India? Which groups, if any, had these freedoms in the past?

Fifty per cent of your population is eliminated at the starting gate: women in India, told so often to hold their tongues, to speak softly, to silence themselves and to know their places, do not have freedom of expression, and barring a very few exceptions, never did. Many Dalits and most members of the scheduled castes and tribes still run the risk of punishment, ostracism, torture and death if they dare to unlock their tongues. Many members of minority—read non-Hindu—religions remain painfully aware that they can say nothing without being judged as representatives of the Muslim or the Christian or Sikh community.

Perhaps the wealthy and the powerful have an untrammelled right to free speech? Not so; even the richest of Indians, the most feared of politicians, would hesitate before they ventured to criticize religion, even if they were free to speak their minds about politics and business. Even the most devout of Indians would hesitate to criticize the towering, and sometimes stifling, institution of the family. It is possible, theoretically, that wealthy and powerful male Brahmin priests might be able to exercise their free expression rights with complete impunity, but I have yet to meet someone who fits this description.

The great Indian epics are ambiguous on the subject of free speech. They include subtle cautions and warnings: the rakshashi Surpanakha's crime is chiefly that she expresses her desire for Rama and Lakshman freely, in a manner that goes against the norms of behaviour they are used to from women. The price she pays for her desire, and her openness, is disfigurement: Lakshman cuts off her nose, and she runs weeping to her brother Ravana. The power of speech is ferocious, not to be taken lightly: Kunti's careless words bring Draupadi four more husbands than she had bargained for, a half-lie—Ashwatthama (the elephant) is dead—kills a mighty warrior, grief-stricken because he thinks that Ashwatthama (the person) has been slaughtered on the field of battle.

Vac, the goddess of speech, is often represented as a benign, womanly deity, her gifts abundantly and freely given, her connection with creation itself stronger than any of the Vedic gods. Vac is rarely worshipped today, but of all the gods and goddesses, her power seems to tower above the rest. 'From this holy sound flow the oceans, by her the four regions of space live, and from her proceeds the ultimate ground in which the entire universe is rooted.'

The earliest myths about Vac tell a cautionary tale, worth repeating. The gods and the asuras were both the children of Prajapati. Claiming their inheritance, the gods chose mind, the asuras speech. At the site of ritual sacrifice, the gods swoop down on Vac, cutting her off from the asuras. They gain possession of the goddess, and offer up to the fire, making her their own. Yajna himself lusts after Vac, seeking union with the goddess of speech—fearful of what might come of this yoking of the goddess with the god of sacrifice, Indra turns himself into a foetus so that no monster may be born of that union.

In one of our inherited ideas of Vac, this is what emerges from the stark telling of the myth. Sacred speech is coveted and desirable, but it is not for everyone—in fact, it will be snatched back from those who may have a just claim to it, but who cannot defend their claim. Speech, sacred as it may be, can be taken into custody and sent up into flames; Vac herself is tamed, forcibly possessed and impregnated, before she regains herself. After all of this, Vac is worshipped, honoured and prayed to. In this version, while the scriptures tell us of Yajna's lust and Indra's quick retrieval of the situation, they remain silent on one subject. Nothing in the sacred texts tells us, in this story about speech, what Vac thinks of all of this.

There is another, far more complex version that I read in a paper on Vac by Asko Parpola, the Finnish Indologist. In this Puranic version, Vac is not captured by the gods—she goes over to the side of the gods on condition, says Parpola, that the ritual offering be made to her before it reaches the sacrificial fire. Behind all of this is a dark tale of incest: Prajapati, overcome by Vac's beauty, unites with his own daughter.

She goes over to the gods, and out of her union with Yajna, bears Rudra, the god of wrath, who will ultimately take revenge on Prajapati with a three-joined arrow. Rudra can only be born through the combined powers of the gods; and Vac's sacrifice and impregnation is revealed to have quite a different meaning. After the sacrifice, after the gods unite and offer their powers to Vac, after Indra allows himself to be reborn as Rudra, after Rudra takes revenge on the father who committed incest with his beautiful daughter, Vac continues, serenely, letting the shared mantle of Durga the warrior goddess slip from her shoulders, and allowing her story to flow into learned Saraswati's story.

Of all the goddess myths I grew up with, Vac's story was rarely told to us. When I finally read enough to uncover it, the lessons were searing. Speech is an act of creation. Speech may be coveted, even dominated or possessed by force, as Prajapati does; but speech has its own ability to win allies, endure the fire, demand nourishment and call up power. Speech will even create its own instruments of justice; but once justice has been served, speech will settle back into the more important and ever-present business of creation.

And perhaps just as important in times of grave censorship: speech does not have to battle in order to be set free. It will create its own salvation. It will eat the offerings meant for the fire, in order to nourish the warrior growing inside its own womb; it will endure and thrive on sacrifice, taking what it needs from the lust of others and turning that to good account. It will settle its own accounts, and find its own freedom, even if it is slightly singed, a little scorched, along the way.

(Based on assorted writings from 2002–2014.)

Postscript

In January 2015, the Tamil novelist Perumal Murugan posted a short note on his Facebook page: 'Perumal Murugan, the writer is dead . . . Leave him alone.' He took this decision after facing escalating protests from local caste-based groups and the RSS over his 2010 novel *Madhorubhagan*.

On 20 February the same year, the Marathi rationalist and politician Govind Pansare died of gunshot wounds he had sustained on the 16th, when two gunmen shot him and his wife when the two were out on their morning walk. The most popular of his twenty-one books remains *Shivaji Kon Hota* (Who Was Shivaji), first published in 1988.

On the morning of 30 August, Kannada scholar and former vice-chancellor M.M. Kalburgi was shot dead when he answered the door to two unknown assailants. Dr Kalburgi's research and his firmly expressed views on the subject of religious orthodoxy and superstition had made him many enemies among Lingayat communities; the VHP and the Bajrang Dal had also burned his effigies.

A week later, the Hindi writer Uday Prakash announced that he was returning his Sahitya Akademi award in protest at the Akademi's silence over the threats to writers. In interviews, he spoke of the many incidents that had preceded the murders of Pansare and Kalburgi: the withdrawal of A.K. Ramanujan's essay from a university syllabus, the trouble over James Laine's biography of Shivaji, the pulping of Wendy Doniger's book, the harassment of the late U.R. Ananthamurthy, among other assaults on writers in India.

Nayantara Sahgal followed Uday Prakash, giving up her award and issuing a powerful statement, 'The Unmaking of India', in memory of the Indians who had been murdered and in support of the right to dissent. Over the next few weeks, about forty-five writers across the country, from Surjit Pattar and Krishna Sobti to G.N. Devy and Chandrashekhar Patil, returned their Akademi (and other) awards; some 300 writers, academics, editors and intellectuals spoke up supporting the protest. As this book goes to press, writers—K.S. Bhagawan, the young Dalit author Huchangi Prasad—continue to be threatened.

In these decades of battles over book bans, censorship and attacks on writers, this marks the first time that so many writers have spontaneously come forward to mark their anger and fear at these changing times. As Anita Desai wrote, 'I was born in an India that enshrined democracy, pluralism and the freedom of speech in its Constitution . . . In an atmosphere where there is no security or support for those who voice dissent, criticism or rational thought, there can be no intellectual or artistic work of any worth.'

Those who write, create and live in India hope for a better ending, and better days ahead, a time when we have as much freedom in the outside world as we do in the lively addas where we meet our fellow writers, in the quiet rooms of our own minds. Earlier versions of 'Hold Your Tongue' and 'Empty Chairs' were subject to constant revisions, each one marking another assault, another dismaying development. This chapter has no closing sentence.

3

Crossing Over

The first home I rented in Goa, for five months' worth of writing time, was in the village of Calvim. It was a large, spacious white-and-blue house in which I rattled around like a ridiculously happy pea in a very big pod, working on my first novel. I lived mostly upstairs, visited by two anxious swifts who had a nest in the broad balcony. The chapters flowed easily here; the writing had gone sluggishly in Delhi, where our friendly home in Jangpura had been overwhelmed by the roar of traffic, of new constructions, of the competing, loud and sadly tuneless late-night bhajan evenings from the nearby gurudwara and temple.

In the Calvim house, I had a rickety, thin-legged table set up near a window. The white egrets would rise up from the river nearby every evening, startling and then beguiling me by soaring so close that their visits felt like benedictions. The house belonged to the writer, poet and artist Margaret Mascarenhas, who lived across the river and lent this out as a residency for people who could handle the peace and quiet of the village. 'It's like going back in time,' said Margaret, taking a long drag from her cigarette, her mischievous Madonna face reflective for a change, 'to Goa the way it was fifteen years ago. And it'll all change when the bridge between Calvim and Aldona comes up.'

The only way to cross over to Aldona was by ferry. I liked the walk down from my house past the Sevros Bakery and the church, down to a concrete jetty frequented by cats and the occasional secretive mongoose; sometimes you had to pause to let a brown snake go by, crossing like a careful old grandmother, it's head anxiously raised, as it slithered from one red-soil covered bank to the other side, where the paddy fields started. The Calvim River was broad, opening out into mysterious, green islands at one end, its black-and-silver waters home to frogs, reedy water snakes and the collective grief of the village.

The buses in Goa had names, a distinguishing characteristic that made me partial to them over other forms of transport. I had a particular fondness for Victor, who rattled down the road from the Aldona side of the ferry halfway up to Mapusa. When I boarded Victor for the first time, I smiled absently at a lady in her fifties who surprised me by giving me a sticky mango, fresh from her tree, after which I found I'd been adopted.

We often took the bus together after that and Wilhelmina told me the best ways to cook bangda—Indian mackerel—and her mother's generations-old recipe for rechad masala and where to get the most superior palm vinegar in Aldona market.

And she told me about the day in February 2012 when a bus called Lucy came down the road on the Aldona side. The driver was going too fast, or perhaps he had handed the steering wheel over to a seventeen-year-old apprentice, this was uncertain. Instead of halting at the bus stand, where we sat as Wilhelmina talked, listening to the peacocks and watching the rain pelt down on the mangrove roots, Lucy had rolled into the river.

The bus went in deep; it took time to find ropes, winches, machinery of the sort that was seldom needed in either Calvim or Aldona. Six people died in the accident. Four of them were children—all schoolgirls who had walked from their homes in Calvim every day down to the ferry to take the bus to the St. Thomas Girls High School in Aldona. On both sides of the bank, families grieved. Both villages were still in deep mourning when I visited Calvim.

It took time for me to understand what this tragedy had meant. I had lived for over twenty years in Delhi, where the city's massive sprawl, the aggression and jostling and busy lives of sixteen million people left no room for individual adversity to be noticed, let alone mourned.

But Goans made time for matters that often went by the wayside in metropolises: for family ties, for the wider community that made up a village. The evening of the bus accident, the council of Panjim announced that they were cancelling the carnival procession, to join Calvim in mourning. Panjim and Calvim were far away from each other, by local standards; one was among the largest cities in Goa, while Calvim was a community of about 115 families.

The loss of the Dias girls was felt in every house and heart. My neighbour, Cecilia often came over to 'help', which was a euphemism for 'rescue the outsider who has no idea how to fix leaking roofs, handle recalcitrant wells or chase spiders out of the kitchen'. It took weeks and months to start to understand how deep the collective grief went, or how the disruption and disaster visited on one family could also be felt in the hearts of fellow villagers. On my evening walks, I often saw the padre making his house calls, offering comfort to his small flock.

Back in Delhi, a friend heard the story and said, 'You must write about this!' He had in mind an investigative report, and there was much to say. The tragedy was used as a reason to press for a bridge to be built between Calvim and Aldona, though the village was divided on whether this would be good or bad.

Cecilia's father was often ill. On one blustery night, in the middle of the monsoons, with the roads flooding and the electricity off all evening, an ambulance had to be called.

The procedure for raising the ferry at night, after 10 p.m., was simple: you stood on one bank or the other, and flashed your torch or called out until the ferry man woke. They took their duties seriously, never complaining about the lateness of the hour. The day charges for a ferry crossing was Rs 7 per passenger. At night, you had to ask for a Special Ferry. We called for the Special Ferry often when my husband dropped in to see how the writing and I were getting along, for which the charges were the magnificent sum of Rs 20. But on this night, the ferrymen had their windows and doors tightly boarded against the

storm, and weren't expecting anyone to be out in the middle of that
furious rain. It took Cecilia and her brother over twenty minutes to
raise the ferry.

Cecilia badly wanted that bridge to be built. She also wanted to
feel less disconnected from the chatter, the evening dinners and dances
that young women of her age could attend in Aldona. The ferry boat
was a marker between Calvim and the rest of the world. It saved the
village from being over-run by the changes that were sweeping across
Goa, but it also kept it stuck in the past.

On some of my walks, I went past the village up to the new road
that had been cut into the hills. It stood out like a fresh red gash,
and went up to the mines. The trucks had to come around the long
way, and Calvim remained untouched by the development that was
changing the face of the hills themselves. One afternoon, idling on
the ferry, watching the fish leap for mayflies, tracking the curve of the
white egrets' triumphant arc around the village, I saw the first of many
mining barges go past. It was a long, flat, ugly platform masquerading
as a boat, and it carried soil in mounds.

'A quarter of a hill,' the ferryboat captain said to me softly. 'Each
time it goes by, it takes some of our hills along.' His voice was neutral.
'The bigger barges can take almost half a hill at a time.' We watched
the red soil of the hills of Goa, floating down the river, until the hills
and the barges rounded the bend.

When I went back to the city, my friend—a bright, ambitious
editor—asked if I'd got started on the Calvim story. I said, not really.
He said, impatient with me already: 'But it's such a great story! You
should tape interviews with the villagers, talk to the families.'

I didn't want to; they were becoming friends. I agreed silently with
him that someone should 'do' the Calvim story for what it said about
small communities binding together in the aftermath of a tragedy, for
the subtext of development and the question marks over the virtues
of progress. The price of keeping a place like Calvim pure and free of
taint by the world of tourists, mining companies, New Age cafes, and
visitors like myself was paid by the families who lived here, and there
was a worth to talking about all of this.

But I didn't want to be the one to write this, to intrude on the griefs and memories of people whom I could no longer report on objectively, because they were my neighbours and my friends. After spending twenty years as an adult content to read other people's books, I wanted to write my own, and for some reason that I could not explain or fathom, I wanted to write about imaginary cat clans much more than anything else in the world.

I tried to write something more serious and literary. There was a story about a butcher who had come over into Delhi at the time of the Bangladesh war, but every time I tackled it, the butcher's life stayed flat and dead on the page. I did not like people who talked about 'the process of being a writer' or said 'Writer' with a capital W, because storytelling is such a basic human skill—everyone has it, once they acquire language. But I was beginning to face the fact that while I knew my reading tastes very well, I knew nothing about what I might be like as a writer.

Ray Bradbury had faced the same problem as a young man, and tackled it by setting down a list of things that fascinated him: the Jar, the Cistern, the Skeleton, the Lake, the Dinosaur. He believed that by making a list of nouns and then asking, what does this noun mean, you would find out what mattered to you. I thought he might be right, but to my mind, this sort of work was what you did after writing something of worth.

I went back to the butcher's book and butchered it some more for a miserable drizzly week, growling at the poor swifts every evening when I was done with my word count. One evening, the swifts came up and perched on the railing, gave me a severe look, and launched into what can only be described as a long complaint, presumably about my temper and growling and general bad manners. I left them some beetles and ants on a leaf the next morning in apology.

The next day, instead of writing, I tried to weed the garden, which had grown into a lush jungle during the monsoon months. The problem was that it was beginning to attract almost too much animal life; mice, snakes, mongooses, tomcats, squirrels and palm-squirrels, and my peaceful writer's house in Calvim was competing with

Jangpura's traffic-filled lanes in the raucousness stakes. One evening, I thought I saw a civet slip out of the gate, its jaws bloody, but it was not easy to see in the dark. The jackfruit trees that overhung the property already attracted cows, who came in every day and held a self-important morning conference before marking the event with manure signatures, much like their human counterparts in the corporate world.

It was pleasant work, cutting down the undergrowth, until I reached a cluster of weeds with delicate stems and tough roots. It took me half-an-hour to dig down to the root of the tallest of the weeds and when I raised it out of the soil, it was astonishingly beautiful — a brown, light corm that felt and looked like a baby armadillo. I raised it up and like tripwires, taproots attached to the corm quivered, and then straightened, showering earth across the small garden. I yanked at them again, and weeds started to collapse and fall over.

When I gently levered each tripwire/taproot up, being careful not to break them, the roots led back to more corms; I had to dig up each one, walking around in a tangle of roots. At the end of the afternoon, I had levered up most of the corms. Then I started to gather up the taproots, starting with the ones at the centre, holding them up like a squarish net of wires, not dissimilar to a football net laid out horizontally. As I tugged, the plants came up, and then I tugged with more force. The weeds rose up around me, almost of their own volition; after that it was easy enough to collect them and place them in a wheelbarrow.

The neighbour was watching with interest. She was a taciturn lady who shuffled by every evening. We had developed an excellent nodding relationship. 'Girl,' she said, 'that was a fine thing to see. Now you go wash off that mud and have a nice cup of tea.'

I still didn't know why I wanted to write about cats, but the more I dug at the root of that thing, the more it snaked away, towards the childhood years of reading Isaac Asimov, Ray Bradbury, Satyajit Ray and Premendra Mitra, Arthur C. Clarke, Nancy Kress, Ursula K. Le Guin and other science-fiction and fantasy greats. When I lifted up those taproots, they went off into another direction; my teenage fascination with dolphin and chimpanzee intelligence, and with that first generation of Artificial Intelligence creations, from the Alicebot onwards. One root said simply, 'Deep sea creatures'; one said 'Neurons'; one said 'Warg'; one said 'Flacon': none of this was either impressive or useful, but I took it as a sign. Late that night, I pulled out the printed pages of the butcher's book, read it through, and dumped it without regret into the recycling bin.

Four days later, I had *The Wildings* fully mapped, in twenty-two chapters. The novel was a romp, and it did not aspire to be the literary heir to *Midnight's Children* or *To Kill A Mockingbird*, but I loved writing it. When the rains stopped, I took my first drafts down to the river and read them to the frogs and the fish, who were a wonderful audience. They never corrected me, and they croaked and splashed at all the right places.

★

Handwriting, in the age of keyboards, is precious because it's becoming so rare.

There's a set of books that has survived the many house-shifts and the frequent culls of our overgrown library. I keep them near my writing table, which is still the dining table, and some days when the writing is stuck, or when I am wondering why I ever thought I could be a writer, they will be brought out.

Harold Pinter signed his collected plays for me at the Edinburgh Book Fair, and we took a moment to discuss our views on the Iraq War—we agreed, though he agreed more unprintably than I did.

Agha Shahid Ali printed out a poem because I said it was one of my favourites and sent it to me, his signature uncurling into an exuberant sentence and then wrapping around the next page.

My sister-in-law who lives in New York got Toni Morrison to sign *Home* for me, and didn't tell me she had. When I opened the package, all I could do was to trace that name over and over again in wonder and disbelief: 'Dear Nila, with pleasure, Toni Morrison.' It is hard for me to act as though these are perfectly normal things, a famous author signing a book for you; I grew up reading Morrison and revering her. This is one of the most precious things I will ever own.

Another is the book with Salman Rushdie's signature embossed in black ink across the page. When I look at that, it brings back the first heady rush of reading *Midnight's Children* or *Haroun and The Sea of Stories*, a time when Rushdie was welcome in his own country. (Perhaps some day, that time will come again, soon.)

Others are signed by writers whom I grew to know through the slender thread of a mutual love of books, which widened into friendships that have in some cases lasted for years: Manjula Padmanabhan, Ruchir Joshi, Margaret Mascarenhas, Jeet Thayil and a host of others.

Many are much better writers than I could hope to be, but that isn't the point. Making the transition from a lifelong reader into someone who is probably a writer because she spends most of her time writing has not been easy for me. At one time, dealing with an incident of old trauma, it felt as though I was riddled with tripwires and dark roots. Speaking out about one sad memory would immediately tug at a host of others, and it took years of patience before all the roots came up at once. But then, becoming a writer is not effortless for anyone. These signatures raise the bar for anyone who wants to write—calling yourself a 'writer' means you're at some level placing yourself in this company, which is a terrifying thought. But they also remind me that of all the vocations and occupations you could choose, this is an amazing, magical tribe to want to belong to.

★

Reading is so easy compared to writing. A friend drops by one day, one of those wonderful people who leaves me awestruck with her multiple talents. She is an artist, a writer, a rider and sports fanatic, intensely politically astute and engaged. She's stuck on her book. It's close to the end, and she is immensely frustrated because she can't explain how delicate this stage is; if she moves one thing in the structure that she's been building slowly over a period of six years, everything could collapse.

She talks about the book as if it's made up of bones and flesh—strong but also so fragile, permeable, breakable. Like this? I ask, and show her a YouTube video that I've been replaying obsessively.

The performer is Miyoko Shida Rigolo. Her props are thirteen dried palm branches. She moves with slow, focused concentration. The balance she's working on, the Sanddorn balance, was created by Maedir Eugster Rigolo, who saw his act as a perfect example of Zen concentration.

Miyoko takes a feather, and balances it crosswise over the palm branch. Then she takes a longer branch and balances it at an angle on the first branch. Then another, and another.

All of her attention is concentrated at the point of intersection between the branches. By the time she gets to the fourth branch, she has to pick the rest up with her foot. The branches are not light; you can see the slight ripple in her biceps as she strains to hold the delicately filigreed structure together. It is as though she is building the skeleton of a boat that rocks in the invisible air. At four minutes in, I find that I am holding my breath. What rises from Miyoko Shida's hands is as fragile as new-blown glass, and as strong as an iron frame, a dinosaur skeleton. At five minutes and forty seconds in, she raises the structure ever so slowly above her head, her face impassive. Then she balances the palm branch balance on her head. And then, using her right foot, she picks up one more branch.

What holds this impossible structure together is concentration and technique, nothing more.

The hardest sticks to place are the final ones. There are only two left to place, but if she gets them wrong, the whole creation, so odd, so beautiful, will tumble down. These last two sticks, coming at the end of the balance when her muscles are already straining and her focus has already been tested, are more important than the fifteen that came before. My friend's book is like that: she has ten or twelve of its branches already placed, and the hesitation comes out of the recognition that she must get the last few chapters precisely right or risk it all tumbling down.

I don't have the craft to write a book like this yet, but I have read books that feel like Shida's beautiful, eerie structure. The keyboard fools you into thinking otherwise, but novels are physical hand-labour. You're going sentence by sentence, a process that becomes apparent if you use index cards, or map out books in diaries and notebooks.

I cannot imagine writing a book without handwriting.

When I started reading, I spent years wondering how it was done. It felt like a conjurer's trick—Oz, and Apu's Nischindipur, the moon of Kahani, Shivpalgunj, all created out of twenty-six alphabets. After my friend has left, I watch Miyoko Shida again and again, understanding that all books are written the same way. You take a form that doesn't exist, balance it on thin air, and pretend that it rests on solid ground. It is magic, and it works.

(Written in 2015-16)

Acknowledgements

Many of these essays began as short columns for *Business Standard*, which is also where many of the short profiles were first published. My thanks to T.N. Ninan, Ashok Kumar Bhattacharya, Tony Joseph, Kanika Datta and other editors at the paper for generously granting permissions—and for creating so much space for books in a business newspaper. Many thanks to Brinda Datta at *Biblio* for permission to reproduce some essays and reviews from the magazine.

The first reading from *The Girl Who Ate Books* was held at the Bellagio Center—immense gratitude to Pilar Palacia, Rob Garris, Claudia Juech and others at the Rockefeller Foundation for the gift of that serene and stunningly beautiful space, where these essays finally started to come together. And to Beatrice Lamwaka, Ben Kiernan and Glenda Gilmore, David and Nancy Grant, Farah Mohamed, Glen MacDonald, Jean-Baptiste Kakoma, Jorge Tacla and Rajeevan Poyil for the gelato, encouragement and goodwill.

Love and gratitude to my parents, Sunanda and Tarun Roy, and my family, readers down to the youngest devourer of books: Tara, JT, Neel, Mia, Rudra, Antara and Arun.

To Kamini Karlekar, Meenakshi Ganguly, Peter Griffin, Prem Panicker, Rahul Bhatia, Ruchir Joshi, Salil Tripathi, Shefaly Yogendra, Sharmistha Roychowdhury; Arjun Nath, Akhil Bhardwaj, Dr Yusuf Merchant and Keshav Palita for reading and commenting on various essays in this book—and for surviving years of my absent-minded geekery. As ever, to David Godwin, for being such a fabulous agent and friend.

Margaret Mascarenhas: thank you for those laidback Goa months and the conversational kintsugi. Anjali Puri: thank you for the Bastora house, and its friendly sub-tenants.

To everyone at HarperCollins India: V.K. Karthika and Krishan Chopra for suggesting this book, and for their immense patience; editors Somak Ghoshal and Arcopol Chaudhuri for understanding how to shape the mess I handed them, for their astute editorial sense and for the style upgrades; art director Bonita Vaz-Shimray and my astonishingly talented friend, Kriti Monga, for the generous gift of the design for the book cover.

Devangshu Datta: as always, thank you for the care and feeding of high-strung authors, and for all the years of letting me steal your books.

Bibliography[*]

I've been heavily influenced and entertained by several books about books and reading. A very short list of some of them:

1. Alberto Manguel, *A History of Reading* (Penguin Books, 1997). *The Library at Night* (Yale University Press, 2008).
2. Amitav Ghosh, *The Testimony of My Grandfather's Bookcase* (Kenyon Review, 1999).
3. Anne Fadiman, *Ex Libris: Confessions of a Common Reader* (Farrar, Straus & Giroux, 1998).
4. Azar Nafisi, *Reading Lolita in Tehran* (Random House, 2003).
5. Elif Batuman, *The Possessed* (Farrar, Straus & Giroux, 2010).
6. Francis Spufford, *The Child That Books Built: A Life in Reading* (Faber & Faber, 2002).
7. Larry McMurtry, *Books: A Memoir* (Simon & Schuster, 2008).
8. Michael Dirda, *Readings: Essays and Literary Entertainments* (W.W. Norton & Company, 2000).
9. Nicholas Basbanes, *A Gentle Madness* (Henry Holt & Company, 1995).
10. Pradeep Sebastian, *The Groaning Shelf* (Hachette India, 2010).

Finding Dean

1. Dean Mahomet, *The Travels of Dean Mahomet: An Eighteenth-Century*

---

[*] Every effort has been made to credit sources and original texts; if any omissions are discovered, they will be corrected in the next edition.

343

Journey through India, ed. Michael Fisher (University of California Press, 1997). *Shampooing; or, Benefits resulting from the use of Indian Medicated Vapour Bath, as Introduced Into This Country by S.D. Mahomet (a native of India),* Brighton (1823).

2. *Mookerjee's Magazine,* ed. Dr Sambhu Chandra Mookerjee (Digital Library of India, 1861 onwards).

3. Amardeep Singh, http://www.lehigh.edu/~amsp/2006/09/closer-look-at-dean-mahomet-1759-1850.html.

4. Arvind Krishna Mehrotra, *The Illustrated History of Indian Literature in English* (Permanent Black, 2003).

5. *The Picador Book of Modern Indian Literature,* ed. Amit Chaudhuri (Picador, 2001).

6. John Timbs, *Clubs and Club Life in London: With Anecdotes of its Famous Coffee Houses, Hostelries and Taverns, from the Seventeenth Century to the Present Times* (John Camden Hotten, 1872).

7. *Hicky's Bengal Gazette: Contemporary Life and Events,* ed. Tarun Kumar Mukhopadhyay (Subarnarekha, 1988).

8. Mushirul Hasan, *Wit and Humour in Colonial North India* (Niyogi Books, 2007).

How to Read In Indian

1. Farhatullah Baig, *The Last Musha'irah of Dehli,* Farhatullah Baig (Orient Blackswan, 2010).

2. Nirad C. Chaudhuri, *Autobiography of an Unknown Indian* (NYRB Classics, 1951).

3. Bankimchandra Chattopadhyay, *Rajmohan's Wife* (Rupa & Co; first serialised in 1864).

4. K.C. Dutt, *A Journal of Forty Eight Hours of the Year 1945* (Kolkata Literary Gazette, 1835).

5. S.C. Dutt, *The Republic of Orissa: Annals from the Pages of the Twentieth Century* (Kolkata Literary Gazette, 1845).

6. *The Dutt Family Album* (first published Longmans, Green & Co, London, 1870).

7. Arvind Krishna Mehrotra, *The Illustrated History of Indian Literature in English* (Permanent Black, 2003).

8. B.S. Kesavan, *History of Printing and Publishing in India:A Story of Cultural Re-Awakening* (National Book Trust, 1985).

9. Meenakshi Mukherjee, *The Perishable Empire: Essays on Indian Writing in English* (Oxford University Press, 2000).

10. *Moveable Type: Book History in India*, ed. Abhijit Gupta and Swapan Chakravorty (Permanent Black, 2008).

11. Rabindranath Tagore, *Nashta Neer* (1901–1902).

12. Johannes Ferdinand Fenger and Emil Francke, *History of the Tranquebar Mission Worked Out From Original Papers* (Tranquebar, Evangelical Lutheran Mission Press, 1864).

13. J.N. Dutt, *The Life and Work of Romesh Dutt* (JM Dent & Sons Ltd, 1911).

14. I. Allan Sealy, *The Trotternama*, (Knopf, 1988).

1857 And All That

1. Edward Money, *The Wife and The Ward; or, A Life's Error* (Routledge, 1859).

2. James Grant, *First Love and Last Love* (Routledge, 1868).

3. Philip Meadows Taylor, *Seeta* (London: Henry S. King & Co, 1872).

4. Flora Annie Steel, *On The Face Of The Waters*, (New York: Macmillan, 1897).

5. G.A. Henty, *In Times of Peril*, (New York: The Mershon Company, 1900).

6. Jules Verne, *The Steam House* (Paris: Pierre-Jules Hetzel, 1880).

The Pioneers

1. *City Improbable:An Anthology of Writings on Delhi*, ed. Khushwant Singh (Penguin, 2004).

2. R.C. Dutt, *Three Years in Europe: 1868-1871*, (Kolkata, S.K. Lahiri & Co., 1896).

3. Behramji Merwanji Malabari, *The Indian Eye on English Life*, or, *The Rambles of A Pilgrim Reformer* (Bombay: Apollo Printing Works, 1895); *The Indian Muse In English Garb* (Bombay: Reporters' Press, 1876); *Gujarat and the Gujaratis* (London: W.E. Allen & Co., 1882).

4. *The Essential Rokeya: Selected Works of Rokeya Sakhawat Hossain (1880-*

1932), ed. Mohammad A. Quayum (Brill, 2013).

5. *Sultana's Dream and Selections from The Secluded Ones by Rokeya Begum*, trans. Roushan Jahan, (The Feminist Press, 1988).

6. Rassundari Debi and Tanika Sarkar, *Words To Win, The Making of 'Amar Jiban'* (Kali For Women, 1999).

7. Mrinalini Sinha, *Specters of Mother India: The Global Restructuring of an Empire* (Duke University Press, 2006).

8. Rokeya Sakhawat Hossein, *Sultana's Dream and Padmarag* (Penguin, 2005).

9. Manjula Padmanabhan, *Escape* (Picador India, 2008); *The Island of Lost Girls* (Hachette, 2015).

10. Suniti Namjoshi, *Mothers of Mayadip* (The Women's Press, 1989).

11. Swami Nikhilananda and Dhan Gopal Mukerji, *Sri Ramakrishna: The Face of Silence* (Skylight Paths Publishing, first published in 1953).

12. Dhan Gopal Mukerji, *Caste and Outcast*, ed. Gordon Chang (Stanford University Press, 2002).

13. Dhan Gopal Mukerji, *My Brother's Face* (Thornton Butterworth, 1935).

14. Dhan Gopal Mukherji, *Gay-Neck: The Story of a Pigeon* (E.P. Dutton, 1927).

15. Raja Rao, *Kanthapura* (Orient Paperbacks, 1970 edition).

16. Raja Rao, *The Meaning of India: Essays* (Vision Books, 1996).

17. Rao Raja and Robert L. Hardgrave, *Word as Mantra* (Katha/Centre for Asian Studies, University of Texas, 1998).

18. G.V. Desani, *All About H Hatterr,* (NYRB Classics, 2007).

Angrezi Devi

1. Shankar Gopal Tulpule, 'A History of Indian Literature', Vol. 9, Part 4.

2. G.N. Devy, 'The People's Linguistic Survey of India', http://www.peopleslinguisticsurvey.org/default.aspx.

3. Rajeshwari V. Pandharipande, 'Minority Matters: Issues In Minority Languages in India', International Journal on Multicultural Studies, Vol. 4, No. 2 (UNESCO, 2002).

4. Sisir Kumar Das, *History of Indian Literature* (Sahitya Akademi, 2002).

5. Dr M.G. Mali, *Savitribai Phule: Samagra Wangmay* (Navayan, 1988).

6. Savitribai Phule: First Memorial Lecture 2008, Dr T Sundararaman (NCERT).
7. Zareer Masani, *Macaulay: Pioneer of Indian Modernization* (Random House, 2013).

Coffee Break

1. Dom Moraes, *A Variety of Absences* (Penguin, 2003).
2. Dom Moraes, *Typed With One Finger* (Yeti Books, 2002).
3. Arun Kolatkar, *Jejuri*, (NYRB Classics, 2006).
4. *60 Indian Poets: 1952–2007*, (Penguin India, 2008)
5. Agha Shahid Ali, *The Country Without a Post Office* (Ravi Dayal Publishers, 1997; Penguin Modern Classics, 2013).
6. Kamala Das, *My Story* (Sterling Publishers, 1976).
7. I. Allan Sealy, *Red: An Alphabet* (Picador, 2006).

The Baba Yaga in the Back Garden

1. Arkady Gaidar, *The School*
2. Olga Perovskaya, *Kids and Cubs*
3. Yuri Olesha, *The Three Fat Men*
4. Victor Dragunsky, *The Adventures of Dennis*
5. Galina Demykina, *The Lost Girl and the Scallywag*

Hold Your Tongue

Many of the ideas and values in 'Hold Your Tongue' were developed over a period of time. Among the many books that have presented histories of censorship and free speech, a brief selection of some of the most influential:

1. Salman Rushdie, *Step Across This Line: Collected Non-Fiction 1992-2002* (Modern Library, 2003).
2. Salil Tripathi, *Offence: The Hindu Case* (Seagull, 2009).
3. *Free Expression Is No Offence*, English PEN (Penguin 2005).
4. 'Censorship in South Africa': J.M. Coetzee (English in Africa, Vol. 17, No. 1).
5. Girija Kumar, *The Book on Trial: Fundamentalism and Censorship in India* (Har-Anand, 1997).

6. Nick Cohen, *You Can't Read This Book: Censorship in an Age of Freedom* (Fourth Estate, 2012).

7. *The Guarded Tongue: Women's Writing and Censorship in India*, ed. Ritu Menon (Sage, 2002).

8. Dubravka Ugresic, *The Culture of Lies* (Penn State University Press, 1995).

Other references

1. 'Vac as a goddess of victory in the Veda and her relation to Durga', Asko Parpola, (Zinbun: Annals of the Institute for Research in Humanities, Kyoto University, 1999).

Index